My Gettysburg

MY GETTYSBURG

Meditations on History and Place

Mark A. Snell

THE KENT STATE UNIVERSITY PRESS

Kent, Ohio

"Casinos and Other Entertainments" first appeared as a guest post on the
Civil War Memory blog on September 12, 2010, with the title "Gettysburg
and Battlefield Preservation: Another Perspective" and appears courtesy
of Kevin Levin. "Music Inspired by the Battle of Gettysburg, 1863–1913" is
reprinted from *Bugle Resounding: Music and Musicians of the Civil War Era,* ed.
Bruce C. Kelly and Mark A. Snell. Copyright © 2004 by The Curators of the
University of Missouri, University of Missouri Press, Columbia, Missouri
65201. "Union Lifeline" is reprinted from *The Ongoing Civil War: New Versions
of Old Stories,* ed. Herman Hattaway and Ethan S. Rafuse, Copyright © 2004
by The Curators of the University of Missouri, University of Missouri Press,
Columbia, Missouri 65201.

Library of Congress Catalog Card Number 2016008085
ISBN 978-1-60635-293-9
Manufactured in the United States of America

LIBRARY OF CONGRESS CATALOGING-IN-PUBLICATION DATA
Names: Snell, Mark A., author.
Title: My Gettysburg : meditations on history and place / Mark A. Snell.
Description: Kent, Ohio : The Kent State University Press, 2016. | Includes
    bibliographical references and index.
Identifiers: LCCN 2016008085 (print) | LCCN 2016009338 (ebook) |
    ISBN 9781606352939 (pbk. : alk. paper) | ISBN 9781631012266 (ePub) |
    ISBN 9781631012273 (ePDF)
Subjects: LCSH: Gettysburg, Battle of, Gettysburg, Pa., 1863.
Classification: LCC E475.53 .S66 2016 (print) | LCC E475.53 (ebook) | DDC
    973.7/349--dc23
LC record available at http://lccn.loc.gov/2016008085

20 19 18 17 16   5 4 3 2 1

For my sisters,

SHIRLEY LEE WOJEWODZI,

a true Civil War buff,

and

MARTHA DARLENE ERNST

(1944–2013),

who couldn't have cared less

Contents

Preface and Acknowledgments

This book is a collection of essays that focuses in one way or another on the Gettysburg campaign, viewed by some historians and laymen as the most decisive campaign of the Civil War. Of course, it was not. In terms of strategic decisiveness, the Vicksburg and Atlanta campaigns were far more important. Gettysburg, however, was bloodier and was fought on northern soil at the chronological halfway point of the conflict. Raids notwithstanding, it marked the last invasion of northern territory by a significant Confederate force. Despite its non-decisiveness, the name "Gettysburg" conjures images of daring bayonet assaults, mounted cavalry charges, and heroic last-ditch efforts by determined gray-clad infantrymen—the "High-Water Mark" of the Confederacy. It has captured the imagination of generations of Americans, North and South and mostly white. As William Faulkner wrote in *Intruder in the Dust,*

> For every Southern boy fourteen years old, not once but whenever he wants it, there is the instant when it's still not yet two o'clock on that July afternoon in 1863, the brigades are in position

behind the rail fence, the guns are laid and ready in the woods and the furled flags are already loosened to break out and Pickett himself with his long oiled ringlets and his hat in one hand probably and his sword in the other looking up the hill waiting for Longstreet to give the word and it's all in the balance, it hasn't happened yet, it hasn't even begun yet, it not only hasn't begun yet but there is still time for it not to begin against that position and those circumstances which made more men than Garnett and Kemper and Armistead and Wilcox look grave yet it's going to begin, we all know that, we have come too far with too much at stake and that moment doesn't need even a fourteen-year-old boy to think This time. Maybe this time with all this much to lose and all this much to gain: Pennsylvania, Maryland, the world, the golden dome of Washington itself to crown with desperate and unbelievable victory the desperate gamble, the cast made two years ago.[1]

Many years after Faulkner penned that extremely long sentence, an African American historian visited Gettysburg and saw Pickett's Charge in a very different light. After viewing the Electric Map in the old, now-razed Visitors Center, he strolled southward down Hancock Avenue, part of the maze of twenty-six miles of tour roads maintained by the National Park Service. "I began with Cemetery Ridge, the site of Pickett's Charge, where on the afternoon of July 3, 1863, some 13,000 Southerners, flags flying, drums rolling, trumpets blowing, had marched up a softly sloping hill toward the waiting Yankee cannon." Continuing, he reflected,

Half of them never made it back to their lines. The spot of their furthest advance is near a monument commemorating Brig. Gen. Lewis Armistead, who had placed a hat on the end of his sword—so that his Virginia lads could look up, see it and be emboldened—and shouted, "Come on, boys, give them the cold steel!" He was mortally wounded in the charge. Had Armistead's admittedly brave men prevailed and the Union lines been broken, slavery might have been preserved in the South for generations. I gazed at his stone memorial and softly cursed his slavery-spreading soul. And for good measure, that of D. Wyatt Aiken, a South Carolina colonel who held my blacksmith ancestor in bondage and commanded one of the South Carolina regiments that had fought half a mile or so way from this spot on the previous day. Then I asked the good Lord to forgive me.[2]

Thus, the Gettysburg Battlefield and the battle itself are viewed in different ways by diverse peoples and generations. Some visitors come to learn, some come for inspiration, some come because they have no choice, such as the countless bus loads of school children who venture onto the battlefield every spring and go running up the observation towers, screaming and laughing while their licensed battlefield guides wait below during a respite from the pandemonium. Some visitors even come to savor the supernatural. An entire cottage industry has sprung up, with costumed guides leading nighttime walks through the streets of "haunted" Gettysburg, their flock of paying customers hoping to spot the shimmering specter of a long-dead Union or Confederate soldier. Boo. Some people, like me, even come to Gettysburg to live and raise a family, although those residents in my population subset will always be considered "outsiders" by the natives.

The following anthology is a modest addition to the extensive historiography of the Gettysburg campaign and is a result of my own particular interests, some of which do not focus on the battle itself but rather on the impact of the campaign on the people who lived during that tumultuous time and those generations who came later. It also is reflective of my interest in what I call the "culture" of the Gettysburg Battlefield and its ever-changing landscape and view-shed. Some of the essays already have appeared in print, either as journal articles or chapters in books. Chapter 1, "My Gettysburg Address—'A Little Lot of Stars,'" is an autobiographical sketch of sorts, relating how I came to live in Gettysburg and my own personal story associated with such a famous place. Chapter 2, "East of Gettysburg: York, Pennsylvania, during the Invasion of 1863," is based in part on a revision of a section of my master's thesis written while a graduate student at Rutgers University. Chapter 3, "Union Lifeline: The Army of the Potomac's Logisticians in the Gettysburg Campaign," originally appeared in the now-defunct journal, *Columbiad: A Journal of the War between the States* and later was included in the anthology *The Ongoing Civil War: New Versions of Old Stories* (Columbia: University of Missouri Press, 2004), edited by my mentor Herman Hattaway and my friend Ethan Rafuse. Chapter 4, "(West) Virginians at Gettysburg," appeared in another form as part of my latest book, *West Virginia and the Civil War: Mountaineers Are Always Free* (Charleston, SC: History Press, 2011). Chapter 5, "'A Hell of a Damned Fool': Judson Kilpatrick, Farnsworth's Charge, and the Hard Hand of History," originally was a presentation delivered at the annual seminar of Gettysburg National Military Park in 2000. Chapter 6, "Music Inspired by the Battle of Gettysburg, 1863–1913," was a chapter in the anthology, *Bugle Resounding: Music and Musicians of the Civil War Era* (Columbia: University of Missouri Press, 2004) which Bruce C. Kelley and I coedited. Chapter 7, "Cadet Gray, Khaki, and Camouflage: The U.S. Army and Gettysburg, Post-1863," is a revision of an article originally published in *Blue and Gray Magazine* in 1990. Chapter 8, "The History of Civil War Reenacting: A Personal Recollection," is only tangentially related to Gettysburg, but there are enough connections to the battle's centennial that allow it to fit into this volume. The epilogue, "Casinos and Other Entertainments," was a guest post on Kevin Levin's very popular *Civil War Memory* blog, concerning the ongoing fight among commercial enterprises, developers, preservationists, local and state governments, the National Park Service, and Gettysburg residents.

In the course of assembling this anthology, many people provided encouragement, assistance and support. My former assistant, Denise Messinger, pushed me to bring my various Gettysburg essays together under one cover. Historian and author Dennis

Brandt allowed me to use his map of York County, and Gettysburg resident Karl Stelly took many of the photographs. Licensed battlefield guide and author John Archer read and checked the manuscript for historical accuracy. Likewise, D. Scott Hartwig, a retired historian at Gettysburg National Military Park and Christopher "Git 'er Done" Stowe of the Marine Corps University offered their insight. My neighbor Kendra Debany provided historical documentation concerning my Gettysburg farm. Several friends and relatives who either have read or listened to me read parts of this book also deserve mentioning, including my sister and her husband, Shirley and Richard Wojewodzi, and my pals Jim Ankrum, Susan Bouvier, Linda Sherman, and Todd Durboraw. The Kent State University Press staff has my appreciation: Director Will Underwood, Managing Editor Mary D. Young, Design and Production Manager Christine Brooks and her assistant manager, Darryl Crosby, Marketing Manager Susan L. Cash, and most especially, Acquiring Editor Joyce Harrison. Finally, I give a hearty thanks to my copy editor, Erin Holman, who through her expertise, guidance, and patience made me look like a much better writer. To all who helped me bring this anthology together, even those that I might have forgotten to mention, I extend my heartfelt gratitude.

My Gettysburg Address— "A Little Lot of Stars"

I AM OFTEN ASKED why I have chosen to live in Gettysburg, Pennsylvania, when I have not worked anywhere near that historic place in the years since I bought a small farm there in 1989. My answer is the same, no matter the audience: "I've always wanted to be the proprietor of my very own Gettysburg address." Some people immediately understand my dry sense of humor, while others just nod and think I'm strange. The truth is that ever since my childhood, I have been fascinated by the Civil War in general and the Battle of Gettysburg in particular, and it had been my fantasy to one day own a house in or near Gettysburg that sported the little bronze plaque proclaiming the structure was a "Civil War House 1863." I was born and raised in York, Pennsylvania, about thirty miles east of Gettysburg. I am old enough to vividly remember the events of the Civil War Centennial. My much-loved childhood toy was the "Marx Blue and Gray Battle Set," and my favorite childhood movie was John Ford's 1959 Civil War film, *The Horse Soldiers.* My personal connection to the Civil War and Gettysburg even predates my own memory. My oldest sister— herself a Civil War buff who relocated to Gettysburg in 1990 and

The standard bronze plaque issued by the Gettysburg Civil War Round Table for buildings that were "witnesses" to the Battle of Gettysburg. (Photo by author)

Martha (eleven), Mark (nine months), and Shirley Snell (twelve) on the base of the Virginia Memorial, summer 1955. (Author's collection)

today lives in the shadow of Little Round Top—has a photograph of me in her album, taken in 1955 when I was less than a year old, being steadied by her and my other sister as I stood on the foundation of the Virginia Memorial on Seminary Ridge.

During the Civil War Centennial, my parents routinely took me to Gettysburg, not because they had an abiding interest in the place but because they knew how much I enjoyed frolicking around the monuments and cannons and also for the reason that we never had enough money to travel to exotic vacation spots. I also remember the quaint little museums that no longer exist, such as the one on U.S. Route 30 just east of Gettysburg that focused on the July 3 cavalry battle, and the souvenir shop/exhibit/snack stand that formerly stood behind the statues of Gen John F. Reynolds and Gen. John Buford near the Railroad Cut. My favorite, now-defunct museum was situated just north of Little Round Top at the intersection of the Wheatfield Road and Sedgwick Avenue. It was owned by the Rosensteel family, the same clan who also were the proprietors of the Electric Map and Museum before the National Park Service purchased it. The Little Round Top Museum's display of artifacts always held my attention, especially the macabre displays of human teeth and bone fragments, left behind when the soldiers' remains were relocated to the Soldiers' National Cemetery in Gettysburg or Hollywood Cemetery in Richmond. To a young boy, those small relics of humanity were tangible proof that something grand and terrible had transpired only a short walk away on the rocky slopes of Little Round Top and among the boulders of Devil's Den.

Also in my memory are the tacky, almost smarmy, tourist traps that seemed to be everywhere around Gettysburg in the 1960s, such as the children's theme park known as Fantasyland that sat astride the Taneytown Road not far from General Meade's Headquarters, or "Fort Defiance," also on the Taneytown Road *directly across* from the Army of the Potomac's command post, the former a stockaded, frontier-era type of fort with costumed cowboys and Indians. (Today, some middle-aged American men might recall that *Playboy* magazine's centerfold for April 1985, Cindy Brooks, was the daughter of Fantasyland's owners. Or perhaps they don't remember. Men only read *Playboy* for the jokes, cartoons, and its compelling writing.) On Steinwehr Avenue (which during the battle was called the Emmitsburg Road) was located the Prince of Peace Museum, complete with its heroic-size plywood Jesus, clad in robes and with arms outstretched, secured atop a huge A-frame support jutting skyward. About a mile to the south, sitting diagonally across the Emmitsburg Road from the famous Peach Orchard—smack dab in the middle of the battlefield—was a

Originally the Prince of Peace Museum, this ugly structure has housed several thematic museums over the years. (Courtesy of Karl Stelly)

turquoise-roofed Stuckey's snack stand and souvenir shop. I also recall billboards hawking the old Peace Light Inn on the Mummasburg Road, where tourists could "eat and sleep on the battlefield." And then there was George Marino's Battlefield Museum, which still exists, holding a collection of artifacts from different wars. But the coolest part of the museum was out back, where George had leased his yard to a group of reenactors who had built a Civil War camp and Petersburg-style trenches and where for twenty-five cents a Yankee soldier would let you shoot a blank cartridge from his musket. Nearby was the surgeon's tent with its barrel-full of gruesome amputated "limbs." For a ten-year-old, that was about as good as it got!

My interest in the Battle of Gettysburg never waned through my adolescence and teenage years, although the normal distrac-

George Marino's Battlefield Museum. (Courtesy of Karl Stelly)

tions associated with a young man's life temporarily took precedence. Upon graduation from high school in 1972, I attended college for a year, ran out of money and joined the Army. (During my two years of service, I continued to further my college education during my off-duty time.) Upon my discharge a few years later, I went back to college armed with a Reserve Officers' Training Corps (ROTC) scholarship and GI Bill benefits. I decided to return home and attend York College of Pennsylvania, but the school was too small to have its own Army ROTC detachment, so Gettysburg College sent young captains and majors, most of them Vietnam veterans, to York College to teach courses in military science. Special events, such as map exercises and marksmanship, were held at Gettysburg College. Although I was not a history major, I did take several electives in that field, including a tremendous Civil War course taught by the late James L. Morrison, himself a retired army officer, Vietnam vet, former first captain of the Virginia Military Institute Corps of Cadets, and West Point professor.

The spring semester of my junior year, I decided to become a "VIP"—an abbreviation for "Volunteers in Parks"—at Gettysburg National Military Park, where I donned a Union army uniform and gave talks about the life of a Yankee infantryman. Sometimes, I even gave presentations about Civil War music, as I was a fairly skilled drummer. The Park invited me to become a "seasonal" uniformed ranger during the summer of 1976—Bicentennial Summer—but I had to decline the offer because the army already had planned for me a six-week "summer vacation" with 82nd Airborne Division and 5th Special Forces Group trainers at Fort Bragg, North Carolina, followed by three weeks of parachute instruction at Fort Benning, Georgia.

After graduating from college in 1977 and accepting a commission—Professor Morrison donned his old dress whites and conducted my swearing-in ceremony—I attended the Ordnance Officer Basic Course at Aberdeen Proving Ground (APG), Maryland. My subsequent assignment took me to Stuttgart, Germany. In my spare time (the little that I had) I traveled to historic sites in France, Belgium, Luxemburg, and the Netherlands, visiting battlefields ranging from Blenheim (1702) to Waterloo (1815) to Verdun (1916), and finally World War II battle sites, including Normandy, Arnhem, and the Ardennes Forest—the last, where my own father had fought. My real interests, however, were the sites associated with the American campaigns of 1918, particularly the Argonne Forest. There, from September 26 through November 11, 1918, the American Expeditionary Forces met a determined German foe. It was the largest campaign ever waged by an American army to that point in history, and it caused nearly 117,000 American casualties, with almost 49,000 dead. Yet few Americans visited those sites to see the grand American memorials dedicated there after the war, or the largest U.S. cemetery in Europe, the Meuse-Argonne American Cemetery in Romagne, France, containing more than 14,000 graves. On the first day of that campaign, a young tank officer named Patton was wounded in action while leading his ponderous armored vehicles on foot after his own tank had broken down. Back in the United States, another young officer named Eisenhower commanded doughboys at Camp Colt, located on the Gettysburg Battlefield. It was the seminal tank-training facility of the U.S. Army, but Ike yearned to see action in France. He would have to wait for another war. Nevertheless, Eisenhower lost almost as many men at Gettysburg as Patton's brigade suffered during the Argonne—Camp Colt counted nearly 160 dead from the Spanish influenza, while the 1st Provisional Tank Brigade sustained 19 killed and 152 wounded, totaling 171 battle casualties.[1]

Upon my return to the United States, I again was stationed at Aberdeen Proving Ground, but in less than a year I was transferred once more, this time to Picatinny Arsenal, tucked away in the mountains of New Jersey. I spent two pleasant years there, an area steeped in the history of the War of Independence. On weekends I volunteered at nearby Morristown National Historical Park as a living-history interpreter, portraying a soldier of George Washington's Continental Army. While living in New Jersey, I was introduced to the historical artist Don Troiani, and we made several trips to the Hudson Highlands to relic hunt army campsites of the American Revolution that Don had researched and for which he had secured the permission of the landowners.

It was also at this time that I decided that I wanted to teach history at West Point, so I gained an interview with the head of the U.S. Military Academy History Department, Col. Roy Flint, and started the long process to be accepted on the faculty. By then—1982—it was time for another transfer, again to Aberdeen to complete the Ordnance Officer Advance Course and then in the summer of 1983 to Fort Benning, Georgia, where I commanded a company in the 197th Infantry Brigade. There are numerous Civil War sites within a few hours' drive of Fort Benning, including Chickamauga and Chattanooga National Military Park and the battlefields of the Atlanta campaign, but my duties as a company commander precluded me from spending much time on Civil War stuff, especially now that I had a little boy waiting at home when I walked through the door about 7:00 P.M. every night. I did, however, find the time to join a reenactor group of expatriate Yankees who lived in the Atlanta area, and we formed the 21st Ohio Volunteer Infantry. (This was not my first reenactment unit, as I had been a member of the 87th Pennsylvania Infantry while attending college, and upon returning from Germany I joined the

1st Maryland Light Artillery and later the 5th New York Infantry, "Duryee's Zouaves.") The 21st Ohio was in great demand at reenactments, as there were few "authentic" Union units in the South. Then, in 1985, it was time for yet another transfer, first to Fort Leavenworth, Kansas, for a three-month staff-officers' course, followed by graduate school at Rutgers University in New Jersey.

The short stay in Kansas allowed me to visit some Civil War sites I had never seen, including Pea Ridge, Arkansas; Wilson's Creek Battlefield and Lexington, Missouri; Mine Run Battlefield and Fort Scott, Kansas; Shiloh, Tennessee; and Corinth, Mississippi. Then, it was back to the east coast and graduate school. At Rutgers, I had never felt so intellectually inadequate in my life. Most of my peers had studied history for their undergraduate degrees, and I was starting from scratch. Many of them were shockingly liberal women—Rutgers was lauded for its women's history program (*her*story, they called it back then)—who stereotyped me as a "baby-killing army guy." One day I entered my office (a cubicle) in the basement of Van Dyke Hall and was shocked to see "BABY KILLER" scrawled in lipstick on the wall. I guess whoever wrote it had seen too many Vietnam War movies. Despite this rude treatment by an anonymous, ignorant, biased, and cowardly graduate student, my exposure to gender studies and women's history made me, in the long run, a more well-rounded historian and a better teacher, although I did not realize it at the time.

After two years of coursework, I was given a choice of writing a masters' thesis or taking a comprehensive examination. My professors and peers told me the test was a breeze, and that no one in the Rutgers history department had written a masters' thesis in decades. However, my soon-to-be boss at West Point, Lt. Col. Casey Brower (who had just taken the helm of the American history division in the Department of History, after serving as President Ronald Reagan's army aide-de-camp), thought otherwise: "You don't have a choice, Captain Snell. You WILL write a thesis." So, my orders in hand, I decided to research and write a social history of York County during the Civil War (see chapter 2 for a very abridged version), focusing on how the county's numerous communities reacted to the calls for volunteers, conscription, and even a Confederate invasion. My advisor was Professor John W. Chambers II, himself an expert on the history of U.S. conscription polices. Spending time in the bowels of the old York County Courthouse, the special collections of the York County Historical Society (now known as the York County Heritage Trust), the Hanover Library, and other small archival depositories across York County proved to be a labor of love. I also made use of records of the Provost Marshal General (Record Group 93) in the National Archives, as well as conscription records of the Commonwealth of Pennsylvania, housed at the Pennsylvania State Archives in Harrisburg. The research and writing of my thesis took about seven months, and it turned out better than my advisor expected. It was the first time in my career that I felt like I was a real historian.

In June 1987, my family and I moved to West Point. The fall semester began in mid-August, after a summer of professor "boot camp" (officially called New Instructor Training), a six-week period when incoming instructors learned how to impart knowledge the "army way." I was slated to teach the U.S. history survey course to first-year cadets, known as "plebes." (When George Meade and R. E. Lee were cadets, the only thing lower than a plebe was a "thing"—a prospective cadet who had not yet passed the entrance examinations, a hurdle that did not survive the nineteenth century.) After completing our training, classes began in mid-August. Most of the first-year instructors immediately came down with what we all called the "crud," an affliction that seemed to come and go for most of that academic year, apparently transmitted from the plebes to the professors. Stress, fatigue, and living day and night in close quarters ensured that once one plebe succumbed to the crud, everyone did. A runny nose, sniffles, and the occasional sore throat were the main symptoms. After that first year, we all became immune to the crud, cadets and professors alike.

The academic departments considered Army-Navy week, or the days leading up to the "big game" in early December, a wash-out.

We were told not to give any "writs" (West Point slang for quizzes) that week—the plebes resembled zombies, having been up most of the night with pep rallies, pranks, and the like. In the history department we showed documentaries on our closed-circuit televisions and instructed the plebes that if they could not stay awake that they were to stand up and assume the "parade rest" position. I had several unfortunate kids zonk while standing and almost fall over. Army had a great football team in the late 1980s, and we took three out of four of the games from the "Squids" while I was on the staff and faculty. (Army even boasted a Heisman Trophy finalist in 1990, record-breaking running back Mike Mayweather.)

I also assisted the military history division when its instructors took cadets to Gettysburg for weekend "staff rides," the term for an intellectually intensive interactive tour. The purpose of a staff ride is for cadets and officers to learn from old battlefields such timeless values as leadership, courage, and selflessness, as well as military-specific knowledge like terrain analysis and the application of the principles of war. (See chapter 7 for an examination of how the U.S. Army has used the Gettysburg Battlefield for training since the end of the Civil War.) During the summers, I was assigned to cadet field training and also assisted with a program that brought civilian professors to West Point. The history faculty taught the civilians—some of whom were much respected scholars—the basics and nuances of military history and historiography. My final summer on the faculty, in the midst of one of those seminars, I was introduced to Dr. Michael Riccards, the president of Shepherd College (now Shepherd University) in Shepherdstown, West Virginia, who had invited the professors and their West Point instructors over to his residence at the end of the Antietam staff ride. Little did I know that my introduction to him would change my life in only a few years.

A normal tour of duty for officers assigned to West Point is three years, but I was allowed to stay another year because I had been selected to become the Executive Officer (XO) of the 1st Battalion, 1st Infantry Regiment, which was an infantry battalion in name only. In reality, the "1st of the 1st" was the U.S. Military Academy sustainment battalion—a collection of units that supported the academy mission. The battalion included an aviation detachment, an airborne detachment, an engineer detachment, a military police company, and a headquarters company. The U.S. Military Academy Band was attached to the battalion, but not assigned. In addition to being the XO, or second in command, I also had two major additional duties: I served as the S-3, or operations/training officer, as well as commander of the U.S. Military Academy Airborne Detachment, which had the mission of training the cadets' sport parachute team.

I had not made a parachute jump since graduating from Airborne School back in 1976, some fourteen years earlier. Accordingly, I received a half-day of refresher training from my noncommissioned officers and was taught how to pack my parachute, which was not the standard military variety but a sport version used by skydivers. One sultry afternoon in September 1990, I lifted off in a 2nd Aviation Detachment "Huey" (UH-1) helicopter, and within minutes I was "out the door" at about eight hundred feet. Since it was my first jump in a long time, the parachute was attached to a static line in the chopper so I did not have to worry about pulling the ripcord. Upon exiting the aircraft, I counted "one-one thousand, two-one thousand, three-one thousand, four-one thousand" and then looked up to check for a successful canopy opening. That's when I noticed that I had a malfunction! My training kicked in and I was able to clear the malfunction but was unable to land in the designated drop zone. Instead, I touched down in a large patch of wild, multiflora roses that shredded my skin and tangled the parachute. I will never forget my senior noncommissioned officer's words: "God damn, Sir! You really f——d up the 'chute!" Sheepishly, I responded, "Thanks, Sergeant Lewis. I'm OK." My two little boys, ages seven and four, who had begged me to bring them along to the drop zone, squealed and yelled, "Do it again, Daddy!" I did, but only once every three months, the minimum number required to maintain "jump status."

My tour at West Point came to an end in the late summer of 1991. My next—and, as it turned out, last—assignment took me back to the Home of Ordnance, Aberdeen Proving Ground (the Ordnance Center and School has since relocated to Fort Lee, Virginia), where I was assigned as a branch chief in the Combat Developments Directorate. While there, I received orders to spend a month of temporary duty in South Korea during the summer of 1992, and soon after my return, I got a phone call from a friend, Scott Hartwig, a senior historian at Gettysburg National Military Park. "Hey Mark," he said, "you wanna be in the movie *Gettysburg?*" During my Korean adventure, Turner Pictures had begun filming just west of Seminary Ridge along Pumping Station Road, not far from Eisenhower National Historic Site. *Of course,* I wanted to be in the movie, so I donned my old blue uniform and joined Scott and his fellow NPS historians, John Heiser and the late John Andrews, and for one day in late August we filmed the July 2 bayonet charge of the 20th Maine Infantry. When the film was released, I could actually find myself on screen—although I was "dead," sprawled over a breastwork. (About a decade later I was asked to be a historical consultant for the *Gettysburg* "prequel," *Gods and Generals.* The director, my friend Ron Maxwell, inquired if my youngest son [who at the time was about seventeen and looked the correct age for a young soldier] and I would like to be in one of the scenes, and by mere happenstance, we came to portray Yankees—once again—in the 20th Maine, this time in their futile attack on Marye's Heights during the Battle of Fredericksburg. As in *Gettysburg,* I was killed.)

In the course of what turned out to be my last duty assignment, the long Cold War finally ended and the military services began their inevitable reductions-in-force. With the prospect of promotion slim to none, I opted for retirement and left the U.S. Army with twenty-one years of active and reserve service. Luckily for me, I got a phone call from an old friend just as I was pondering the return to civilian life.

It seems the president of Shepherd College was looking for a qualified candidate to fill a new position, the director of a Civil War research center. When none of the candidates who had been vetted by the history department met his liking (the faculty was more concerned with hiring a candidate that specialized in a field such as Asian or African history with a secondary "interest" in the American Civil War), President Riccards remembered a young army major who had impressed him during the Antietam staff ride a few years earlier. The timing could not have been more perfect. My friend, Capt. (now colonel, retired) Jim Scudieri, a colleague from the USMA history department, had been informed of the opening and urged me to apply. After an interview with the college's dean of arts and humanities and Riccards, I was notified a few weeks later that I was accepted for the position, with the provision that I eventually finish my PhD. (In defiance of the president, the history department faculty members boycotted their scheduled interview with me, since I was not one of the candidates whom *they* had recommended for the position, portending a rocky relationship with the department that lasted the first half of my career at Shepherd.)

Back when I still was stationed at West Point, I was privileged to make the acquaintance of Professor Herman Hattaway, who from 1990 to 1991 was the academy's visiting professor of history. Herman and I became good friends, and he asked me to apply to the doctoral program where he taught, the University of Missouri at Kansas City. I applied in 1990, was accepted, and began my studies. Because I was serving on active duty, I took summer and weekend courses as well as independent study. Luckily, my next job, at Aberdeen Proving Ground, required me to regularly travel to St. Louis and Kansas City, making class attendance a bit easier. Balancing the demands of military service, academic study, and family life was quite grueling, and my retirement from the Army did not make matters any easier. Nonetheless, I persevered, finished my course work in 1995, fulfilled the foreign language requirement, took my comprehensive exams in 1996, completed and defended my dissertation in 1998, and was granted the doctor of philosophy degree in 1999.

Writing the dissertation was the best part of earning the PhD. I originally had planned to conduct research and then write about the short-, mid-, and long-term effects of the Battle of Gettysburg on the Gettysburg community and its environs, especially the role of the U.S. government in the town's recovery and eventually the administration of Gettysburg National Military Park by the U.S. Army and later the National Park Service. Such a topic would blend my major field, U.S. history, with my minor field, public administration. However, something unexpectedly fell into my lap and I quickly changed topics.

As a native of York, Pennsylvania, I always had been interested in the career of another "Yorker," Maj. Gen. William B. Franklin, the first commander of the Army of the Potomac's Sixth Corps, from May 1862 through early 1863. Unfortunately, his personal papers had not seemed to survive the hand of time, aside from a tiny collection in the Library of Congress and his postwar business correspondence in the Connecticut State Library. However, through a little sleuthing and some serious good luck, I was able to track down his living descendents, who still possessed a treasure trove of Franklin's personal papers, including his wartime letters to his wife, several diaries, and other correspondence. It was a "no brainer" for me to change dissertation topics, and Professor Hattaway readily agreed. The dissertation garnered the Outstanding Dissertation Award from Missouri and also landed a book contract with Fordham University Press.

While still assigned to West Point and just prior to becoming a doctoral student, we bought a small farm in 1989, about five miles south of Gettysburg, ostensibly as my "retirement" home, thus bringing to reality what had once been only a pipe dream. I started restoring the old farmhouse about a year later, and when I received transfer orders to Aberdeen in 1991, I reluctantly decided to make the 164-mile daily commute from Gettysburg to

APG and back. Then, upon accepting the position at Shepherd, my family and I remained at our farm in Gettysburg, and from that time until my retirement from the university I made the 94-mile round trip on a daily basis, except for a four-month hiatus, when I served as the visiting senior lecturer of war studies at the Royal Military Academy (Sandurst) in England during the fall semester of 2008.

Since my retirement from the army and during my tenure at the university, I watched my two sons grow up in historic Gettysburg. They first attended the old Meade Elementary School, until it closed; then were transferred to Keefauver Elementary School (since razed), located on the edge of Cemetery Hill and Culp's Hill; and later went to nearby Gettysburg Middle School, just off Baltimore Street. They both graduated from the new Gettysburg High School, situated near Barlow's Knoll. I cheered them in high school football at Warrior Stadium in the shadow of East Cemetery Hill and helped to coach my oldest son when he played Little League and Teener League baseball on the site of the World War I cantonment, Camp Colt. For someone like me, with a lifelong interest in American history, I was (and still am) living my dream.

But what about my own "Gettysburg Address"? My house was built about 1832 in Cumberland Township by William Conover and sold in 1843 to Henry B. Cromer. One of Henry's sons, William, served in an emergency cavalry unit (100-days' service), Warren's Independent Cavalry Company, during Jubal Early's raid in the summer of 1864. William Cromer later married Elizabeth Sandoe, the sister of the first Union soldier killed at Gettysburg. (William and Elizabeth took over the farm when Henry died and raised their own family in the house where I now reside.) Elizabeth's brother, George Washington Sandoe, met his demise on June 26, 1863, when Confederates passed through town on their way to York. On the Baltimore Pike just south of town, George took a shot at a Reb cavalryman but missed. The southern trooper had better aim. George was a soldier in an earlier emergency unit, Captain Bell's Independent Cavalry Company, which later became Company B, 21st

Elizabeth Ann (Sandoe) Cromer, sister of the first Union casualty at Gettysburg (June 26, 1863). She was nineteen years old at the time of her brother's demise. (Author's collection)

Pennsylvania Cavalry. (Sandoe is buried in the graveyard of Mt. Joy Lutheran Church, only a few feet away from Elizabeth and her husband, and within sight of the Cromer homestead.) Cromer descendants retained the farm until 1925. Several other families had owned it before I came to purchase the property back in 1989 and systematically restore the house and barn to a semblance of the way they might have looked during the nineteenth century.

Is my house haunted? Mark Nesbitt, a former National Park Service ranger who now owns Gettysburg Ghost Tours, seems to think so. A partial chapter in one of his *Ghosts of Gettysburg* volumes discusses the supernatural happenings at my residence. I gladly shared my "unexplained experiences" surrounding the farm with the understanding that he not use my name in the book. Mark agreed. You can imagine my surprise—and chagrin—when I read what he wrote: "The owner is a historian and former professor at West Point and is currently [1995] director at the Center for the Study of the Civil War."[2] Geez, who might that be?

I consider myself privileged to be the temporary custodian of a piece of history. Every day when I walk out my front door to sit on the porch, cup of coffee in hand, I gaze upon fields of corn, wheat, and soy or, in winter, snow-covered stubble and can see Big Round Top in the distance. I sometimes allow my mind to drift back to the summer of 1863 and ponder on the thoughts of the young 11th Corps soldiers marching through Henry Cromer's farm, trampling his fields along their way, as they hurried onward to the flat land north of Gettysburg and a bloody defeat on July 1. Many spoke German as their first language, and for some of the so-called Dutchmen, that morning would be their last few hours

Replacement gravestone for George Washington Sandoe. Both the original marker and its replacement erroneously state that he was a soldier in Company B, 21st Pennsylvania Cavalry. In reality, Sandoe was a member of Captain Bell's Independent Cavalry Company. Later in the campaign and after Sandoe's death, the unit was redesignated as Company B of the 21st. It was an emergency regiment that answered Governor Andrew Curtin's call for six-months' regiments to stem the Confederate invasion of the Commonwealth. (Photo by author)

of mortality. *"Guten Morgen"* or *"Wie geht es Ihnen?"* the soldiers might have shouted to the Cromer clan as they rushed by, their accoutrements, canteens, and tin cups banging against their sweaty bodies as they veered left to take a shortcut through planted fields, much to Mr. Cromer's dismay. During the three-day battle, Henry, then aged fifty-four, his wife Harriet, fifty, and their eight children, ranging from three to twenty-three, undoubtedly trembled in terror as the cacophony of combat thundered a mere two miles away.[3] Afterward, survivors of Col. Adelbert Ames's command of the same hapless 11th Corps camped the night of July 5 on the Cromer farm, using his fence rails for firewood and flattening more crops, causing further damage, to the tune of $1,087 (by Cromer's estimate). At the time of the battle, the Cromers were growing Indian corn, rye, wheat, sweet potatoes, white potatoes, hay, grass, and flax. They also produced silk, soap, and candles. Cromer never received compensation for his losses, despite filing postwar claims with the state and federal governments.[4]

Nearly a century later, an old soldier who became the thirty-fourth president, and who also came to the battlefield to retire, tried to improve his newly purchased fields and pastures. Concerning his challenge, the former commander of Camp Colt reflected, "One of the attractions about the place . . . was the rundown soil. This was a chance, I thought, to . . . restore land to its original fertility. The challenge outweighed certain obvious faults. Although we haven't achieved the greatest success . . . there are enough lush fields to assure me that I shall leave the place better than I found it."[5] And so he did.

Now, more than sixty years after Ike and Mamie purchased their farm some three miles from my own homestead, I have come to live on this ground with similar hopes of leaving it better than I found it. I have dubbed my bit of paradise "Crescent-Chapel Farm," in memory of the crescent-moon insignia worn by the long-ago visitors of the 11th Corps and in recognition of the little church that sat on a corner of the farm when Henry Cromer's family lived there.[6] When I attended the world premiere of *Gods and*

Generals in February 2003, I was especially touched by Ron Maxwell's selection of George Eliot's remarkable quote in the film's opening credits. Her thoughts on the meaning of land, place, and home fittingly capture the emotions that I feel for my personal *Gettysburg Address* and its own "little lot of stars":

> A human life, I think, should be well rooted in some area of native land where it may get the love of tender kinship from the earth, for the labors men go forth to, for the sounds and accents that haunt it, for whatever will give that early home a familiar unmistakable difference amidst the future widening of knowledge. . . . The best introduction to astronomy is to think of the nightly heavens as a little lot of stars belonging to one's own homestead.[7]

2

East of Gettysburg

York County, Pennsylvania, during the Invasion of 1863

Situated on the west bank of the Susquehanna River with what was later to be known as the Mason-Dixon line as its southern border, the area that was to become York County was first settled by white men and women in the late 1720s, when English settlers and Maryland squatters ventured into the area. Large numbers of Germans followed thereafter, settling in the eastern part of the county near the Susquehanna River. Welsh and Scots-Irish pioneers began arriving around the middle of the eighteenth century, many of them making their home in the extreme southeastern and southern areas of the county. The town of York, the county seat, was laid out in 1741 by order of the Proprietors and has the distinction of being the first Pennsylvania town west of the Susquehanna. York played host to the Continental Congress from 1777 to 1778 while British forces were occupying Philadelphia, and it was during this time that the rebel congress drafted the Articles of Confederation.[1] (In later years, York would take pride in boasting that it was the home of the "First Capital of the United States."[2]) In 1800, Adams County (named for the second U.S. president), with Gettysburg as its seat, would be created from the western half of York County.

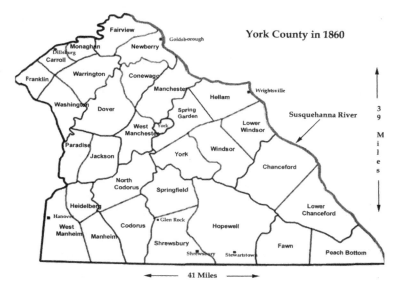

York County, Pennsylvania in 1860. Gettysburg was twenty-nine miles
west of the borough of York. (Map by Dennis Brandt)

With its fertile, rolling land and proximity to the Susquehanna
as major attractions, York County continued to attract settlers
from other states and counties, as well as from abroad. By 1860,
the county had a population of 68,200 in its thirty townships and
several largest boroughs and towns. The borough of York was by
far the most populated area, with 8,605 residents clustered within
its five wards. The only other boroughs of significant size at that
time were Hanover, located at the extreme southwest corner of
the county, with a population of 1,630, and Wrightsville, which
sat on the bank of the Susquehanna River and had 1,294 residents.
The inhabitants of the county in 1860 included many foreign-
born men and women, with the German-speaking immigrants
the most prominent. There also were 1,204 African Americans
living in the county at that time, which was only 1.8 percent of
the total population. The ratio of men to women, both black and
white, was roughly equal.[3]

The three dominant religious groups in the county during the antebellum period were the Moravians, the "plain people" (pietistic denominations such as the Brethren, Mennonites, and Amish), and the "church people" (Lutheran, Reformed, United Brethren, and Evangelical faiths).[4] *The York Gazetteer and Business Directory for 1856* listed thirteen churches within the borough of York, including a Roman Catholic church, a Quaker meeting house, and an Episcopal church, with the remaining houses of worship consisting of the various Protestant denominations. Hanover had four churches in 1856, and Wrightsville had five. Many other churches and religious meeting places were scattered throughout the different townships and villages of the county.[5]

York's concern for its children was evident in the number of public schools located throughout the county. In 1855 York County had 279 free schools, which operated an average of five months; during that year 8,737 boys and 6,688 girls were enrolled, with an average countywide student attendance of 9,602. With 293 teachers employed, the average student to teacher ratio was approximately thirty to one. There were numerous private schools in the county, including boys', girls', and coeducational institutions, and one charitable school for black children.[6]

Antebellum York was very active socially, at least from a white man's point of view. York Borough had one Masonic and three Odd Fellow lodges, five volunteer fire companies, two beneficial associations, a men's temperance society, a mechanics' order, and a Young Men's Christian Association. The boroughs of Wrightsville and Shrewsbury also had Odd Fellow lodges, and many of the other boroughs and towns in the county had at least one volunteer fire company where the menfolk could gather and socialize.[7] York and Hanover also had two active militia companies each, which, during peacetime, were more like clubs than military organizations.

The economy of York and its environs was rooted in agriculture, with much of the county's somewhat limited industrial capability tied to farming products as well. The 1856 directory estimated that "the amount of flour and grain received and shipped by

forwarding merchants, during the year ending March 1, 1856, may
be rated thus, viz: flour, 50,000 barrels, wheat, 135,000 bushels,
rye, 34,000 [bushels], corn, 200,000 bushels, oats, 45,000 bushels,
buckwheat, 6,500 bushels, buck wheat meal, 255,000 pounds." In
addition to the grain market, it was estimated that 1.5 million feet
of lumber were produced and sold in the county annually. One of
York's foremost business firms was P. A. & S. Small, which, among
its other interests, owned one of the largest flour-milling operations in southern Pennsylvania. Other businesses in the county
were also dependent upon agricultural products, with the most
prevalent types being distillers, tobacconists, tanners, and pro-
ducers of leather goods. There were also nine agricultural imple-
ment factories listed in the 1856 directory.[8]

Although York was undeniably a farm town, it also had its share
of mechanized industry. In addition to the factories that made
farm implements, there were three railway car factories (which
produced over a thousand cars in 1855 alone), four brass foundries, three iron foundries, two ornamental iron-railing factories,
five machine shops, a platform-scale factory, and numerous ma-
chinists who plied their trade individually.[9] When the Civil War
began, York County had a total of 589 retailers selling many of the
products that had been grown on county farms or produced in its
factories and industrial establishments.[10] Thus, by 1861, York was
beginning to feel the effects of the Industrial Revolution.

Tantamount to York's gradual departure from a rural economy
was the advent of the railroad. The Baltimore & Susquehanna Railroad began construction in 1829 on a line running from Baltimore
to York, which was completed by 1838. It was extended in 1843 to
Wrightsville, in 1850 to Harrisburg, and in 1852 to Hanover.[11] When
the Baltimore & Susquehanna was taken over by the Northern
Central Railway Company in 1854, service to many of the major cities of the Northeast became a reality. (By 1861, the Northern Central, like the Baltimore & Susquehanna before it, fell victim to hard
times, losing 28 percent of its stock and much of its internal control
to the Pennsylvania Railroad.) Not only did the railroad open up

new markets for York County industry, business, and agriculture, it would also have strategic significance during the war, hauling troops and supplies from the camps and arsenals of the North to the theater of war in Virginia and points south.[12]

The railroad tied York County's economic interests to the South before the war, and for this reason some county inhabitants were reluctant to voice opposition to slavery and the southern way of life. County residents, however, had more in common with the South than just a penchant for southern money. They also shared many of the same social values and political ideals of their southern neighbors.

A survey of York County's voting record in presidential elections from 1812 (the first time statistics were compiled and recorded in the county) through 1860 reveals an unbroken pattern of countywide Democratic victories.[13] York's strong sense of loyalty to the Democratic party can be traced back to the 1790s, when county residents felt extreme dissatisfaction with Federalist policies, especially the excise tax on whiskey. Not only did inhabitants of the region detest this tax (which affected many who made their living as distillers), they also were appalled by the central government's assertion of power with the presence of troops in the area during the Whiskey Rebellion. This and similar Federalist actions stuck in the minds of many Yorkers, who eventually would take out their grievances at the polls by voting for the party that deemphasized a strong federal government and claimed to support the goals of the "common man."[14]

Two historians who studied the voting trends of nineteenth- and twentieth-century York determined that county residents continued to vote Democratic through the first half of the nineteenth century even when the party became the pro-slavery party as well as pro-laissez-faire. The study also reveals other reasons why Yorkers continued to cast their ballots for the Democrats. York County voters were hesitant to jeopardize their trade links with the southern states, one of which sat immediately below the county line. Many county inhabitants also were aware that the

Republican party was a direct descendent of both the Federalist and Whig parties, which traditionally had favored a strong central government. Finally, with the state of affairs becoming increasingly tumultuous in the 1850s, many Yorkers saw the Democratic party as the only established national political party. In this time of crisis, the Democrats seemed likely to have the best chance of keeping the nation from being torn asunder.[15]

There were fears among many York citizens that southern secession or the abolition of slavery might lead to a flood of freedmen northward across the Maryland line and into south-central Pennsylvania. Such a migration would create an excess of unskilled labor, depriving many white men of their jobs. There were additional concerns that former slaves might become "the white man's burden" in York County, with its residents footing the bill to keep the freedmen fed, clothed, and sheltered. On February 5, 1861, one of York's Democratic news organs ran the following story:

> FREE NEGROES—Sixty free negroes from North Carolina, bound North, passed through Maryland the other day. Cause: the Southern secession excitement. We may expect hundreds and thousands of such visitors before long. Let our abolition philanthropists make their arrangements accordingly. Shall the poor negro, unless he be a fugitive slave, be allowed to starve? What says Parson Beecher?[16]

On the same day and page that this story appeared, another commentary under the headline "Free Labor and Free Homes," opined on the "negro problem":

> The people, so long blindfolded, will see the guilty demagogues who have used the negro for the destruction of white men. They will mark those who have sung of negro freedom only to destroy the white man's liberty to earn bread for his starving family, and when they see all the terrible consequences of negro freedom

and equality, the result will shake northern society to its very
foundations.[17]

Not all of York's residents were so inclined, as there were many
who literally took the law into their own hands by helping to smug-
gle fugitive slaves northward through the Underground Railroad.
Numerous stations were located throughout the county, with many
of York's most influential citizens providing either overt or covert
support, financially and otherwise. One of the more famous activ-
ists in this organization's early years was a young professor at the
York County Academy, who would later become famous in both
Lincoln's and Johnson's administrations as the most outspoken
Radical Republican in Congress—Thaddeus Stevens.[18]

The majority of York County's citizens, however, did not believe that the slavery issue and its accompanying ramifications
were worth going to war over, a conclusion substantiated by the
results of the 1860 presidential election. Of 11,761 votes cast in the
county, 6,059 went to the Democratic candidates, with only 5,128
going to Lincoln (Bell of the Constitutional Union Party received
562 votes), giving the Democrats the decided edge, with almost 52
percent of the county's popular vote.[19] But the members of York
County's Republican "Wide-Awake" clubs were not to be disappointed, as Lincoln carried Pennsylvania by more than 90,000
votes, and won fifty-three of the state's sixty-five counties. Besides losing the presidency to the Republicans in November, the
Democrats failed a month earlier when they lost the Pennsylvania
governorship to Andrew G. Curtin, with York County again on
the losing side.[20]

Even after the election of Lincoln and the subsequent secession of the Deep South, many residents still favored a compromise to avert a civil war. On February 16, 1861, members of the
Democratic County Committee met in York to approve the action
of the Democratic State Central Committee, which favored adop-
tion of either the Crittenden or Guthrie Compromise or "any fair

and equable compromise, that is satisfactory to our sister border slave-holding states." This conciliatory action, they hoped, might convince the seceding states to reconsider.[21]

The Democratic meeting came one month after an earlier "Union Meeting," when "a large number of the citizens of . . . [York] Borough and County had assembled in the Court House [on Jan. 8] . . . , for the purpose of considering the present condition of our National affairs." During this meeting, the members of the committee (most of whom probably were Republicans) approved of the Crittenden Compromise but further resolved to "support . . . the National administration in vindicating the Constitution, in enforcing the laws . . . [to] deny the right of any State to secede at pleasure from this Union, and to carry with it the property of the United States within its limit."[22]

In the Democratic meeting a month later, the loyal party members were careful not to condemn secession, while putting the fault squarely on the shoulders of the Republicans:

> The Republican party, by disregarding the warning voice of Washington, and the voice of reason and patriotism against sectional parties by electing sectional candidates, on a sectional platform, to the highest office in the Republic, and by declaring for "an irrepressible conflict," has filled the minds of the people of the South with excitement and alarm, driven them to desperation, and caused them to embrace the desperate alternative of abandoning the Union, and forming a new government for their protection.[23]

This sort of debate would go on for another two months in York County, with the Democrats seeking compromise and peace at any price. York's Republicans, however, were not as worried about trying to soothe the South's ruffled feathers, and they openly condemned any state that seceded. Even when secessionists began seizing United States forts and arsenals in the South, York County's Democratic newspapers tried to justify and play down these hostile actions:

Until the pending negotiations going on in Congress, and in the Peace Convention . . . have ended, and the people of the North have decided upon what is to be done in the present emergency, it makes very little difference who holds possession of the forts and arsenals. They were built to defend the country from foreign aggression, and as long as they are in the hands of the Southern people they are in possession of the members of one family. It is all nonsense, therefore, to talk of resorting to coercion for their recovery until it is decided by the voters of the Northern States whether there is really to be a Union or not. Until the question is settled the forts and arsenals will do very well where they are.[24]

On April 12, 1861, when Fort Sumter was taken by force of arms, interparty bickering would be put aside, at least for a short time, as the inhabitants of York County prepared to send their sons to war.

The initial euphoria soon wore off. Casualty lists became longer, and York County soldiers contributed to those long lists. A U.S. Army general hospital was established on the town commons in the Borough of York, with its amputee patients a visible reminder to civilians that the Civil War was not going to be short and relatively sterile. By the summer of 1862, the northern states resorted to a militia draft because young men were not as willing to enlist as they had been in the spring of 1861. Making matters even worse, northern victories in the eastern theater were few and far between. By June 1863, York County residents were becoming accustomed to the two-year conflict with no end in sight and the prospect of a Confederate victory seeming more likely every day. County newspapers were hurling epithets at one another on a regular basis, with the Democratic organs blaming the war on the "Black Republicans" and the Republican papers slinging mud-loaded euphemisms at the "Copperheads." In January 1863, the pride of the county, York native Maj. Gen. William B. Franklin was relieved of his command in the Army of the Potomac in the flurry of events surrounding the Fredericksburg fiasco and the removal of Ambrose Burnside as its commander. Another Union disaster at the Battle of Chancellorsville only added to the gloom, with the crippled remnants of what had once been healthy, young Union soldiers arriving by the trainload for treatment at York's military hospital. To cap it off was Lincoln's announcement of a new, federal conscription law, which would only supply more cannon fodder for what looked like a hopeless situation.

Yet the people of York were doing their part on behalf of the war effort. Calls for charity by the Ladies' Soldiers' Aid Society in the weekly newspapers usually met with success, with money, clothing, toilet articles, and food items among the most common donations.[25] A soldier from Allentown who was passing through York with the other members of the 128th Pennsylvania Volunteer Infantry in August 1862 commented on the goodwill and patriotism of the townsfolk of York. To his family, he wrote that the citizens "gave three cheers for us," and he seemed elated that "many a young fair lady could be seen standing [in her] door with the stars and stripes in her hand." Before departing York for Baltimore, the 128th was "marched to the Soldiers' Relief Association," where, according to this young soldier, "we took breakfast which was the finest received since we left home."[26]

After Second Bull Run and Antietam in the late summer of 1862, the secretary of war issued urgent requests for volunteer surgeons to proceed to the battlefields to help minister to the wounded, and on each occasion a number of county physicians answered the call.[27] York's "Soldier's Relief Fund," organized at the beginning of the war, continued to solicit donations in an effort to care for widows, orphans, and crippled soldiers, as well as to provide for the welfare of the families of soldiers who still were serving. The various communities also showed pride in their fighting men by publishing in the newspapers the names of soldiers from their townships or boroughs who already were in the service of their country, or by honoring them upon their return to York with parades, speeches, and banquets.

Many of York's businesses were profiting from the war by selling goods directly to the government or by taking advantage of the constant flow of troops passing through York on their way south. The mills of P. A. & S. Small supplied large quantities of flour to the government throughout the war, and advertisements in the weekly newspapers attest to the numerous businesses, not to mention taverns, that were selling their wares or services to the Union troops.[28] For example, the classified section of the November 4, 1862, issue of the *York Gazette* included advertisements ranging from attorneys soliciting military pension claims services to a store selling "MILITARY GOODS! such as War Blankets, Woolen Over-Shirts, Under-Shirts, Drawers, Blouses, Caps, &c., &c." In addition to these ads were one for a substitute agent, one hawking war bonds, and one taking subscriptions (although a bit prematurely) for a book titled *The Pictorial History of the War for the Union.*

The white male citizens also served their country in other ways. During the invasion scare of 1862, eight emergency companies of infantry, one of cavalry, and one battery of artillery were organized to meet the threat, which never materialized.[29] In addition to these companies, home guards and border guards were organized at the beginning of the war and drilled sporadically throughout, just in case an emergency might arise. These units, however, were not even considered organized militia, and the men who numbered among their rank and file most likely felt self-assured that the chances they would ever see action were slim. Any real fighting by York County's residents would be done by members of the volunteer and regular units that comprised the Union army, and two years into the war most men who wanted to fight already had enlisted.

By June 1863, few county residents had been touched, let alone hurt, by the war. Certainly wartime inflation had cut into most people's pocketbooks. The families that had sent their sons or husbands off to the battlefields only to have them never return or come home as invalids were acutely aware of the conflict's costs. But to the majority of Yorkers, the war was becoming a real nuisance, like a burr under the saddle, especially now that the Democratic papers kept harping that ever since the Emancipation Proclamation the real goal of the conflict had become freeing the slaves.

Actual hostilities, however, would touch almost every York County resident personally in the summer of 1863, for the Army of Northern Virginia was bringing it right into their own kitchen gardens and farmyards. On the morning of June 27 at roughly ten o'clock, a Hanover farmer ran through his town yelling, "The enemy will soon be here. They are now in McSherrystown."[30] Moments later the vanguard of Gen. Jubal Early's forces entered Hanover, and for the first time in its history, York County was being invaded by an armed enemy.

Rumors that the rebel forces were approaching had been circulating through the county for days, and many of its residents had resorted to burying their household treasures in their gardens or yards to prevent them from being confiscated by the Confederates. Governor Curtin had ordered the residents of York and neighboring counties to remove their horses, cattle, and valuables to the eastern side of the Susquehanna River so they would not fall into rebel hands, and the county's banks followed suit by transferring their money and important documents to Philadelphia and New York. By then, many of the citizens had packed up and left for safer areas.[31] Those who did not heed Curtin's warning learned the hard way. One Confederate soldier later wrote, "We gave the old dutch in Penn. fits. Our army left a mark everywhere it went. Horses, cattle, sheep, hogs, chickens, spring houses suffered alike. They cried peace, peace most beautifully everywhere we went."[32]

Military preparations to resist the enemy, and particularly the defense of the bridge over the Susquehanna at Wrightsville fell under the jurisdiction of the newly created Department of the Susquehanna, under the command of Maj. Gen. Darius N. Couch.[33] Other than a few entrenchments and rifle pits thrown up near Wrightsville, few actions were taken by the York County citizenry or Couch's Department to enable them to actively resist the Confederates on the western side of the river. In a June 15 letter to his brother, York resident James Latimer summarized the minutes of a borough meeting that was held that evening "to devise measures for the defense of the town and respond to the very earnest call for volunteers which Governor Curtin telegraphed over today." Latimer opined, "Nothing definite was done, and it is likely nothing will be done."[34] A few days later, he disgustedly reported, "There is not the least excitement here. No one is alarmed. Everyone seems indifferent as if there were no rebels within a thousand miles."[35]

As it turned out, little *was* done to obstruct the Confederate advance, and the southern forces succeeded in destroying portions of the Northern Central Railroad, cutting telegraph lines, and almost capturing the bridge at Wrightsville before militiamen assigned to the Department of the Susquehanna put the torch to it. There was a minor skirmish at Wrightsville between Brig. Gen. John B. Gordon's Confederates and Yankee militiamen on June 28 prior to the bridge being burned, and Hanover was the scene of a cavalry fight between Brig. Gen. Judson Kilpatrick's Union troopers and Maj. Gen. Jeb Stuart's rebel cavalrymen on June 30, but this is all the actual fighting that York County would see.[36]

York County, and specifically the borough of York, was to suffer a more ignominious but less devastating fate than neighboring Adams County and its county seat, Gettysburg. Although York County would escape the terror of two huge armies locked in combat and all its accompanying horrors, it would be unable to escape the occupation of its soil by Confederate troops who took any provisions that they needed (sometimes paying for them in worthless Confederate currency) before marching on to meet the Army of the Potomac. The sight of the rebels trooping through the county while confiscating livestock and supplies without anyone attempting to stop them was insulting to many county residents and would not be lived down for years to come.[37] A few days before the Confederates entered York, Latimer wrote,

> There is the most extra-ordinary apathy with regard to this invasion. If the information we have is reliable we may have an attack on Harrisburg in a day or two, and yet nothing is being

Major General William B. Franklin, former commander of the Sixth Corps, Army of the Potomac. He graduated from West Point in 1843, first in his class. Unfairly blamed for the Union defeat at Fredericksburg in December 1862, he subsequently was relieved of command and was at his home in York awaiting orders during the Confederate invasion. He wisely evacuated to Philadelphia rather than risk capture. (Library of Congress)

done here. We have sent *one* Company. I have put my name down to another but it fell through. If men won't go to the defense of their own State they don't deserve to be called patriots. I am ashamed of myself and my town.[38]

Even an anonymous appeal by General Franklin, home on leave awaiting orders after his relief from the Army of the Potomac, did little to motivate the men of the county to answer the call to arms.[39] What, however, could be done? How could a few home guards and militiamen stop an enemy army that rarely was defeated in battle? Apparently, this attitude was reflective of most of the county residents, who opted to stay in their homes, relying on the mercy of the Confederate soldiers for their safety rather than fleeing across the river. Additionally, the strong Democrat tradition in the county probably had some influence on many of the citizens, who by this phase of the war were not all that convinced that the Union was worth fighting for anymore.

When portions of the Army of Northern Virginia finally did enter the county, its residents, apathetic as they were, were no doubt expecting the worst to happen. As it turned out, the Confederate soldiers were, for the most part, well behaved, and the wanton destruction of private property, which was so prevalent in Virginia when Union soldiers entered a town, did not occur. The rebels' restrained behavior can be directly attributed to General Lee's issue of General Orders No. 72, which stated: "No private property shall be injured or destroyed by any person belonging to or connected with the army, or taken, excepting by the officers hereinafter designated."[40] On June 27, Lee followed up this order with General Orders No. 73, which was a sermonlike reminder to his men of what he expected of them:

> It must be remembered that we make war only upon armed men, and that we cannot take vengeance for the wrongs our people have suffered without lowering ourselves in the eyes of all whose abhorrence has been excited by the atrocities of our enemies, and offending against Him to whom vengeance belongeth, without whose favor and support our efforts must all prove in vain.[41]

As the Confederates approached the town of York on June 26, the Committee of Safety held a meeting and determined that because of the enemy's overwhelming strength, the town would offer no resistance. The *York Gazette* reported that "Chief Burgess Small and . . . members of the Committee . . . went out to meet the [Confederate] advance, to inform them of the decision of the Committee, and ask the protection of the private property and the unarmed citizens." They were met by General Gordon of Jubal Early's Division, the former assuring them that their request would be honored.[42] One of the invaders, Capt. William Seymour of the famed "Louisiana Tigers" recalled,

> The surrounding country was in a high state of cultivation, and from our camp presented a beautiful appearance with its immense fields of golden grain that flashed in the sunlight—dotted

here and there with neat little cottages and large substantially built barns that were literally bursting with wheat, oats, & corn. Most of the barns in this section are larger and more finely built than the dwellings of the farmers; the Dutch lords of the soil invariably bestow more care and attention on their crops and stock than they do on their families.[43]

When the main body of Confederates entered the town on the twenty-eighth, most of the civilians decided to come out on the streets to gawk, while a minority of the residents thought it was wiser to remain indoors. James Latimer observed, "The whole town, men, women & children were on Main St. when the Rebs came in. People turned out en masse to receive them. There was no expression of sympathy as they marched thro' town except in a very few instances."[44] Young Cassandra Small, who was living with her parents in York at the time of the invasion, described the events in a letter to her friend: "Sunday morning Mother, Mary and I dressed for church; all the rest expected to stay at home. Just then the bells rang, the cry was heard, 'They are coming!' Oh, Lissy, what did we feel like? Humiliated! disgraced! Men who don't often weep, wept then. They came with loud music, flags flying." Continuing, she wrote,

> Then came General Gordon's [Brigade]; they halted in the square and took down our flag . . . , but didn't put one of their own up. . . . Then they came up the street; General Gordon stopped his horse at our door, came up to the pavement and said, 'Ladies, I have a word to say. I suppose you think me a pretty rough looking man, but when I am shaved and dressed, my wife considers me a very good looking fellow. I want to say to you we have not come among you to pursue the same warfare your men did in our country. You need not have any fear of us, whilst we are in your midst. You are just as safe as though we are a thousand miles away. That is all I have to say.' He bowed and turning his horse rode away.[45]

Latimer commented, "Some of the Copperheads were very much alarmed . . . [while] others gave them all the aid and comfort in their power." He then related that

> Reb. officers said that they had many sympathizers here; that they could get any information they wanted. One Copperhead, hearing a Union man asked by an officer for a map of York Co. which was of course refused, volunteered to take him to his house and give him a map. . . . I think the Rebel visit to this county will have a wholesome effect on the Copperheads. The Rebs made no distinction. The worst Copperhead Townships such as the Codoruses and Dover suffered most heavily in horses. Men who joined the "K.G.C." [Knights of the Golden Circle] & paid their dollars to learn the signs which were to save their property, found them of no avail.[46]

Cassandra Small also noted how some of the civilians openly fraternized with the enemy and when writing to her friend about their behavior said, "There will now be a dividing line drawn here." Of the ladies whom she saw waving handkerchiefs and collecting Confederate uniform buttons she wrote, "they will never be recognized again."[47]

The Confederates also exacted a requisition for food, clothing, shoes, and $100,000 in Union greenbacks. The *Gazette* reported that "every effort was made to fill the requisition," out of the fear, no doubt, that Early would take what he wanted anyway and then destroy the town for spite.[48] Latimer wrote that "Ward Committees were appointed to collect money, P. A. & S. Small furnished the groceries and flour, and the hatters and shoemakers were called on for the shoes and hats." According to Latimer, this was done "with the understanding that the Boro' would assume the debt & repay the money & pay for the supplies."[49]

The Committee of Safety scraped together all of the supplies and provisions that could be obtained but only came up with a little more than $28,000. The *Gazette* acknowledged that the committee "had done the best in their powers to do, [and] General Early signified his satisfaction and agreed to accept their offer."[50] The Confederates also destroyed portions of the railroad yard and some of the rolling stock, but generally little damage was done within the borough.[51] Cassandra Small was distressed by the condition that the Confederates had left the partially evacuated military hospital, writing, "Our beautiful hospital! I would be ashamed to tell you all they did there."[52]

Throughout the county, the Confederate invasion had affected most of the residents in one way or another. Livestock and supplies had been confiscated from many of the farmers, buildings in Wrightsville and Hanover had been damaged from the skirmishing, and most residents had been scared out of their wits, if nothing else. On the morning of June 30, Early and his command departed York, having received orders the day before to rejoin the rest of the Army of Northern Virginia. They left hurriedly because the Army of the Potomac had crossed the Potomac River and was now in a position to threaten the main Confederate force. Stuart's Confederate cavalry engaged Union horse soldiers in Hanover on the same day, but as of July 1 the eyes of the nation would no longer be focusing on York County. They turned instead to neighboring Adams County.

During the great battle at Gettysburg, Latimer reported that the "cannonading could be heard here."[53] York's military hospital was quickly reopened and began receiving hundreds of crippled soldiers from the battle—so many that tents had to be erected to accommodate them.[54] Hanover also became the site of three small military hospitals, with townswomen tending to the wounded and furnishing the hospitals with food and supplies. That little town, situated fourteen miles from Gettysburg, thus experienced the tribulations of the battle even more than York. According to the *Hanover Spectator*,

> The terrible cannonading at the series of Battles near Gettysburg, was heard with awful distinctness in this place, as also was the

Major General Jubal Early, commanding a division in Ewell's
Corps. (Library of Congress)

musketry firing. The ground was fairly shaken by the concussion, and the whole country for miles around was filled with the terrible sounds of warlike strife. Some persons even assert that in the evening the flight of the shells, thrown by the contending armies, could be distinctly traced in their course through the air.[55]

Curious York citizens ventured to the battlefield after the departure of Lee's army, and the macabre scenes they witnessed only added to their distaste for war that the recent invasion had already ingrained in them. Cassandra Small wrote that some of York's women went to the battlefield to serve as nurses, and hundreds of wagons filled with provisions were sent to Gettysburg for the wounded soldiers and the hapless townspeople.[56] A former York police chief, Samuel Wehring, made the trip to the Gettysburg and while collecting firearms from the field was accidentally killed when one of his battle trophies discharged. In eastern York County, tragedy struck closer to home. A resident of East Prospect brought home a Confederate artillery projectile left over from the

Wrightsville skirmish. His two children played with the shell and rolled it into the fireplace where it exploded, mortally wounding them both.[57]

The Confederate incursion and the Battle of Gettysburg had a profound effect on York County's citizens, with some even becoming more determined to defeat the Confederacy, while others were convinced that the slaughter should be stopped regardless of the Union's plight. The invasion created more issues and animosities for Copperheads and Black Republicans to quarrel about and gave young men additional reasons to either enlist or evade. To a farmer who had his livestock or provisions commandeered, the war might have taken on a character of personal revenge, or it might have convinced him that he had suffered enough from the war's depredations, and to ask him or his sons to risk their lives in combat was requesting too much. Likewise, the restrained conduct of the Confederate invaders might have reinforced an attitude that the southern boys were not that bad after all; if they really wanted to leave the Union, why not allow them? However, the humiliation of having the national flag disgraced and their soil occupied by an armed enemy was more than others could stand, and it made them all the more anxious to enlist and defeat the rebellion. The war was far from over, and these men would get their chance.

There would be one more invasion scare, when in 1864 a raid by Jubal Early's force would make it all the way to Chambersburg, which was burned, and to Hagerstown and Frederick, Maryland, and even the outskirts of the nation's capital, but nothing during the entire war could compare to the events of the summer of 1863. A York man who experienced the events of that short period of time later wrote, "No one but those who were eyewitnesses to the occupation of York can have any conception of the extent of anxiety and suspense of our people during the two days of occupation."[58]

3

Union Lifeline

The Army of the Potomac's Logisticians in

the Gettysburg Campaign

NINETEENTH-CENTURY MILITARY theorist Baron Antoine Henri Jomini defined logistics as "the practical art of moving armies." He submitted that logistics also included "providing for the successive arrival of convoys of supplies . . . [and] establishing and organizing . . . lines of supplies." In other words, logistics was defined as the "practical art of moving armies and keeping them supplied."[1] As important as logistical operations are to a successful military campaign, there have been very few studies that focus on this neglected aspect of military history. Successful logistical operations should be so well planned and calculated that the re-supply of an army while it is on campaign will seem routine and uneventful. Unfortunately, books about logistical operations do not necessarily make for interesting reading, so little has been written on this subject—especially in the cases where logisticians have done their jobs well. This is true even in the field of Civil War scholarship, where almost everything has been studied several times over. Most of the inquiries into this topic are concerned with operational or strategic logistics, or the movement of troops and supplies within a given theater of war or between theaters.

Few Civil War studies focus on tactical logistics, defined as the movement and supply of troops in a given campaign or battle.[2]

An examination of logistical operations during the Gettysburg campaign could fill an entire lengthy volume when one considers the magnitude of moving and supplying the 163,000 soldiers who comprised the two participating armies. This essay, therefore, merely will function as a primer to familiarize students of the war with the missions and staff functions of logisticians serving the field armies, using the Army of the Potomac's logisticians as a case study. The three staff functions examined are the roles of the quartermaster general, the commissary of subsistence, and the chief ordnance officer.

Before jumping ahead to the summer of 1863, it first is necessary to understand the historical background of the U.S. Army's supply departments. When the Rebellion began in the spring of 1861, the army departments responsible for arming, supplying, moving, and feeding U.S. soldiers found themselves in a terrible predicament. Not only were the Quartermaster, Subsistence, and Ordnance Departments ill-prepared for a large-scale conflict, these agencies also suffered the loss of some key officers who resigned to join the Confederacy.

The Quartermaster Department, created in 1812, was responsible for land and water transportation; billeting and tentage; providing uniform items, other clothing, and shoes; and procuring horses, mules, and forage. In 1861 the department had an authorized strength of thirty-seven officers and seven military storekeepers. Almost one-fourth of the department's officers, including the quartermaster general, Brig. Gen. Joseph E. Johnston, resigned to cast their lot with the South.[3]

The Subsistence Department had similar difficulties. Organized in 1818 and charged with feeding the troops, the department had an authorized strength of only twelve officers when the war began. Secession brought the immediate resignation of four officers, a loss of one-third of the department. Congress remedied the situation by passing legislation in August 1861 that added twelve more officer positions, for a total of twenty-four. This was still too small of an officer corps to oversee the procurement and issue of food for hundreds of thousands of men, so a year and a half later the department again was enlarged to twenty-nine officers, still only a modest increase.[4]

The Ordnance Department probably had the most difficult assignment of the three logistical departments in 1861: it was responsible for the manufacture and procurement of small arms and edged weapons; field-, garrison- and siege-artillery; ammunition; and accoutrements (scabbards, cartridge boxes, et cetera) used by the land forces. In addition, the department was responsible for storage and accountability of ordnance supplies at all Federal arsenals, for maintaining those weapons once they were with the field armies, and for issuing and transporting the ammunition. Complicating matters was the fact that the U.S. government owned only two small-arms manufacturing facilities when the war began. The U.S. Armory at Harpers Ferry was captured immediately by Confederate forces and its machinery dismantled and transported south, leaving the Springfield Armory as the lone government-owned small-arms–producing facility in the Union, thus making it necessary for the Ordnance Department to contract with private gun-makers both at home and abroad. The end result was that many different makes and calibers of small arms saw service in the Union army for the first two years of the conflict. Artillery, accoutrements, and ammunition were manufactured at several government-owned facilities, among them Allegheny Arsenal in Pittsburgh; Watervliet Arsenal, near Albany, New York; Frankford Arsenal in Philadelphia; Rock Island Arsenal, on an island in the Mississippi River between Illinois and Iowa; and Watertown Arsenal, Watertown, New York. The Ordnance Corps originally had been part of the Corps of Artillery, but in 1832 Congress passed legislation to make it an autonomous department. Still, the department had only forty-one officers when the conflict began.[5]

Some, like Benjamin Huger, would resign to join the Confederate army, while others, such as Oliver Otis Howard and Jesse Reno, would take field commands in the Union army.

Although the supply departments of the U.S. Army were ill-prepared and undermanned before the outbreak of hostilities, the men leading them quickly would have to overcome any obstacles and adapt to the pressing needs of the service once the shooting began. Most of the logistical officers of the Regular Army were West Point graduates who had several years, if not decades, of experience in their respective specialties. The rapid expansion of the Union army in 1861, however, would mean that untried and inexperienced volunteers would fill the ranks of the Quartermaster, Ordnance, and Subsistence departments for the war's duration.

By the late spring of 1863, when the Army of Northern Virginia embarked on its second invasion of the North, the logistical officers of the Army of the Potomac had gained a wealth of experience since the opening salvos two years earlier. During the time since First Manassas, the officers and enlisted men of the three supply departments had moved the entire Army of the Potomac to the Virginia Peninsula and back again, they had armed the soldiers with adequate small arms and artillery—albeit of many different types and calibers—and they had supplied the troops by water, rail, and overland transportation. (Rail transport was the responsibility of the director of military railroads, initially a civilian-run operation, but the Quartermaster Department was responsible for all procurement activities of that organization.[6])

The Army of the Potomac's logisticians had learned valuable lessons about locating forward supply depots too close to the front lines, such as at Savage's Station, just east of Richmond. There, on the Richmond and York River Railroad during the Seven Days' Battles the year before, hundreds of thousands of dollars in army supplies were torched, lest they be captured by the advancing Confederates.[7] During that same campaign, the logisticians learned the hard way about the proper organization

Major General Montgomery Meigs, quartermaster general of the Union armies. (Library of Congress)

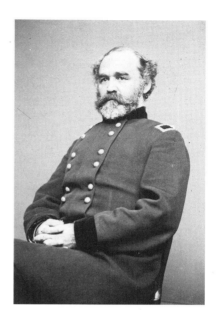

and coordination of wagon train movements, for when Maj. Gen. George B. McClellan ordered the change of his army's supply base from the York to the James River, confusion reigned, and it was every wagon-train master for himself. The result of the haphazard movement from the supply base at White House on the York River, to Harrison's Landing on the James, was the loss of almost half of the Army of the Potomac's five thousand wagons.[8]

By the third summer of the war, the men responsible for supplying, arming, and moving the Army of the Potomac had become seasoned veterans. Army regulations had streamlined to some extent the troops' baggage trains, which now were organized, moved by schedule, and left far to the rear when a battle was imminent. In addition, the standardization of ammunition calibers finally was bearing fruit, and the soldiers normally were well clothed and fed. The men in Washington charged with overseeing these functions also had come a long way since 1861. The most prominent was Quartermaster General Montgomery C. Meigs. Meigs had not been a quartermaster before the war but had served his entire career in the Corps of Engineers. For much of the previous decade, he had been assigned with the rank of captain as the chief engineer in charge of the construction of the new Capitol dome in Washington. The unscrupulous secretary of war, John B. Floyd, relieved him of this position in 1859, but after Abraham Lincoln took office, he was appointed the quartermaster general. Meigs was a brilliant engineer and extremely detail-oriented. His aggressive management of the Quartermaster Department's operations and his strong belief in the Union were the driving factors behind his success.[9]

When the war began, the head of the Subsistence Department was Col. George Gibson, an old man who had been an invalid for many years. Running the day-to-day operations of the department was Lt. Col. Joseph P. Taylor, who became the commissary general of subsistence when Gibson died in September 1861. (Joe Taylor was the son of late president Zachary Taylor and brother of Confederate general Richard Taylor.) The commissary general's mission was as daunting as the tasks charged to Montgomery Meigs. Unlike European wars, where the troops generally were expected to live off the land, most food for the Union forces was purchased in the major metropolitan areas of the North and then packed and shipped to field depots. From there the foodstuffs were issued to the commissary officers of the field armies and then transported to the troops. The exception to this procedure was the procurement of flour and beef, both commodities usually being purchased in the areas where the armies were operating. Much of the fresh beef was transported in herds that followed the forces in the field, and then slaughtered as needed.[10]

The chief of ordnance when the war began was another elderly gentleman, Col. Henry Knox Craig, then seventy years of age. Deemed unsuitable to manage the wartime demands that would be placed on the department, he was replaced in April 1861 by Lt. Col. James W. Ripley, who at sixty-seven was no young man himself. Yet Ripley was equal to the assignment, and he certainly had the experience to run the department, having previously served in several important ordnance positions including stints as commander of Watertown Arsenal and Springfield Armory. His most important duty would be to properly arm the hundreds of thousands of men entering the Union army. Although some historians have greatly criticized the Ordnance Department for failing to arm the troops with the most modern weapons then available, a closer examination reveals that Ripley and his officers accomplished a monumental task just ensuring that most of the front-line troops were armed with rifled muskets, regardless of their make, caliber, or the end of the barrel from which they were loaded. By 1863, domestic production of first-quality rifled muskets had made it possible to begin replacement of all but the best European-made arms, such as the Enfield, then in the hands of the troops.[11]

Nonetheless, the Army of the Potomac's infantrymen carried a variety of different long arms onto the field of battle at Gettysburg, including .54, .577, .58, and .69 caliber muskets, and a few regiments carried breech-loading Sharps rifles. (The .577 and .58 caliber were interchangeable, and most of the .69 caliber weapons were smoothbores.) Cavalry troopers were armed primarily with .52 caliber Sharps carbines, although a few other makes and calibers could be found. The horse soldiers also were armed with .44 or .36 caliber single-action pistols. Union artillery was limited to "twelve-pounder" smooth-bore cannon that fired spherical ammunition, three-inch rifled pieces that fired elongated conoidal ammunition, and some larger rifled pieces.[12] The greater the variety of ammunition required, the more wagons were required to haul it (only one type of ammunition was authorized per wagon), and the greater the chance that the wrong caliber of ammunition would be issued during the heat of battle.

All three supply departments had experienced problems with crooked contractors and corrupt politicians early in the war, which was exacerbated in part by a lack of qualified officers who could stop the dishonesty and fraud. Legislation expanding the departments remedied the situation somewhat, but the small number of Regular Army officers filling critical positions hampered the

Brigadier General Rufus Ingalls, chief quartermaster of the Army of the Potomac. (Library of Congress)

efficiency of the logistical departments for the war's duration. Since ordnance, quartermaster, and subsistence officers also were authorized on army, corps, division, and sometimes brigade and regimental staffs, it became obvious there would not be enough qualified officers to go around. Thus, these staff positions usually were filled by line officers, who normally were volunteers themselves. When officers were placed in logistical staff positions but were not assigned to the respective supply departments, they were designated as "acting," such as "acting assistant quartermaster" or "acting commissary of subsistence." The majority of the logistical officers in the Army of the Potomac fit this bill.

In the summer of 1863, however, the three chief logisticians of the Army of the Potomac were Regular Army officers holding commissions in their respective departments, and they all had a good deal of field experience in their areas of expertise. Key among the Army of the Potomac's logisticians was its quartermaster general, Brig. Gen. Rufus Ingalls, an 1843 graduate of West Point and a classmate of U. S. Grant. A Maine native, Ingalls originally was commissioned a dragoon officer and saw service during the Mexican War. He became a quartermaster in 1848, so by the time of the Civil War he had thirteen years of experience under his belt.[13] Ingalls was promoted to quartermaster general of the Army of the Potomac at the close of the Peninsula campaign in the summer of 1862. He was a little more than a month away from his forty-fourth birthday when the Battle of Gettysburg was fought.[14]

The chief commissary of subsistence was Col. Henry F. Clarke of Pennsylvania. Like Ingalls, Clarke was an 1843 graduate of West Point. He finished twelfth in the class of 1843, ahead of both Ingalls and Grant. His friends gave him the nickname "Ruddy," apparently because of his rugged complexion. He was commissioned in the artillery and served in the 2d U.S. Artillery in Mexico, where he was wounded in action and brevetted for gallantry.[15] After the Mexican War, he was assigned as a mathematics professor at West Point, where he formed close friendships with future Union generals George McClellan, William Franklin, and Fitz John Porter, as well as future Confederate general Dabney Maury.[16] Clarke transferred from the artillery to the Subsistence Department in 1857 and served as the chief commissary of subsistence for the Mormon Expedition that same year. In 1861, he married the daughter of Joseph Taylor, the commissary general of subsistence of the U.S. Army. She also was the granddaughter of the late President Zachary Taylor. Clarke became the chief commissary of subsistence for the Army of the Potomac when his friend McClellan took command in the summer of 1861.[17] Ruddy Clarke was forty-two years of age in the summer of 1863.

Capt. Daniel Webster Flagler was the Army of the Potomac's chief ordnance officer. A native of New York State, he graduated from the U.S. Military Academy in June 1861 and was commissioned directly into the Ordnance Corps. He served as an acting aide-de-camp to Col. David Hunter at the first battle of Bull Run and subsequently became an aide to Brig. Gen. Irvin McDowell, a position he held from the end of July until December 1861. During

Captain Daniel Flagler, chief ordnance officer of the Army of the Potomac. (Gettysburg National Military Park)

Maj. Gen. Ambrose Burnside's expedition to the North Carolina coast, Flagler was assigned as the chief ordnance officer for the entire operation. When Burnside's command joined the Army of the Potomac in the late summer of 1862, Flagler served as an assistant ordnance officer and aide-de-camp on Burnside's staff and became the Army of the Potomac's chief ordnance officer on November 21, 1862, when Burnside was elevated to its command.[18] At age twenty-eight, Captain Flagler was the youngest of that army's three supply chiefs.

Ingalls, Clarke, and Flagler were the primary staff officers of their respective logistical functions in the Army of the Potomac, but they could not possibly supply and move the army by themselves. They were assisted by officers and enlisted men filling similar staff positions all the way from corps down to regimental level. The staff officers in the echelons below army level—normally "acting commissaries," "acting quartermasters," and "acting ordnance officers"—consolidated requests from their subordinate units, ensured the paperwork was filled out properly, and forwarded the requests to the next higher command. When the requisitions were filled, these men ensured that the correct number and type of supplies were picked up, transported, and issued to their subordinate commands. For example, the chief commissary of subsistence for the First Division of V Corps would have provided staff supervision for the requisition, transportation, and issue of food for the three brigades assigned to his division. The brigade chief commissaries had similar responsibilities and provided staff supervision of the regimental quartermasters. This setup was similar for the chief quartermasters, but ordnance officers were not authorized any lower than division-level staffs.

Since the regiment was the basic building block of the army's organizations, most of the hands-on logistical work occurred at the regimental level. In the majority of instances, the lieutenants serving in these logistical functions were line officers of their respective branches (i.e., cavalry, infantry, or artillery). At the regimental level, the quartermaster also served as the commissary officer, but he was assisted by a quartermaster sergeant and a commissary sergeant. Ordnance officers were not authorized at the brigade and regimental level, but most regiments were authorized an ordnance sergeant who issued weapons and ammunition and made minor repairs on his unit's small arms. Still, many brigade and regimental commanders chose to have an officer oversee their units' ordnance supply and transportation, so they appointed a line officer to this position as an extra duty. At the company level, each infantry unit was authorized a wagoner; and each cavalry company was authorized two farriers, one saddler, one quartermaster sergeant, one commissary sergeant, and two teamsters. Each artillery battery was authorized a quartermaster sergeant, two to six artificers (repairmen), and a wagoner.[19]

During the Chancellorsville campaign in the spring of 1863, the main supply base of the Army of the Potomac was at Aquia Creek, a tributary of the Potomac River about twenty-five miles southwest of Washington. On June 14, that depot was ordered to be abandoned, but Quartermaster General Meigs was adamant that as much government property should be saved as was possible. During the next three days, more than ten thousand wounded and sick soldiers were moved, as were five hundred carloads of army and railroad property. With its base of supply closed down, the Army of the Potomac marched westward to the Orange and Alexandria Railroad, which became its main line of supply.[20]

Once the high command had determined that Robert E. Lee intended to strike across the Potomac River into Maryland and Pennsylvania, General Ingalls decided to locate the Army of the Potomac's main supply base at Baltimore, an obvious choice with its improved harbor, rail lines, and extensive road network.[21] While the Union force groped northward in search of Lee's army, Ingalls, Clarke, and Flagler saw to it that the vast supplies of the army were stockpiled at strategic locations and several days worth of food, ammunition, forage, and other essentials accompanied the troops. To accomplish this, long wagon trains followed in the rear of the forces or moved on alternate roads. As supplies were consumed, empty wagons were sent back to the forward supply depots for replenishment and returned with full loads. Ingalls later reported, "Our transportation was perfect, and our source of supply same as in . . . [the Maryland] campaign. The officers in our department were thoroughly trained in their duties. It was almost as easy to maneuver the trains as the troops."[22]

The forward depots of the Army of the Potomac during the Gettysburg campaign normally were adjacent to a rail station, since the railroad was the main means of transportation for the bulk supplies. Once enlisted men and civilian laborers had offloaded the freight from the cars, supply officers and civilian clerks of the Quartermaster Department established storage areas, with the different commodities organized by type or category. The officers and clerks maintained a careful inventory so they would know how many days of supply, by item, they had on hand. Issues were made from these stocks to the supply officers assigned to the various corps of the Army. As the stores began to dwindle, telegrams were sent to the respective bureaus in Washington, where orders were issued to release stocks from the main depots, such as Washington Arsenal.

Complicating matters was that the Army of Northern Virginia destroyed railroad bridges, rolling stock, and sections of track as it moved through enemy territory. To the rescue came Herman Haupt, a brilliant engineer who always seemed at his best during crisis situations. A native of Pennsylvania, Haupt graduated from West Point in 1835 along with George Meade, who had taken over command of the Army of the Potomac on June 28, 1863. Haupt resigned his commission shortly after graduation from the academy and went to work for the railroads. He taught civil engineering for a while at Pennsylvania College in Gettysburg and in 1851 published a book titled *The General Theory of Bridge Construction*, considered a significant contribution to the engineering profession at the time. Haupt held several other important positions during the antebellum period, including general superintendent and later chief engineer of the Pennsylvania Railroad, and chief engineer in charge of construction of the Hoosac Tunnel in Massachusetts. He had served the War Department since the spring of 1862, and his accomplishments under incredibly adverse conditions enabled him to acquire almost dictatorial authority over the military operations of the railroads in the eastern theater. One historian of Civil War railroads has said that Haupt

> took pleasure in surmounting difficulties, and was delighted to find a badly tangled situation which he could clear up with his magic touch . . . this humorless man was responsible for developing not only the general principles of railroad supply operation, but also detailed methods of construction and destruction of railroad equipment. To this capable engineer and brilliant organizer is due most of the credit for the successful supply of the Army of the Potomac.[23]

Haupt took control of the situation on June 27 when, in Special Orders No. 286, General in Chief Henry Halleck authorized and directed him "to do whatever he may deem expedient to facilitate the transportation of troops and supplies to aid the armies in the field in Virginia, Maryland, and Pennsylvania."[24]

Even if Haupt could repair the tracks and keep the trains moving, it took wagons, mules, horses, and teamsters to convey the supplies from the forward depots to the army, and the Army of the Potomac had an abundance of wagons during the Gettysburg campaign—3,652, not counting ambulances. Normally, 4 horses or mules were required to pull an army wagon, sometimes 6 animals if the wagon was overloaded, so a *minimum* of 14,608 animals were required just to move the supplies and baggage of the Army of the Potomac.[25] Transportation and supply reforms earlier in the year were supposed to decrease the number of wagons accompanying the army on campaign. General Ingalls estimated that "one wagon to every 50 men ought to carry 7 days' subsistence, forage, ammunition, baggage, hospital stores and everything else"; this was a standard of 20 wagons to every 1,000 men. During the Gettysburg campaign, there was one wagon for every 25.6 men, which translates to roughly 39 wagons per 1,000 men. If the transportation reforms had been adhered to, the Army of the Potomac would have required only 1,870 wagons, 1,782 fewer than were actually employed.[26]

The total number of horses and mules used by the Army of the Potomac at the Battle of Gettysburg has been estimated at 43,303. Ingalls not only was accountable for the horses used by his own trains, he also was responsible for the replacement of horseflesh for the artillery and cavalry.[27] For example, Gen. Alfred Pleasonton's Cavalry Corps had been exceptionally active the month of June, and the wear and tear on the horses was beginning to tell. Ingalls telegraphed Pleasonton on June 26 to inform him that 700 horses were being shod at Alexandria and were ready for issue.[28]

The supply of forage for the beasts of burden was Ingalls's responsibility, too. In the same telegram he sent to Pleasonton on

June 26, Ingalls queried if "fifty wagons, laden with forage" had yet reported to his command. Since these animals normally required 12 pounds of grain and 14 pounds of hay or grass per day, almost 520,000 pounds of feed and 606,000 pounds of hay had to be supplied daily to the Army of the Potomac if the horses were going to remain healthy. Grazing would reduce the amount of feed and forage required to keep the horses fit, but the great number of Union and Confederate horses (more than 72,000 combined) quickly devoured the grasses and other edible vegetation in the area. Comments by the soldiers of the cavalry and artillery about their worn-out horses indicates that the poor brutes probably were not eating well, but it is no wonder that forage constituted the largest single commodity of supply during the Gettysburg campaign.

Those men not lucky enough to ride horses had to walk, and the wet weather and macadamized roads of Maryland and Pennsylvania were taking their toll on the footwear of the Union soldiers. On June 28 Ingalls wired Meigs that at least 10,000 pairs of shoes and socks were needed at Frederick to issue to soldiers as the various corps of the Army of the Potomac passed through the town. Ingalls telegraphed back the same day that the "bootees and socks have been ordered, and will be sent as soon as a safe route and escort can be found." Then Meigs followed with a terse message:

Last fall I gave orders to prevent the sending of wagon trains from this place to Frederick without escort. The situation repeats itself, and gross carelessness and inattention to military rule has this morning cost us 150 wagons and 900 mules, captured by cavalry between this [place—DC] and Rockville.

Yesterday morning a detachment of over 400 cavalry moved from this place to join the army. This morning 150 wagons were sent without escort. Had the cavalry been delayed or the wagons hastened, they could have been protected and saved.

All the cavalry of the Defenses of Washington was swept off by the army, and we are now insulted by burning wagons 3 miles outside of Tennallytown.

Meigs ended his missive with a sarcastic conclusion: "Your communications are now in the hands of General Fitzhugh Lee's brigade."[29]

The troopers of Jeb Stuart's cavalry had captured the wagon train in question as it was making its circuitous ride around the Army of the Potomac. Ingalls shot a telegram back, stating that it was unfortunate that the train was captured, but he did not even know about the Union cavalry force leaving earlier in the day, nor did he feel that any ordinary guard force could have prevented the train's capture.[30] Shortly after sending this message, Ingalls received another telegram, this one from his assistant, Lt. Col. Charles G. Sawtelle, who said he had just seen General Meigs, who in turn told him there was to be an investigation concerning the loss of the wagon train.[31]

Now Ingalls was incensed, to say the least. He telegraphed Meigs that he did not understand how the quartermaster general could hold *him* responsible, since he had nothing to do with the escort.[32] Meigs apparently settled down and became more rational. In a follow-up message to Ingalls he mentioned that 25 teams of mules sent later in the day to Edwards Ferry, Maryland, also had been captured, yet he did not lay fault this time. In fact, he told Ingalls that he was sending 20,000 pairs of shoes and socks instead of the 10,000 pairs ordered, and that 600,000 pounds of grain had been loaded on a train, ready for him if needed.[33]

Ingalls obviously had better things to do than engage in a war of words with the quartermaster general. The Army of Northern Virginia was somewhere in Pennsylvania, and the Union army desperately was trying to ascertain its whereabouts. To prevent the clogging of roads by the Army of the Potomac's supply trains as the forces approached Gettysburg, Ingalls ensured that combat elements always had the right-of-way. He later wrote that "on this campaign . . . our trains, large as they were necessarily, never delayed the march of a column, and, excepting small [arms] ammunition trains, were never seen by our troops. The main trains were conducted on roads to our rear and left without the loss of a wagon." Once the battle opened on July 1, Westminster, Maryland, was selected as the forward supply base of the Army of the Potomac. In his official report written months after the battle, Ingalls described the logistical scenario as the battle unfolded:

> The wagon trains and all *impedimenta* had been assembled at Westminster, on the pike and railroad leading from Baltimore, at a distance of about 25 miles in the rear of the army. No baggage was allowed in front. Officers and men went forward without tents and with only a short supply of food. A portion only of the ammunition wagons and ambulances was brought up to the immediate rear of our lines. This arrangement, which is always made in this army on the eve of battle and marches in the presence of the enemy, enables experienced officers to supply their commands without risking the loss of trains or obstructing roads over which the columns march. Empty wagons can be sent to the rear, and loaded ones, or pack trains, brought up during the night, or at such times and places as will not interfere with the movement of troops.[34]

General Ingalls was not the only supply chief busy on the eve of the battle. At 10:00 P.M. on June 30, from his tent at Headquarters, Army of the Potomac, then located near Taneytown, Maryland, Col. Ruddy Clarke scribbled a hurried report to his father-in-law, Commissary General Joseph Taylor, informing him that the army had seven days of rations on hand except for the cavalry, which apparently had outdistanced its supply wagons. Clarke forecasted his subsistence requirements and requested 300,000 rations of hard bread, coffee, and sugar; 100,000 rations of pork or bacon; 100,000 rations of candles; 150,000 rations of salt; and 50,000 rations of soap be loaded on rail cars in Washington or Baltimore and kept ready to be sent forward. He stipulated that if hard bread could not be supplied, then flour must be substituted and demanded that the coffee was to be roasted and ground. He then told his chief that one of his assistants had been sent to the main supply base at Baltimore to arrange matters for the army's future food supply, but that he had not yet arrived, the Army of Northern Virginia having destroyed a section of the Baltimore & Ohio Railroad on which his assistant was traveling. After informing the commissary general that the Army of the Potomac "was well off for beef cattle" which were following in herds behind the supply trains, Clarke concluded, "It is necessary I should be kept informed of the arrangement made by the [Subsistence] Dept. to supply this army in so far as I have requested and otherwise."[35] The situation rapidly changed. Two and a half hours later, at 12:30 A.M. on July 1, Clarke sent an urgent telegram to Taylor, which read, "Send three hundred thousand (300,000) marching rations to Union Bridge on the Westminster Rail Road as soon as possible."[36] Battle was imminent.

Captain Flagler, the chief ordnance officer of the Army of the Potomac, sent few messages back to Washington during this time period. Since the infantry and artillery had not been engaged for several weeks, enough ammunition was on hand for any imminent confrontation. The cavalry had been in contact with the enemy several times in June, but the status of their ammunition supply on the eve of the Battle of Gettysburg is not known. General Orders No. 20, Headquarters, Army of the Potomac, dated March 25, 1863, dictated that infantry divisions must constantly have on hand 140 rounds per man, and cavalry must have 100 rounds carbine and 40 rounds pistol ammunition per man. Both of these figures included the rounds that soldiers carried in their cartridge boxes. For the artillery, 250 rounds per gun were required to be on hand, including what was carried in the limber's ammunition chest.

These same general orders dictated that the wagons carrying a division's reserve ammunition would be marked by a six-inch-wide horizontal stripe painted on the canvas. Artillery ammunition had a red stripe, cavalry a yellow stripe, and infantry light blue. To prevent confusion in a combat situation, the wagons had to be "distinctly marked with the number of the corps and division" to which they belonged, as well as the type and caliber of the ammunition they carried.[37] Captain Flagler apparently was so

unmoved by the events transpiring on July 1 that he took the time
that day to fulfill one of the Ordnance Department's bureaucratic
requirements: he sent to the chief of ordnance in Washington the
Army of the Potomac's quarterly disbursement and accounts current reports for the second quarter of calendar year 1863.[38]

By July 2, the flow of supplies was coming into Westminster
without much difficulty. The major supply artery between Baltimore and Westminster was the Western Maryland Railroad. It
had only a poorly constructed single track, no telegraph line, and
no adequate sidings. Its main station was at Westminster, and the
terminus was at Union Bridge. Herman Haupt was at Westminster
on July 1. He immediately brought order to a confusing situation,
since the line was being operated off schedule to prevent capture
of the trains. After assessing the situation, Haupt sent for construction supplies, tools, lanterns, and 400 laborers. He also bor-
rowed rolling stock from several other railroads. Since there was
only one track and no acceptable sidings, Haupt sent the trains to
and from Westminster by three convoys a day, five or six trains at
a time, with ten cars per train. Haupt calculated that by keeping
to this schedule, he could move 1,500 tons of supplies a day from
Baltimore and return with 2,000 to 4,000 wounded soldiers. Two
other rail lines, the Northern Central from Baltimore to Hanover
Junction, and the B & O to Frederick, also were available for use
at this time.[39] Most supplies traveled over the Western Maryland
Railroad, however, since the route through Westminster was the
most direct path to Gettysburg.

Meanwhile, General Ingalls moved with army headquarters
and directed resupply operations from Gettysburg. He arranged
to issue supplies at Westminster and eventually at Frederick and
ensured that telegraphic communications were open between
these two towns and Baltimore and Washington. He then established communications with Westminster and Frederick by sending relays of cavalry couriers every three hours.[40]

At 7:00 A.M. on July 3, Ingalls wired Meigs that "at this moment the battle is raging as fiercely as ever. . . . We have supplies at

Westminster that must come up to-morrow if we remain here." He concluded by correctly predicting that "the contest will be decided today, I think."[41] Only ammunition wagons and ambulances had been allowed to accompany the Union corps to Gettysburg, and after three days of fighting, Ingalls knew that the Army of the Potomac soon would have to be resupplied. His extraordinary efforts had made the situation appear routine, but on July 3 he personally had a close brush with death or injury. While Ingalls was conversing with General Meade and Dan Butterfield (Meade's chief of staff) during the artillery duel that preceded Pickett's Charge, a shell from a Confederate gun exploded so close to the trio that it knocked down and wounded General Butterfield, but neither Ingalls nor Meade was hurt.[42]

Back in Westminster, the rations Colonel Clarke had requested in the early morning hours of July 1 finally began to arrive on July 2. Pvt. James Terry, a teamster assigned to Company A, 7th Wisconsin Infantry, noted in his diary that "100 teams came from Washington with rations for the troops. We are 25 miles from them [the troops at Gettysburg]."[43] Late the next day, July 3, orders were received in the army's wagon parks in Westminster to proceed to Gettysburg with fresh rations. The magnitude of this task was daunting; in the Third Corps alone, which had only two divisions rather than the customary three, 60,000 rations and 250 head of cattle were sent on the Baltimore Pike toward Gettysburg.[44] Hundreds of wagons headed northward and offloaded their supplies, most of which began arriving during the early morning hours of July 4. A First Corps soldier who had been captured on July 1 and had escaped the morning of July 4 remembered that he had just returned to the Union lines in the morning when the commissary wagons began arriving. "We soon filled our haversacks with coffee, sugar, pork, and hardtack, the standard articles of a soldier's diet," he wrote.[45]

In Washington, General Meigs prepared for the battle's aftermath. He sent messages to quartermasters in Philadelphia and Harrisburg directing them to purchase as many wagons and horses as possible to replace expected losses in the Army of the Potomac. On July 4 Meigs telegraphed Ingalls to buy or impress all the serviceable horses that were within the range of his foraging parties. Priority for fresh mounts went to the combat arms: he directed Ingalls to "refit the cavalry and artillery in the best possible manner" and also sent instructions to the quartermaster at Baltimore to redirect all remounts to Frederick as replacements for the cavalry. As if to underscore his priorities, Meigs sent a message to Herman Haupt at Westminster: "Let nothing interfere with the supply of rations for the men, and grain for the horses." On July 6, Meigs telegraphed his counterpart in the Army of the Potomac that 5,000 horses would be headed by rail for Frederick from depots across the East and Midwest.[46]

The soldiers of the Army of the Potomac and their horses needed sustenance, but the men required ordnance, too. One historian has estimated that the Union soldiers probably expended more than 5.4 million rounds of small-arms ammunition during the three days of fighting. Captain Flagler estimated that at least 25,000 artillery rounds also had been fired or lost as well. The situation was serious enough that General Meade issued a circular order on July 5 urging his corps commanders to be cautious in expending both their small-arms and artillery ammunition. "We are now drawing upon our reserve trains," the circular stated, "and it is of the highest importance that no ammunition be exhausted unless there is reason to believe that its use will produce a decided effect upon the enemy."[47] Additionally, Brig. Gen. Henry Hunt, chief of artillery, commented on the destructiveness of the Confederate cannons on the Union artillery during the July 3 bombardment: "The night of the 3d, like the previous one, was devoted to repairs and reorganization. A large number of batteries had been so reduced in men and horses that many guns and carriages, after completing the outfit of those which remained with the army, were sent to the rear and turned in to the ordnance department."[48]

On July 6, Captain Flagler wired General Ripley at the Ordnance Bureau. After informing his chief that a wagon train of ammunition was standing by at Frederick, he requested the following ordnance supplies be sent to Gettysburg: 800,000 cartridges, caliber .574; 100,000 .69 caliber rifled-musket cartridges; 200,000 .54 caliber cartridges; 200,000 .69 caliber smooth-bore cartridges; and 30,000 Sharps rifle cartridges. For the artillery, he initially requested 2,500 12-lb. rounds; 2,500 rounds for 3-inch rifles, and 1,500 rounds for ten-pounders. Shortly after his request was sent, Flagler found out that the Army of Northern Virginia had begun to withdraw. Since the Army of the Potomac soon would be in pursuit, Flagler requested that the ammunition be sent to Frederick instead of Gettysburg. He also asked if his earlier request for artillery ammunition could be increased to 4,000 rounds each of 3-inch and 12-lb. rounds. The telegraph operator made a mistake, however, and requested 40,000 rounds each. Upon arriving in Frederick, Flagler discovered the error, took what he needed from the supply train, and sent the rest back to Washington Arsenal.[49] Considering the vast amount of ammunition expended during the Battle of Gettysburg, Flagler's requests *were too low,* both for small-arms and artillery ammunition.

When the Army of Potomac marched southward in pursuit of Lee's army, some of the ordnance officers remained in Gettysburg to oversee the collection and classification of ordnance matériel. More than 24,000 muskets were collected in the immediate aftermath of the battle, as well as thousands of bayonets, cartridge boxes, and other accoutrements.[50] Some of these items would be reissued to the troops, while many were sent back to Washington Arsenal for repair. Similarly, General Meigs sent Capt. Henry C. Blood of the Quartermaster Department from Washington on July 6 to assist with the collection of government property and oversee the burial of the dead. During the first week after his arrival, Blood's time was occupied with supervising the temporary interments of the fallen. Thousands of horses on both sides had been killed, and their carcasses also had to be disposed of. After a quick return to Washington, by July 16, Blood was back in Gettysburg, where he spent much of his time administering the collection of equipment from the battlefield and the confiscation of U.S. property from the citizens of Gettysburg who had picked it up on the field. Wounded and worn-out horses that were wandering aimlessly about the battlefield or had been taken by civilians also were rounded up. In fact, Meigs received word from Gettysburg on July 18 that more than 350 horses and mules had been recovered and, with proper care and medication, could be made ready for service in a very short time. The Quartermaster Department's recovery of equipment at Gettysburg would continue through the end of August.[51]

As the Army of the Potomac moved farther from the Gettysburg area in its pursuit of General Lee, the supply trains that had been assembled at Westminster were ordered to rejoin their respective corps by way of Frederick so they could restock from the forward depot that had been established there.[52] The badly wounded had no choice but to remain in Gettysburg, and arrangements had to be made for their care. Colonel Clarke ordered 30,000 rations brought to Gettysburg on July 4 to be issued specifically to the hospitals, and he requested more to be delivered after the army departed.[53] When the army moved west from Frederick, once again only ammunition and ambulance trains were allowed to accompany their commands. Supply and baggage wagons were to remain in the Middletown Valley on the evening of July 9, but the trains would be left without guards. The severe manpower losses the Army of the Potomac sustained at Gettysburg required every able-bodied man to be in the ranks. While Meade's command was taking up positions around Williamsport from July 10 to 13 to attack the Confederate army, the trains remained in Middletown Valley and supplied the army from there.[54]

The planned Union attack came too late, and the Army of Northern Virginia escaped across the Potomac on July 13–14. With this unexpected change in the operational situation, General Ingalls thus ordered his logisticians to replenish the army's supplies from depots that recently had been established at Berlin and Sandy Hook, Maryland, and Harpers Ferry, West Virginia. Three days' cooked rations were issued to the troops, and those men who needed replacement uniform articles received them. In addition, fresh horses and mules were issued to commands that needed them, though probably not in the required numbers, as it would take some time for the horses that Meigs had ordered sent to the army to actually arrive. Once the army crossed the Potomac, Ingalls made the necessary arrangements to resupply the command via the Orange and Alexandria Railroad.[55] Thus ended the Gettysburg campaign from the logistical perspective.

The logisticians of the Army of the Potomac had accomplished a herculean task, but the soldiers and animals were worn out. Muddy roads from heavy rains made resupply difficult as the Union force pursued Lee through Maryland, making tired men and horses even more exhausted. The campaign had taxed the transportation assets of the army to its fullest, and food and forage were running low.[56] Ammunition supplies had been replenished, but it is doubtful that the Army of the Potomac had as much ordnance on hand as it did when the battle began, especially in light of the modest requisitions Flagler had made earlier—almost 3 million small-arms rounds fewer than what was expended.

The major logistical lesson that was learned—actually reinforced—from the Gettysburg campaign was that large supply trains degrade the tactical mobility of an army. To reduce the number of wagons accompanying the Army of the Potomac on campaign, General in Chief Halleck issued a general order on August 21, 1863, that instituted, for the *entire* Union army, the transportation recommendations made earlier by General Ingalls: no more than 20 wagons would be allowed per every 1000 men— even though Ingalls had not enforced his own orders during the Gettysburg campaign.[57] Although Ingalls had done a magnificent job in resupplying the army while at the same time keeping the ponderous wagon trains out of harm's way—and out of the way of the combat elements of the army—the logistical umbilical cord had been stretched very thin, perhaps explaining why he did not stick to his own regulation. The horrific three-day battle was the largest and most intense that had ever been fought on American soil, and the supply of military necessities could not keep up with the demand, especially ammunition. From purely a tactical point of view, Meade should have counterattacked Lee on July 4 or 5. When the element of logistics is factored into the equation, Meade was probably right in his decision not to attack.

And what happened to the men who orchestrated the supply efforts of the Army of the Potomac during the Gettysburg campaign? Ruddy Clarke remained the chief commissary of subsistence of the Army of the Potomac until the spring of 1864. At his own request, he was transferred to a commissary post in New York. Clarke was brevetted to major general on March 13, 1865, for faithful and meritorious service during the war. When the conflict ended, he stayed in the army and served in several commissary positions, including chief commissary under Gen. Phil Sheridan in the Division of Missouri. Henry Francis Clarke died on May 10, 1887.[58]

Daniel Flagler became ill shortly after the battle and took sick leave from the army. Once he had recovered, he was reassigned to inspection duty at the West Point Foundry, from October 1863 until May 1864, and he finished the war as an assistant in the offices of the Ordnance Bureau in Washington, DC. He was brevetted to lieutenant colonel in March 1865 for distinguished service in the field and faithful service to the Ordnance Department. After the war, he had a number of different ordnance assignments, his most notable as commander of Rock Island Arsenal, Illinois, for fifteen years. He was promoted to brigadier general in the Regular Army and appointed the chief of ordnance in January 1891. He still served in this capacity during the Spanish-American War. General Flagler died on March 29, 1899.[59]

Rufus Ingalls remained the Army of the Potomac's quartermaster general for the duration of the war. At the end of the conflict, he was brevetted major general for faithful and meritorious service during the war. Like his two other fellow logisticians, he, stayed in the Regular Army and was promoted to increasing positions of responsibility, becoming quartermaster general of the U.S. Army in February 1882. Ingalls retired on July 1, 1883, twenty years to the day after the Battle of Gettysburg began. He died nine-and-a-half years later, on January 15, 1893.[60]

The men who moved, armed, fed, and supplied the Army of the Potomac are a shining example of logisticians at their best. Although no monuments were dedicated at Gettysburg to honor their memory, it is obvious that their efforts were critical to the success of the Army of the Potomac during the first week of July 1863. If nothing else, these men certainly deserve more attention from historians than they have received in the past.

4

(West) Virginians in the Gettysburg Campaign

WHEN THE COMMONWEALTH of Virginia seceded from the Union in the spring of 1861, political leaders primarily from the northwest region of the state began the process of reorganizing a government that would remain loyal to the United States. Ultimately, the "Restored" (or "Reorganized") Government of Virginia would give its consent to create a new state, West Virginia, with Abraham Lincoln signing the statehood bill on December 30, 1862. Six months later, on June 20, 1863—in the midst of the Gettysburg campaign—West Virginia officially became the thirty-fifth star in the Union flag.

The legality of West Virginia's statehood has been deliberated ad nauseam ever since the idea to create a new state was conceived, back in 1861. Even Abraham Lincoln questioned the constitutionality of the process, but he relented nonetheless and signed the West Virginia Statehood Bill while recognizing it as a necessary wartime measure. "The division of a State is dreaded as a precedent," Lincoln wrote. "But a measure made expedient by a war, is no precedent for times of peace. It is said that the admission of West-Virginia, is secession, and tolerated only because

Waitman Willey, author of the Willey Amendment to the West Virginia Statehood Bill. (Courtesy of Richard Wolfe)

it is our secession. Well, if we call it by that name, there is still difference enough between secession against the constitution, and secession in favor of the constitution." In conclusion, Lincoln conceded, "I believe the admission of West-Virginia into the Union is expedient."[1]

However, West Virginia would enter the Union as a *slave* state, although a provision to gradually end slavery within its borders was added to the statehood bill by Senator Waitman T. Willey, one of the senators representing the Restored Government of Virginia. The Willey Amendment stated:

> The children of slaves born within the limits of this State after the fourth day of July, eighteen hundred and sixty-three, shall be free; and all slaves within the said State who shall, at the time aforesaid, be under the age of ten years, shall be free when they arrive at the age of twenty-one years; and all slaves over ten and under twenty-one years, shall be free when they arrive at the age of twenty-five years; and no slave shall be permitted to come into the State for permanent residence therein.[2]

Thus West Virginia, like the other border states—Maryland, Kentucky, Delaware, and Missouri—would continue to allow human bondage while sending regiments to fight for the Union. The new state, however, would become the *most* divided in that Union.

Historians have long debated the number of troops from those counties comprising West Virginia who volunteered or were conscripted to fight for the Union and the Confederacy, with a high of approximately 32,000 Union troops credited to West Virginia and a low of roughly 7,000 Confederates. Recent scholarship has adjusted these figures, with historians estimating approximately 20 to 22,000 fighting for each side. If any state can claim the dubious honor that the Civil War pitted family members and friends against each other, West Virginia can most certainly do so.[3] The discrepancy between the Union low figure of approximately 20,000 to the "official" high of 32,000 can be explained by the fact that thousands of enlistees in West Virginia's Union regiments were natives of Pennsylvania and Ohio and crossed the state border to enlist because they either found it more convenient or, at least in 1861, because they were turned away by recruiters in their own communities since the Keystone and Buckeye states already had exceeded their enlistment quotas set by the Federal government. Additionally, reenlistments were included in the finally tally of 32,000.[4]

After four years of war, the State of West Virginia was credited with contributing to the Union cause fifteen infantry regiments, two "veteran" infantry regiments, one independent infantry battalion, eight light artillery batteries, seven cavalry regiments, and one veteran cavalry regiment. In addition, 133 personnel of the U.S. Navy and Marine Corps are credited to West Virginia, as well as 196 African Americans, serving primarily in the 45th U.S. Colored Infantry. West Virginians also served in the Potomac Home Brigade, which is attributed to the State of Maryland. (West) Virginians serving with the Confederate army—mostly in units with "Virginia" designations—comprised all or part of thirteen infantry regiments, three infantry battalions, one mounted infantry battalion, one sharpshooter battalion, twelve artillery batteries, fifteen cavalry regiments, six cavalry battalions (including mounted infantry and partisan rangers), and one independent company of partisan rangers. Some (West) Virginians also served in Confederate units attributed to Kentucky. Only two men from West Virginia counties can be credited to the Confederate States Navy.[5]

As a result of the divided loyalties within West Virginia, family members, friends, and neighbors sometimes found themselves on opposite sides of the firing lines, including during the Gettysburg campaign.[6] Following the Battle of Chancellorsville—which saw the mortal wounding of another (West) Virginian, Clarksburg native Thomas "Stonewall" Jackson—the Army of Northern Virginia's cavalry division, under the command of Maj. Gen. Jeb Stuart, was preparing for its own campaign, the precursor of the invasion of Pennsylvania by the rest of its army. Located on a remote station of the Orange and Alexandria Railroad near Culpeper, Brandy Station was the scene of a grand review and parade of the gray-clad troopers on June 8, 1863, with General Lee himself in attendance as the reviewing officer. Nearby, the rest of the Army of Northern Virginia was bivouacked around Culpeper, about six miles to the southwest of the cavalry camps, the soldiers' moods in high spirits after their recent victory at Chancellorsville. Originally scheduled for June 5, the review included mounted charges and battle simulations, but Lee was unable to attend, so a more modest event was carried out on June 8 in the commanding general's presence. The next day, Stuart's command would head northward, with the mission of screening the movements of the Confederate infantry during its trek toward Pennsylvania. Stuart and his troopers, and General Lee, for that matter, had no inkling that a Union cavalry force with attached infantry was poised for a surprise attack on the very morning that Stuart's command was to begin its mission.[7]

The Army of the Potomac's Cavalry Corps had a new leader in Maj. Gen. Alfred Pleasonton, replacing the previous commander, George Stoneman, whose raid during the Chancellorsville campaign bore little fruit and resulted in his relief. Pleasonton's plan called for a crossing of the Rappahannock River on June 9 and then surprising the Confederates in their camps. Directly on the other side of the river was William E. "Grumble" Jones's cavalry brigade, just recently returned from the so-called Jones-Imboden raid into West Virginia, with the rest of the Army of Northern Virginia's cavalry division nearby. When Pleasonton's command crossed the river at Beverly Ford and Kelly Ford on the morning of the ninth, they believed the Confederates were camped at Culpeper Court House, some ten miles away. Thus, both sides were surprised.[8] "At daylight, the report of small-arms in the direction of Beverly Ford indicated a serious attack," Grumble Jones wrote in his official report. The 6th Virginia Cavalry, manning a picket line at the ford, along with the 7th Virginia Cavalry, acting as the "grand guard," stubbornly resisted the Yankee cavalrymen to allow the horse artillery, parked nearby, to withdraw and set up a defense near a little brick house of worship, St. James Church. The artillerymen were joined by the 11th and 12th regiments of Virginia Cavalry and the 35th Battalion, Virginia Cavalry.[9] The 7th, 11th, and 12th regiments included troopers recruited from ten (West) Virginia counties.[10] In the most recent and authoritative study of the battle, historian Eric J. Wittenberg asserts that "the irascible Jones and his troopers bore the brunt of the fighting at Brandy Station."[11]

Brig. Gen. John Buford, who as a brigade commander had led the 1st West Virginia Cavalry in a charge at the Second Battle of Manassas, was now a division commander and responsible for the attacking force that had crossed at Beverly Ford. After ordering a charge against the Confederate artillery and cavalry at St. James Church, Buford tried to flank the Confederates on their left, but as the Union troopers under Gen. David McMurtrie Gregg in the other wing, the one that crossed at Kelly's Ford, had not yet made it to the battlefield, Buford was fought to a standstill.[12] Only one small squadron of West Virginia cavalry accompanied the Union cavalry that day, Companies A and C of the 3rd West Virginia, which sustained a slight loss, only three men wounded.[13]

Although the Union cavalry indeed had caught the Rebel troopers off guard, the uncoordinated assault allowed the southerners to react, regroup, and push the blue-clad troopers away from the battlefield. Jasper Hawes, a native of Hardy County, West Virginia, of the 11th Virginia Cavalry recorded in his diary, "The fight was probably the most desperate of any Cavalry fight of the war & continued with varied success until near sundown when the Yankees were driven back across the Rappahannock."[14] Nonetheless, the fight was a near-run thing, instilling confidence in the heretofore somewhat luckless Union horse soldiers—who would stand their ground many times over during the upcoming campaign.

On June 10, the Army of Northern Virginia was on the move, heading northward through the Shenandoah Valley, using the Blue Ridge Mountains to the east to conceal its movements. In the van of the army was Brig. Gen. Albert Gallatin Jenkins's brigade of western Virginians, recently attached specifically for the northern invasion, which now joined other units from the soon-to-be thirty-fifth Union state, including the old Stonewall Brigade, now assigned to Lt. Gen. Richard Ewell's command, known as the 2d Corps.[15] (General Lee had reorganized the Army of Northern Virginia after the death of Stonewall Jackson, creating three corps out of the existing two and transferring regiments and brigades from other military departments. Gen. James Longstreet retained command of the 1st Corps, while Ambrose P. Hill assumed command of the new 3rd Corps.) As the Confederate 2nd Corps (approximately 23,000 men) approached the town of Winchester, another battle was about to pit Confederate (West) Virginians against Union West Virginians assigned to Maj. Gen. Robert Milroy's 8th Corps of the U.S. Army's Middle Department, which included Battery D, 1st West Virginia Light Artillery; Company K, 1st West Virginia Cavalry; companies D and E, 3rd West Virginia Cavalry; and the 12th West Virginia Volunteer Infantry.[16]

During the Second Battle of Winchester, June 14–15 (the first battle was fought more than a year earlier, during the beginning of Jackson's Valley campaign), Maj. Gen. Jubal Early's division and

Maj. Gen. Edward "Allegheny" Johnson's division enveloped the Union defenders and inflicted 4,443 casualties (including 4,000 prisoners) at a cost of only 269 Confederate casualties, Ewell's Corps also captured a significant amount of supplies, along with 300 horses and 23 cannons.[17] Capt. John Carlin, commander of Battery D, 1st West Virginia Light Artillery, reported, "[I] was ordered to spike my guns, destroy what ammunition was on hand, cut up the harness, and take nothing away but the saddles and bridles, with the horses, with the men mounted on them, which order I complied with." Carlin obviously believed he could have saved his cannons, limbers and other ancillary equipment, because in the next sentence he contemptuously wrote, "Had I been allowed to do so, I could have taken my guns and equipment out when the order was given to evacuate, and, in my opinion, could have rendered good service in covering the retreat."[18] Carlin informed the editor of Wheeling's *Daily Intelligencer* on June 25—five days after statehood was achieved—that the "boys almost cried when the order came to evacuate and spike the guns, which latter job was done most effectually, and the harness cut into a thousand pieces." The young battery commander tried to console the families of the artillerymen who were missing in action: "Capt. Carlin desires us to state that the friends of the missing battery boys need feel no alarm about their safety," the *Daily Intelligencer* reported. "He feels confident that they will yet turn up, and report themselves at this point [Wheeling]."[19]

One human-interest story from the Second Battle of Winchester rises above all others. John Wesley Culp had been a resident of Gettysburg, Pennsylvania, before the war but moved to Shepherdstown, (West) Virginia, when his employer relocated his business there in 1856. "Wes," as he was known, joined the Shepherdstown militia, named the "Hamtramck Guards." Most of the militiamen in this unit, including Wes and Maj. Henry Kyd Douglas, a staff officer on Stonewall Jackson's (and later Ewell's) staff, enlisted in Shepherdstown in Company B, 2nd Virginia Infantry at the war's beginning. The same day of Wes's enlistment, his brother,

William Culp, and one of Wes's old Gettysburg friends, Johnston "Jack" Skelly, joined a three-months' regiment of the Union army; eventually both would become members of Company F, 87th Pennsylvania Volunteer Infantry. A first cousin, David Culp, also joined that unit. During the fighting at Winchester, Jack Skelly was wounded and captured. Hearing that prisoners from Gettysburg were being held, Wes went to see them and found Jack, who gave him a note to send to his family and his sweetheart back in Gettysburg, young Virginia Wade, nicknamed "Ginnie." Wes had no clue that he soon would be back in Gettysburg, but he and the Stonewall Brigade arrived there during the evening of July 1, 1863. Wes was killed in the early morning of July 3, never having the chance to deliver the note to Ginnie from Jack, who already had died of his wounds. That same day, Ginnie Wade (today known as "Jennie" Wade) became the victim of a stray bullet, the only civilian killed during the three days of fighting at Gettysburg.[20]

After the Second Battle of Winchester, Ewell's Corps continued its northward advance, crossing the Potomac River from Jefferson County into Maryland at Shepherdstown's Pack Horse Ford on June 18. One young Confederate, John King of Mercer County, (West) Virginia, who only a few weeks earlier had joined Company B, 25th Virginia Infantry, remembered many years later, "We moved on down the valley to Shepherdstown and here we met a company belonging to one of our regiments [undoubtedly Co. B, 2nd Virginia Infantry] that had secured a leave of absence and were staying at their own homes in town . . . someone would go to a dear old mother and speak gently, she would clasp her hands and loft her eyes to heaven, touched with grief, for she knew the ground had closed over her sunny haired southern boy forever."[21] Jefferson County had done its fair share of supplying men for the southern cause: five infantry companies, four cavalry companies, and a battery of horse artillery. "Many joined other commands," recalled Charles Town's (Jefferson County) Roger Preston Chew, the commander of the horse artillery battery. As a result, he noted that the "county was about depopulated of young men."[22] Confederate congressman Alexander Boteler, whose home, Fountain Rock, sat on the southern edge of Shepherdstown, already had lost most of his slaves after they ran off to the Union lines across the Potomac earlier in the war. In June 1863 he saw his remaining, supposedly last loyal slave, "Uncle Louis," also desert the family when the Army of Northern Virginia crossed the river. "So we don't own a negro in the world, and indeed very little else," noted one of Boteler's daughters.[23] Major Douglas recalled that the day before the river crossing, "we encamped near Shepherdstown and I visited my home across the Potomac and saw the desolation of war. My beautiful home [known as Ferry Hill Place] was a barren waste and a common, and the blackened walls of the burnt barn stood up against the sky as a monument of useless and barbarous destruction." He wondered how he would feel when he finally marched across the Pennsylvania state line: would he retaliate?[24]

General Lee, however, would ensure that no intentional reprisals would occur when he issued General Orders No. 72, followed by a similar warning in General Orders No. 73, which stated

> We make war only upon armed men, and that we cannot take vengeance for the wrongs our people have suffered without lowering ourselves in the eyes of all whose abhorrence has been excited by the atrocities of our enemies. . . . The commanding general therefore earnestly exhorts the troops to abstain with most scrupulous care from unnecessary or wanton injury to private property, and he enjoins upon all officers to arrest and bring to summary punishment all who shall in any way offend against the orders on this subject.[25]

Romney (Hampshire County) native John Casler, 33d Virginia Infantry, Stonewall Brigade, would be disappointed by Lee's orders: "When we crossed the Potomac we thought we would have a fine time plundering in the enemy's country, and live fine; but General Lee had orders read out that we were not to molest any of the citizens, or take any private property, and any soldier caught plundering would be shot." These orders, however, only applied to the soldiers in the ranks, since the Army of Northern Virginia's quartermasters took anything and everything they needed, paying for it in Confederate money or writing out receipts for later payment. "They would take the citizens' horses and wagons and load them up with provisions and goods from the stores." Despite Lee's strict instructions, Casler admitted that "some of the soldiers [of the 33d] would strike out into the country, before they had time to put out a guard, and would come back loaded with 'grub.'"[26]

As the Confederate infantry, artillery, and supply trains lumbered into "enemy" territory, the gray- and butternut-clad cavalry troopers screened their movements by providing security in the gaps of the Bull Run and Blue Ridge mountains. In addition, they protected the Loudon Valley between those two ranges to prevent Union cavalry from ascertaining the movements of the Army of Northern Virginia. In a series of bloody clashes from June 17 to 21 fought near the towns of Aldie, Middleburg, and Upperville, the Confederate horsemen stood their ground and inflicted severe losses on the Union cavalry regiments. For example, at the Battle of Aldie on June 17, (West) Virginians in the 1st and 5th regiments of Virginia Cavalry, part of Thomas Munford's brigade, punished four regiments of Union horsemen, who suffered 305 casualties, compared to a Confederate loss of 119.[27] The Union cavalry may have come of age, but it was being wasted by inept leadership at the highest levels of command.

In the midst of this momentous campaign, West Virginia joined the Union on June 20, 1863, with newly elected Parkersburg resident Arthur Boreman its first governor. The gravity of the Confederate invasion of the North was not lost on the editor of the *Daily Intelligencer*, who wrote:

> Let us not forget that our New State, which we inaugurate today amid happy auspices, will be destroyed, the liberty it protects overthrown, and the hopes it inspires blasted, if the federal government is not able to sustain itself and enforce its authority.

Our fate and the fate of our national Union must be the same. We go on together to prosperity, or we go down together to ruin. *Even now the enemies of the country threaten to invade our homes, and the citizen soldiery is under arms for their defense.* Let us each and all vow to-day, in turning this new leaf of our history, undying hostility to this atrocious rebellion which seeks the destruction of the rights of men, and fealty to the government and Union, in and under which alone life, liberty and property are secure. As citizens we are of the State, but as patriots we belong to the whole country.[28]

The warning was ominous: the Union must prevail—especially in the current campaign—or the new state would cease to exist.

By the last day of June, the Army of Northern Virginia was converging on Cashtown, Pennsylvania, about eight miles west of Gettysburg. Fourteen miles to the east of Gettysburg, in York County, Union cavalrymen in Brig. Gen. Judson Kilpatrick's division fought elements of Jeb Stuart's cavalry division in the streets of Hanover, Pennsylvania, once again pitting West Virginians against each other. On June 30, 1863, Brig. Gen. George Custer's brigade of Michigan cavalry, along with Brig. Gen. Elon Farnsworth's cavalry brigade—which included the 1st West Virginia Cavalry Regiment—met, among other Confederate brigades, Col. John Chambliss's command, whose regiments included the 9th Virginia Cavalry, which was recruited partly in Roane County, (West) Virginia. Two soldiers of the 1st West Virginia who were killed in action or died of wounds—George Collins and Garrett Selby—were interred later in Gettysburg National Cemetery. Although the engagement was indecisive, it forced Stuart's division farther away from linking with the main body of the Army of Northern Virginia, which would blunder into Brigadier General Buford's Union cavalry division just west of Gettysburg the very next day.[29]

The same two companies of the 3rd West Virginia Cavalry that had participated in the Battle of Brandy Station were still attached to Buford's command in Col. Thomas Devin's brigade when the momentous Battle of Gettysburg opened shortly after 7 A.M. on July 1, 1863. On McPherson's Ridge west of town, Buford's troopers stymied Maj. Gen. Henry Heth's infantry division for several hours until the Army of the Potomac's 1st Corps arrived on the battlefield and took over the fight. A month later, when Colonel Devin wrote his after-action report for the Gettysburg campaign, he singled out two soldiers in the 3rd West Virginia, Cpl. John W. Shumaker, who was captured at Gettysburg when scouting the Confederate positions, for distinguished service and personal bravery; and Assistant Surgeon Thomas Morton who, according to Devin, was "entitled to special mention for active service on the field, and unremitting and efficient discharge of duty in his care of the [brigade's] wounded."[30]

Despite the tenacious defense of the Union cavalry, as well as that of the soldiers of the 1st and 11th Corps of the Army of the Potomac, the Army of Northern Virginia scored a clear-cut victory on July 1, 1863. Mercer County's John King, whose 25th Virginia Infantry passed through the battlefield after the fighting was over, recalled, "We reached Gettysburg on the evening of the 1st of July. There had been hard fighting before we arrived. We saw some gruesome sights near the railroad cut where Gen. [John] Reynolds [commanding the 1st Corps, Army of the Potomac] was killed. Men's heads were torn from the bodies, legs and arms torn asunder and horses lying around mutilated."[31]

Hoping to retain the initiative, General Lee opted to continue the battle the next day. His plan called for a two-pronged offensive on the flanks of the Union position, with General Longstreet's command making the main attack on the Army of the Potomac's left flank while General Ewell's troops struck the Union right in a diversionary assault. A series of delays prevented the battle from beginning until mid-afternoon, and nothing seemed to go as planned. On the Union right flank at a place called Cemetery Hill, the battle raged late into the night. On the eastern face of the hill, Confederate brigades broke the Union line and were in the midst of capturing several Union cannons, but Col. Samuel Carroll's "Gibraltar Brigade" of the 2nd Corps was sent to the rescue, attacking the victorious Confederates with a bayonet charge that thwarted the rebel breakthrough. One of Carroll's regiments was the 7th West Virginia Infantry. "On arriving there we found the battery about to be taken charge of by the enemy, who were in large force," reported Col. Jonathan Lockwood of the 7th, "whereupon we immediately charged . . . and succeeded in completely routing the entire force and driving them beyond their lines, capturing a number of prisoners, and removing their dead and wounded in order to establish our line on the line previously occupied by the enemy." During the action, Lockwood himself was slightly wounded.[32]

Not far from East Cemetery Hill, perhaps a mile to the southeast, the Stonewall Brigade and the rest of its division had taken the abandoned breastworks of the Union 12th Corps on an adjacent promontory called Culp's Hill (all but one brigade of the 12th Corps had moved southward in an attempt to reinforce the Army of the Potomac's left flank). That lone Federal brigade, however, would prevent the Rebels from taking the crest of the hill. John Casler of the 33rd Virginia Infantry remembered, "The enemy had every advantage of position, and would repulse every charge that was made. Our troops would at different points drive them from their works, but could not hold them for want of proper support."[33] Early the next morning, John Wesley Culp of the 2nd Virginia Infantry was killed near the hill that bore his family's name, and on the same day, Major Douglas was wounded nearby. "I had a severe and ragged wound in the left shoulder," Douglas recalled, "the ball having taken with it a clipping from my coat, shirt, and undershirt, which it cut out in its haste and lodged with its accessories under the clavicle, cutting also some muscles and paralyzing for a time my left arm." He concluded, "My duty in that battle was over."[34]

On Friday, July 3, General Lee planned on renewing the attacks on the Union flanks, but again things went awry, so he decided instead to assault the center of the Union line—on Cemetery Ridge.

Bolstered by the arrival of Maj. Gen. George Pickett's division of Virginians and Jeb Stuart's cavalry on July 2, Lee intended to strike the Union center with three infantry divisions, including Pickett's command (all told some 12,000 soldiers), while Stuart's cavalrymen demonstrated in the rear of the Union position where they could be poised to pursue the Army of the Potomac if the infantry attack on Cemetery Ridge was successful. Prior to the assault, Confederate artillery would bombard the Union defenses on Cemetery Ridge and Cemetery Hill. At 1 P.M., Confederate gunners opened fire with 163 cannons. Some 119 Union guns eventually replied, and for the next two hours the fields of Gettysburg sounded and looked like Hell on earth.[35]

Battery C, 1st Virginia Light Artillery was under the command of an Ohioan, Capt. Wallace Hill. The artillerymen in Battery C had been recruited primarily from Marion, Wirt, Mason, and Ohio counties in West Virginia; Washington County, Ohio; and even Culpeper County, Virginia; but the battery's soldiers hailed from six other West Virginia counties as well. Battery C had been hotly engaged during the Chancellorsville fight and was in the thick of the July 2 battle. On July 3, it dueled with Confederate batteries on Seminary Ridge.[36] Captain Hill remembered, "Shortly after engaging the enemy [on July 2], I had the misfortune to lose Stephen J. Braddock, one of my cannoneers, and on Friday afternoon, Charles Lacey [*sic*], a driver, fell mortally wounded." Hill's command suffered two additional casualties with slight wounds, and lost five horses. During the battle, the battery fired 1,120 rounds of ammunition. Concluding his after-action report, Hill noted, "I have just cause to feel proud of the part my men sustained during the entire terrible engagement."[37] Charles Lacy was one of the soldiers from Washington County, Ohio, who had enlisted at the beginning of the war, when he was twenty-one years old. He had been born in Leitrim, Ireland, and most likely came to the United States during the Irish potato famine. He had brown hair, blue eyes, a light complexion, and listed his occupation as a farmer. He died on July 4, 1863, and is buried in the West Virginia section of Gettysburg

National Cemetery, not far from where he suffered his mortal wound.[38]

About two hours after the bombardment began, Confederate infantrymen prepared for the assault across nearly a mile of open ground checkered with snake-rail and post-and-rail fences that would slow their advance and make them better targets for the Union infantry and artillery anxiously waiting on Cemetery Ridge. Regiments that would make the charge were partly recruited from (West) Virginia—namely Mercer and Monroe counties—included the 7th and 24th regiments of Virginia Infantry, both assigned to Brig. Gen. James Kemper's brigade, Pickett's Division, Longstreet's Corps. Both regiments suffered heavy losses during what came to be known as Pickett's Charge, with the 24th Virginia losing approximately 40 percent of its men, its worst loss of the war.[39]

While Pickett's Charge raged in the fields between Seminary Ridge and Cemetery Ridge, Jeb Stuart's cavalrymen likewise were engaged in a series of dismounted and mounted attacks about three miles to the southeast near the Hanover Road. Trying to get in position to pursue what they hoped would be a vanquished foe, the gray-clad troopers instead ran into a resolute Union cavalry division under the command of Brigadier General Gregg and its attached brigade under Brigadier General Custer. Stuart's command included Brigadier General Jenkins's brigade of Virginia cavalry (most of its regiments were recruited in [West] Virginia counties), as well as the 1st, 5th, and 10th Virginia Cavalry, which contained soldiers from West Virginia's Jefferson, Berkeley, Randolph, and Roane counties. Jenkins—a former U.S. congressman from Cabell County on the Ohio River—would miss this battle, as he had been wounded on July 2.[40] Next to the Battle of Brandy Station, this encounter was the second largest cavalry fight of the war. This time, however, the Union cavalry prevailed.

On July 3, while the bulk of Stuart's Division was fighting east of Gettysburg, Grumble Jones's brigade, which included the 7th and 11th Virginia regiments and supported by Chew's Virginia Battery, routed a Union cavalry force in the farm fields near Fairfield,

Pennsylvania. These three commands were composed in part by (West) Virginia soldiers from Berkeley, Jefferson, Hardy, Hampshire, and Pocahontas counties.[41] Lt. John Blue of Hanging Rock, near Romney in Hampshire County, recalled that the Yankee cavalrymen "were stubborn fighters, rather inclined to be mulish and hard to drive." However, once the Rebels got the best of them, he recalled, "their running qualities were fully equal to their fighting."[42] Another action involving cavalry, this time Union troopers battling with Confederate infantry, occurred on the southern part of the Gettysburg battlefield, about a mile and half south of the area where Pickett's Charge was repulsed. In an attempt to strike the Confederate army's right flank after the main Rebel infantry assault was defeated, Judson Kilpatrick ordered Elon Farnsworth's brigade and Wesley Merritt's attached brigade to attack, with Merritt making a dismounted probe while Kilpatrick foolishly directed Farnsworth to make a mounted charge.[43]

First to assail the Confederates, in column formation, was the 1st West Virginia Cavalry, commanded by Indiana native Nathaniel P. Richmond. Without performing a proper reconnaissance of the terrain over which the charge would take place, Kilpatrick instructed Farnsworth to send his brave troopers toward the Confederates, who had the protection of stone walls along their defensive positions. The horsemen drove their mounts over broken, rocky ground, bisected by ravines, a creek valley, and multiple fencerows. Nonetheless, the West Virginians braved Confederate artillery—that was pounding them with case shot and canister—and galloped forward. A private in the 1st Texas Infantry, who was on the receiving end of the charge, wrote that "the ground trembled as they came." James Dean, a trooper in the 1st West Virginia, recalled, "The booming of cannon, the rattle of musketry, the clank of sabers, parrying the bayonet, together with the cheering of the men made it seem as though all the powers of hell were waked to madness." The West Virginians were forced to slash their way back to the starting point; they lost five killed and four wounded. Farnsworth futilely committed his other regiments to no avail; during the last assault, the young general himself was killed, and Richmond took command of the brigade, leaving Maj. Charles Capehart in command of the 1st West Virginia. It was an inauspicious end to the Army of the Potomac's great victory at Gettysburg, but the campaign was far from over.[44]

General Lee began his withdrawal from Pennsylvania on July 4, 1863. The long train of ambulances—measuring seventeen miles from front to end—was first to leave, guarded by Brig. Gen. John Imboden's cavalry brigade. Union cavalry aggressively pursued the Army of Northern Virginia as it made its way across South Mountain and toward the Potomac River crossing sites near Williamsport, Maryland. Union militia that had been mobilized for the crisis and troops in other commands, namely the garrison at Harpers Ferry and Brig. Gen. Benjamin Kelley's Department of West Virginia, were ordered by the War Department to assist in bagging the Army of Northern Virginia before it could escape across the Potomac.[45]

During the night of July 4–5, in the midst of a terrific rainstorm, Kilpatrick's cavalry division caught the rear guard of Richard Ewell's wagon train as it crossed South Mountain at Monterey Gap, Pennsylvania. On a narrow path, according to the 1st West Virginia's surgeon, Henry Capehart (brother of the new regimental commander), "flanked on one side by woods and underbrush; and on the other side by a precipice, at the foot of which, hundreds of feet below at some points, rushed over rocks and fallen timber a torrent, swollen, noisy, and angry," the 1st West Virginia charged the enemy train, gaining the gap and then pursuing the fugitives down the other side of the mountain.[46] "The night was one of inky darkness," Charles Capehart wrote in his after-action report, "nothing was discernible a half dozen paces ahead." He continued,

As the advance came up to the train, they received a heavy volley of musketry, which at once showed the exact position of the enemy. Onward they dashed, and a hand-to-hand conflict ensued. The scene was wild and desolating. The road lay down a mountainside, wild and rugged. . . . The road was interspersed with wagons and ambulances for a distance of 8 miles, and the whole train was taken—300 wagons, 15 ambulances, together with all the horses and mules attached. The number of prisoners taken was 1,300, including 200 commissioned officers. The casualties of this regiment were 2 killed and 2 wounded.[47]

Many years later, Romney's John Casler recalled this incident, writing that the Federal troopers "turned about twenty wagons over and down the mountain side. The citizens would run out into the woods in some places and cut the spokes of the wheels, until one or two of them got killed for their trouble, when they ceased."[48] For his bravery and resolute leadership that rainy night, Charles Capehart earned the Medal of Honor.[49]

Meanwhile, West Virginia regiments assigned to Benjamin Kelley's Department of West Virginia were futilely attempting to cut off Lee's retreat route, but instead found themselves relegated to provost marshal duties. George W. Morehead of Company I, 12th West Virginia Infantry, who had survived the Second Battle of Winchester a few weeks earlier, wrote in his diary on July 5, "We received the order to fall in and go 12 miles to a town called Mercersburg [Pennsylvania] to bring in 500 Rebble prisoners." The next day he recorded, "The cavilry had captured a large train of 200 waggons. Our regiment drove them to Louden and the other regiments brought in the prisoners who was a hard looking set of men."[50] Undoubtedly, these were the same prisoners Kilpatrick's division had captured a day earlier.

The 1st West Virginia took part in engagements at Smithsburg, Hagerstown, and Williamsport as the Confederate retreat continued through Maryland. In a mounted charge that one squadron made through the streets of Hagerstown, the regiment lost two killed, four wounded, and fourteen missing.[51] Confederate cavalrymen from (West) Virginia, serving in the brigades of Grumble

Jones, John Chambliss, Fitzhugh Lee, John Imboden, and Milton Ferguson (in temporary command for Albert Jenkins, who had been evacuated with the rest of the ambulatory wounded) likewise experienced tough combat during the withdrawal from Pennsylvania, at times even fighting the 1st West Virginia Cavalry. Despite the Union cavalry's efforts to stop them, the Army of Northern Virginia made its escape across the Potomac River on June 13–14. The Gettysburg campaign was over, and the United States had added another star to its flag, that of the Mountain State—West Virginia.[52]

Several decades later, when it came time to memorialize the valor of its native sons on the old battlefields, only the Mountain State's Union military organizations would be remembered in granite and bronze—not unusual, since the Confederate regiments from its counties had been trying to *prevent* its statehood. In 1897, the West Virginia Legislature approved the expenditure of $2000 for the procurement and erection of four monuments at Gettysburg National Military Park, one for each of its Union units that fought there: Battery C, 1st West Virginia Light Artillery on Cemetery Hill; the 7th West Virginia Infantry Regiment on East Cemetery Hill; the 3rd West Virginia Cavalry (Companies A and C) on Oak Ridge; and the 1st West Virginia Cavalry Regiment behind Cemetery Ridge next to the Taneytown Road. All of the monuments were placed where the units had fought, except for that of the 1st Cavalry.[53] (In addition to the Gettysburg monuments, West Virginia also appropriated funds for a 4th West Virginia Infantry memorial at Vicksburg National Military Park.)

On November 28, 1898, in the aftermath of the United States' victory over Spain earlier that summer, the official dedication of the monuments took place. Presiding at the ceremony in front of the 7th West Virginia Memorial was West Virginia governor George W. Atkinson, but also in attendance were the adjutant general of West Virginia, Maj. Gen. John W. M. Appleton (who had served as an officer in the 54th Massachusetts Colored Infantry and had fought at Fort Wagner, South Carolina); Theodore

Lang, Civil War veteran and author of *Loyal West Virginia: From 1861–1865*—the "official" history of its Union regiments; Lt. Col. John G. Kelley and Maj. Isaac Brown, veterans of the 7th West Virginia Infantry; Pennsylvania governor Daniel Hastings and other dignitaries; National Guardsmen of the 2nd West Virginia Infantry who had been mobilized for the recent war with Spain; and

Granite and bronze memorial to the 7th West Virginia Infantry on East Cemetery Hill. The soldier is looking toward the direction of the Confederate attack launched during the evening of July 2. (Courtesy of Karl Stelly)

Bronze replica of the veteran's medal, issued to survivors of the regiment, which is affixed to the memorial. (Courtesy of Karl Stelly)

even Confederate veterans from West Virginia.[54] The veterans' society of the bloodied 7th West Virginia Infantry even struck regimental medals for its members: a large, bronze replica of this medal is attached to its Gettysburg Battlefield memorial. The medallion itself is in the shape of the 2d Corps insignia—a trefoil— with the words "7 W. VA. ROMNEY TO APPOMATTOX." The trefoil is suspended with a ribbon of red, white, and blue that is attached to a bar over which is superimposed a symbolic golden horseshoe (an award that dated to the colonial era, presented to early Virginians who had joined an exploratory expedition west of the Appalachians) and inscribed "We Have Crossed the Mountains." Today, these monuments—and the lack of Confederate (West) Virginia memorials—stand in mute testimony to the divided loyalties in West Virginia during that tragic era.

5

"A Hell of a Damned Fool"

Judson Kilpatrick, Farnsworth's Charge, and
the Hard Hand of History

BRIGADIER GENERAL JUDSON Kilpatrick's decision to launch a
mounted assault with Elon J. Farnsworth's cavalry brigade against
the right flank of the Army of Northern Virginia during the late
afternoon of July 3, 1863, has been characterized by historians as
reckless, fruitless, tragic, ill-conceived, and doomed.[1] The results
have been called a fiasco, a sacrifice, and a senseless slaughter.[2]
Kilpatrick has been accused of ordering the assault because of his
own self-indulgence and his desire to gain eternal glory.[3] What
has come to be known as "Farnsworth's Charge" has even been
compared to the charge of the Light Brigade at Balaclava.[4] Two
well-respected historians simply called the charge a display of
bad generalship.[5] Another claimed that Farnsworth's Charge
marked the downturn of Kilpatrick's career and stood out as the
darkest stain on an already blemished record.[6]

Certainly it is easy to find fault with Judson Kilpatrick. He
was vain and self-centered. He sought favors from politicians.
He boasted and sometimes lied. His modern biographer has concluded that the view held by Kilpatrick's many detractors was
probably close to the truth, in that he was "an egotistical, lying,

sadistic, philandering, thieving miscreant whose lofty reputation had been won by words, not deeds."[7] After Kilpatrick's transfer to the Army of the Cumberland, even William Tecumseh Sherman allegedly referred to him as "a hell of a damned fool," but with the caveat that *that* kind of man was just the sort of cavalry commander he was seeking.[8]

Unfortunately, it is easy to cast aspersions on someone like Kilpatrick based on his character flaws. Likewise, it is tempting to draw simple conclusions about certain events as a result of our own historical hindsight. Because Farnsworth's Charge was repulsed, because Elon Farnsworth was killed, because some of Kilpatrick's decisions in later campaigns were faulty, and because Kilpatrick was egotistical and overbearing, one might be apt to make a superficial assessment about the effectiveness or even the necessity of Farnsworth's Charge. Kilpatrick's ill-fated decision is thus interpreted as yet another bad call by a general officer who had made many unsound decisions during his military career.

Have historians treated Judson Kilpatrick fairly or unfairly—at least in respect to his decisions on July 3, 1863? What if Kilpatrick's decision to order Farnsworth's Charge is examined and objectively evaluated within the context of his orders, the tactical situation, the cavalry's organizational structure, the terrain, the enemy, the timing of the attack, and the results? Did Kilpatrick make a sound decision based on the information he had available to him *at that time?* Could the cavalry assault have succeeded, or was it nothing more than a forlorn hope? After close scrutiny, will it be apparent that the aforementioned historians have been correct all along in their assessment of Kilpatrick's generalship?

Hugh Judson Kilpatrick was born in Deckertown, New Jersey, on January 14, 1836. He attended two preparatory schools in his youth and was admitted to West Point in 1856. At that time, the U.S. Military Academy curriculum was based on five years of academic study. Kilpatrick graduated 17th of 45 cadets in May 1861. Although he was commissioned in the Regular Army as a second lieutenant of artillery, Kilpatrick sought service with a volunteer

The 5th New York Infantry at the Battle of Big Bethel. (*Harper's Weekly*, June 29, 1861)

organization and was able to wrangle a captain's commission in the 5th New York Volunteer Infantry, more commonly known as Duryee's Zouaves. On June 10, 1861, one month and four days after graduating from West Point, Captain Kilpatrick was wounded at the Battle of Big Bethel—the first Regular Army officer to be wounded in the Civil War.[9]

After his convalescence, he was placed on recruiting duty and shortly thereafter gained a commission as lieutenant colonel of the newly recruited 2nd New York Cavalry Regiment. Kilpatrick remained with the 2nd New York throughout 1862, participating in several raids and skirmishes during the Valley campaign and Second Manassas. During that time, neither he nor his command did much to distinguish either Kilpatrick himself or his regiment.[10]

Kilpatrick was arrested and incarcerated for three months in the fall of 1862 for allegedly confiscating civilian property and selling it for his own personal gain, but the evidence was inconclusive, and he was released from jail and the charges dropped. Upon his return from prison, Kilpatrick was promoted to full colonel in December 1862 and given command of the 21st New York Cavalry.[11] When

Major General Alfred
Pleasonton. (Library of
Congress)

Maj. Gen. Joe Hooker took command of the Army of the Potomac
in the winter of 1863, the cavalry was reorganized into a corps of
three divisions and a reserve brigade, all under the command of
Maj. Gen. George Stoneman.[12] Kilpatrick was again elevated, this
time to brigade command in Maj. Gen. Alfred Pleasonton's division.[13] Apparently, Kilpatrick was at the right place, at the right
time. There is no evidence that he ingratiated himself to his supe-
riors, but there also is no evidence that he did not.

Judson Kilpatrick's first tactical mission as a brigade commander came during the Chancellorsville campaign, when he and
much of the rest of the Army of the Potomac's cavalry participated
in "Stoneman's Raid." During this foray deep into Confederate territory, Kilpatrick and 450 Union troopers rode southward, close to
Richmond, and tore up sections of the Richmond, Fredericksburg
and Potomac Railroad and the Virginia Central Railroad.[14] In early
June 1863, Pleasonton replaced Stoneman as the Army of the Potomac's overall cavalry commander, and Brig. Gen. David Gregg

took command of Pleasonton's old division. Days later, Kilpatrick and his brigade fought in the Battle of Brandy Station, briefly driving Confederates from key terrain known as Fleetwood's Hill before being forced back by a Confederate counterattack. Kilpatrick was promoted to brigadier general shortly after this battle. During the middle of June, in the opening moves of the Gettysburg campaign, Kilpatrick's brigade pushed away a stubborn Confederate force from Aldie, Virginia, but at the cost of approximately 300 casualties, compared to only 119 for the southerners. Kilpatrick's inexperience as a brigade commander was readily noticeable during this battle, as he continually fed his units piecemeal into the fighting.[15] On June 21 during the Battle of Upperville, Kilpatrick's aggressive nature resulted in his own capture. Luckily, Union troopers rescued him in short order. Later during the fighting, Kilpatrick risked his life to rescue the wounded commander of the 5th North Carolina Cavalry. The Confederates withdrew from Upperville that evening, giving the Union cavalry another opportunity to claim victory.[16]

Judson Kilpatrick had compensated for his lack of experience with his aggressiveness and courage in combat, something Pleasonton had been seeking in his commanders. One week after the Battle of Upperville, Kilpatrick again was elevated, this time to division command. When Gen. George Meade replaced Joe Hooker as commander of the Army of the Potomac on June 28, he gave Pleasonton permission to reorganize the cavalry corps, which only a day earlier had gained Brig. Gen. Julius Stahel's cavalry division from the Department of Washington. With the subsequent reorganization, Judson Kilpatrick took command of Stahel's division, officially designated the 3rd Division, Cavalry Corps, Army of the Potomac. The 3rd Division comprised two brigades, both of which also would receive new commanders—Elon J. Farnsworth took over the 1st Brigade, and the 2nd Brigade went to George A. Custer. Farnsworth and Kilpatrick had been members of Pleasonton's staff, and both had the military attributes that Pleasonton found appealing. Farnsworth was a good officer, but he also was

Wesley Merritt after he had been promoted to major general later in the war. (Library of Congress)

the nephew of Congressman John F. Farnsworth, Pleasonton's political patron. Custer only recently had been promoted to captain, and now both he and Farnsworth would be jumped four grades to brevet brigadier generals. Wesley Merritt, another young captain and, like Custer and Kilpatrick, a recent graduate of West Point, assumed command of the Cavalry Corps' reserve brigade. Merritt likewise was promoted to brevet brigadier general.[17]

The young generals would have little time to shake out their new commands. Most of the Army of Northern Virginia already was tramping through Pennsylvania. On June 30, Kilpatrick's division encountered Maj. Gen. Jeb Stuart's cavalry division at the small town of Hanover, Pennsylvania. Stuart and his troopers had lost contact with the Army of Northern Virginia's infantry columns. They were trying desperately to find them when advance elements of Confederate colonel John R. Chambliss's brigade engaged a rear guard of Farnsworth's brigade on the outskirts of Hanover sometime after 10:00 A.M. on June 30. The fighting quickly escalated. The early part of the battle was characterized by mounted charges, sometimes through the streets of town. Stuart himself narrowly escaped capture as the battle intensified. Both sides by this time had brought up horse artillery.

Farnsworth eventually deployed his entire brigade—consisting of the 18th Pennsylvania, 5th New York, 1st Vermont, and 1st West Virginia—in the center of Hanover and extending south and east of the town. General Kilpatrick and Custer's brigade, comprised entirely of Michigan regiments, soon galloped into Hanover and extended Farnsworth's line to the northwest. Union troopers barricaded Hanover's streets with boxes, hay bales, fence rails, and overturned wagons. Stuart, meanwhile, stabilized his position on the southern edge of Hanover and extended his line to the southeast. More Confederate horse artillery was deployed, which immediately opened on Farnsworth's troops in the streets of Hanover and east of town. Custer decided to silence the Confederate artillery that had been firing from high ground west of Hanover. The guns were captured and then retaken by a Confederate counterattack, but Custer's Michigan men rallied and tried again. Although unable to seize their objective, Custer's soldiers continued to threaten the Confederate left flank. Concerned with the danger to both flanks and also his rear, which was being threatened by slow-moving Union infantry, Stuart waited until darkness and withdrew from Hanover, moving to the east, farther away from the Army of Northern Virginia. Union casualties at the Battle of Hanover were fewer than 200; Confederate casualties also were slight, approximately 150.[18]

Although the fight at Hanover soon would be eclipsed by the Battle at Gettysburg, the engagement nonetheless had far-reaching ramifications. As a result of the Union cavalry resistance, Stuart was forced to take an even wider detour to link up with his infantry counterparts. If Stuart had not been preoccupied with finding the main body of the Confederate army, he might have trounced Kilpatrick. As it stood, Judson Kilpatrick could notch his first victory as a division commander, and a very important one at that. Nevertheless, Kilpatrick squandered his triumph by failing to pursue Stuart. Then he reported faulty intelligence—that the main body of the Army of Northern Virginia was near East Berlin, Pennsylvania. By pushing his division from Hanover toward East Berlin, Kilpatrick not only completely lost contact with Stuart, he also had put his command far from Gettysburg when Brig. Gen. John Buford's cavalry division opened the Battle of Gettysburg on July 1. Kilpatrick and his division were approaching Gettysburg on July 2 when they again encountered part of Jeb Stuart's division, this time as the Confederates passed through Hunterstown, northeast of Gettysburg, after their long eastern detour. The subsequent skirmish at Hunterstown was a minor affair, with each side believing it had stopped an attack against its main army's flanks and rear.[19]

At eleven that evening, Kilpatrick received orders to move his division to Two Taverns, about five miles south of Gettysburg on the Baltimore Pike. By daylight on July 3, Kilpatrick's division had arrived at its destination. At 8:00 A.M., Kilpatrick received new orders to move to the left flank of the Union line and attack the right and rear of the Army of Northern Virginia, positioned near an eminence known locally as Big Round Top.[20] Farnsworth's brigade and the division commander already had begun their ride toward Big Round Top when a courier from General Pleasonton found General Custer, who had not yet departed. Pleasonton ordered Custer and his brigade to occupy ground near the intersection of the Hanover and Low Dutch roads, due north of Two Taverns about three miles away. Kilpatrick would not discover Custer's detachment until later.[21] In his official report, Kilpatrick stated, "By some mistake, General Custer's brigade was ordered to report to General Gregg, and he did not join me during the day."[22] It was not a mistake; it was faulty communications, or what Prussian military theorist Carl von Clausewitz called the "fog of war." Pleason-

ton somewhat compensated for the detachment of Custer's brigade by attaching Wesley Merritt's brigade to Kilpatrick. Now the
stage was set for one of the most controversial actions of the Battle
of Gettysburg.

According to the after-action reports of Pleasonton, Kilpatrick,
and Merritt, Kilpatrick's mission was to attack the right and rear
of the Army of Northern Virginia.[23] Although Kilpatrick did not
know it at the time, his adversary on that part of the field would
be elements of Maj. Gen. John B. Hood's division, specifically regiments from Brig. Gen. Evander Law's brigade, Brig. Gen. Jerome
Robertson's brigade, and Brig. Gen. George Anderson's brigade.
(Hood had been wounded on July 2, so the division was under
Law's temporary command.) These units were supported by bat-
teries from Maj. M. W. Henry's artillery battalion, including Capt.
William Bachman's German Artillery (South Carolina), Capt.
James Reilly's Rowan Artillery (North Carolina), and Capt. A. C.
Latham's Branch Artillery (North Carolina).

The ground occupied by the Confederates over which Kilpatrick's brigades would attack was, to say the least, formidable.
The Confederates held the lower part of Seminary Ridge where it
crossed the Emmitsburg Road, the rocky high ground between the
Bushman and Slyder farms, the western slope of Big Round Top,
and Devil's Den. Any attack against the Confederate right flank
most likely would have to pass under the guns of Confederate artillery—especially Bachman's and Reilly's batteries—on Warfield
Ridge (the extreme southern wing of Seminary Ridge). Boulders,
fences, and farm buildings provided the Confederates protection
from enemy fire and also helped to conceal their positions. Trees
and other vegetation hid them from the prying eyes of Union cavalrymen. However, Farnsworth's men enjoyed only briefly the
cover and concealment offered by the wooded slopes of Big Round
Top and the surrounding knolls and ravines. Once an assault began they would lose this protection. Merritt's soldiers, however,
would benefit from the cover of some woods during their advance.

The same terrain features that provided the Confederates with cover and concealment proved to be major impediments to Kilpatrick's force. The Union cavalrymen faced natural and manmade obstacles that included boulders, fences, stands of timber, and steep creek banks, making an assault by mounted cavalry highly hazardous. Kilpatrick's avenues of approach for a mounted attack were limited. On horseback, his men could push north and east along the Emmitsburg Road or across the pastures of the Slyder and Bushman farms. Dismounted, he had more options, as his troopers then could take advantage of the terrain and vegetation to mask their movements and protect themselves. However, in a dismounted attack, a quarter of the cavalrymen would be out of action as horse holders, and carbines were no match for the longer-range rifled muskets used by the Confederate infantry.

Although Kilpatrick's orders did not specifically state the exact time of attack, it seems implied that the attack would be made as soon as all his forces had arrived on the scene. Perhaps a better word to use would be *timing*. According to Dennis Hart Mahan in his tactical manual, *An Elementary Treatise of Advanced, Out-Post, and Detachment Service of Troops* (originally published in 1847 and republished in 1861), when mounted troops were given a mission to attack infantry, "Cavalry should . . . either wait patiently . . . until the infantry has become crippled and exhausted by being kept in action for some time; or else, watching its opportunity, make a charge whilst the infantry is in motion, so as to surprise it before it can form to receive the attack."[24] (Mahan had been a professor at West Point when Kilpatrick was a cadet.) In other words, attack the enemy infantry while it is moving, or soon after it has taken a beating.

Custer's detachment left Kilpatrick with Farnsworth's 1,925 men and Merritt's 1,321 troopers, plus two batteries of horse artillery (one for each brigade).[25] In charge of these horse soldiers were a brand-new division commander and two neophyte brigade commanders who only a few days earlier had been staff officers with the rank of captain.

As Farnsworth's brigade approached the eastern slope of Big Round Top late in the morning of July 3, Wesley Merritt and his brigade were getting under way from Emmitsburg, Maryland. On the approach to Gettysburg via the Emmitsburg Road, Merritt detached one of his regiments, the 6th U.S. Cavalry, to capture a Confederate forage train that was reported to be in the vicinity of Fairfield, Pennsylvania. So, minus the 6th U.S., Merritt's brigade came in sight of the Confederate right flank about the time that the artillery bombardment that preceded Pickett's Charge was getting under way. Merritt's dismounted troops skirmished with soldiers of the 9th Georgia Infantry of Anderson's Brigade while his horse artillery began to shell the Confederate positions. The 5th U.S. Cavalry made a mounted charge and drove in the Confederate defenders, but reinforcements were brought forward to stop Merritt's advance. Rather than continue with a mounted assault and thereby take advantage of its speed and shock, Merritt dismounted part of his command and pressed forward. The slow pace of the attack allowed the Confederates to bring up additional reserves. In addition, the guns of Reilly's and Bachman's batteries opened on Merritt's cavalrymen. Now, outgunned and outmanned, Merritt pulled back.[26]

Meanwhile, Kilpatrick and Farnsworth had been probing the Confederate positions between Big Round Top and the east side of the Emmitsburg Road. Dismounting most of his troopers, Farnsworth began to test the Confederate defenses, while placing Lt. Samuel S. Elder's Battery E, 4th U.S. Artillery on a small knoll southwest of Big Round Top. Kilpatrick next ordered a squadron of the 1st Vermont Cavalry to charge down a lane leading to the Bushman Farm. The Vermonters scattered a small rebel outpost and took possession of the farm buildings. Kilpatrick rode forward and told the troopers to hold on for as long as possible. The arrival of the 1st Texas Infantry ended the Vermonters' stay, however, forcing a retreat back to the main Union cavalry line.[27]

While Kilpatrick, Merritt, and Farnsworth probed the Confederate positions, Lt. Gen. James Longstreet's Grand Assault was occurring on the Union center. Around 5:00 P.M., Kilpatrick received word that the charge had been repulsed. A company commander in the 1st Vermont Cavalry was near Kilpatrick when "an Aide came down and Kilpatrick sprang his saddle and rode towards him." According to the captain, "The verbal order I heard delivered was: 'Hood's division is turning (or pressing) our left; play all of your guns; charge in their rear; create a strong diversion.'"[28] (In reality, Hood's troops were not pressing the Union left; they merely were being shifted, but the Union commanders had no way of knowing this at the time.) To Kilpatrick, as Mahan put it, the question of *timing* now seemed more critical than ever: *"Cavalry should . . . either wait patiently . . . until the infantry has become crippled and exhausted by being kept in action for some time; or else, watching its opportunity, make a charge whilst the infantry is in motion, so as to surprise it before it can form to receive the attack."* So far, Kilpatrick's thrusts were uncoordinated and mostly dismounted, and the Confederates had been able to react easily. It was time to use the shocking power of a cavalry charge. His orders were clear, and Kilpatrick sprang to action. Now things really began to go wrong.

If a mounted assault was going to be made anywhere, the most likely place was in General Merritt's sector, where the terrain was a bit more favorable. But Kilpatrick had been having difficulty coordinating with Merritt all afternoon, and timing was now a critical factor. So Kilpatrick decided to strike with Farnsworth's brigade, a command that actually was *assigned* to his own division rather than just attached, like Merritt. Could Kilpatrick really have believed that a mounted charge would garner success? The squadron from the 1st Vermont Cavalry had made some headway earlier in the afternoon, and Merritt's advance initially had been successful. Perhaps Kilpatrick believed that a mounted assault with a larger force would roll up the enemy flank, so he ordered the 1st West Virginia Cavalry to charge toward the Bushman Farm. The assault, however, would have to be made over terribly rough ground, and the charge would carry the West Virginians directly into the fields of fire of Reilly's and Bachman's batteries. Nevertheless, the orders were given, and the charge was made.

The 18th Pennsylvania Cavalry was on the extreme left of Farnsworth's line; the 1st West Virginia was to its right, followed by the 1st Vermont. The 5th New York was in the rear, in support of Elder's battery. Earlier reconnaissance by Farnsworth and some of his commanders convinced them that the terrain was less than desirable for a cavalry charge.[29] Kilpatrick sent the regiment forward anyway. The West Virginians struggled through the woods and over the rocky ground. They had to jump their horses over several fence lines, and when they finally broke into the open they were greeted by soldiers of the 1st Texas Infantry who had taken cover behind a stone wall. They took fire from Reilly's and Bachman's batteries. One West Virginia cavalryman wrote, "The booming of cannon, the rattle of musketry, the clank of sabers parrying the bayonet, together with the cheering of the men, made it seem as though all the powers of hell were waked to madness." After riding completely through the Texans, the West Virginians found themselves surrounded, and their commander ordered a withdrawal. Now they had to fight their way back the same way they came.[30]

While this episode was taking place, Kilpatrick ordered Farnsworth to attack with the 1st Vermont Cavalry. Farnsworth protested to his division commander but to no avail. Capt. Henry Clay Potter of the 18th Pennsylvania Cavalry recalled that

Farnsworth and Kilpatrick had been discussing their options for quite a while, but finally Kilpatrick jumped up and impatiently but in a low voice said, "Farnsworth, if you don't charge that battery, I will." No one except myself and the bugler could possibly have heard the conversation between Kilpatrick and Farnsworth, and all stories about other people having heard it are pure imagination and not true. [Potter was reacting to stories that the two generals were engaged in an argument over the proper course of action, and that Kilpatrick allegedly said that he would lead the charge himself if Farnsworth was afraid.

This supposedly led to another heated exchange between the generals.] There was no order given to charge; but as soon as Kilpatrick made the remark, Farnsworth got up, passed me, and beckoned to his orderly to bring up his horse, met it half way, mounted and ordered the troops to file out.[31]

Farnsworth personally led forward a battalion of the 1st Vermont, in columns of fours, while another battalion from the same regiment charged to his right. Then Kilpatrick sent the 18th Pennsylvania into the fray, but this regiment was quickly repulsed.[32] The 1st Vermont suffered the same fate as the West Virginians. During the charge, Farnsworth rode a circuit around the Bushman and Slyder farms. On the way back, the battalion of Vermonters that he led was caught between two lines of Confederate infantry from Law's brigade. The enfilading fire broke Farnsworth's battalion into three groups. Two of these rode through the 1st Texas and picked up a bag full of prisoners; Farnsworth's group of about fifty men made a desperate charge to break through the 15th Alabama's position, but Farnsworth was killed in the attempt.[33] Contrary to legend, Farnsworth was killed by Confederate infantry, not by turning his revolver on himself.[34]

And so ended a sad chapter in the history of the Battle of Gettysburg. For this short but violent episode, historians would brand Kilpatrick as a blunder-head, a glory seeker, and a fool. For example, in 1910, A. T. Cowell, author of *Tactics at Gettysburg*, wrote, "An attack was made on the right of the Confederate line by Farnsworth's and Merritt's brigades of cavalry. The ground was wholly unsuited for cavalry and the attack was a sacrifice. Farnsworth was killed."[35] In 1956 Edward Stackpole published *They Met at Gettysburg*. Concerning Farnsworth's Charge, he opined,

> Kilpatrick, who was under the impression or at least chose to believe that Meade was about to make a major counterattack, ordered Farnsworth to send the First West Virginia Regiment of his brigade to attack a Texas regiment in his front. . . . Dis-

Farnsworth's Charge, July 3, 1863 (Robert Underwood Johnson and Clarence Clough Buel, eds. *Battles and Leaders of the Civil War*, vol. 3 of 4 [New York: Century, 1887–88], 393)

satisfied with the meager results, Kilpatrick directed General Farnsworth personally to lead a final charge. . . . Farnsworth's charge was equally fruitless. . . . It was a brief and thrilling performance, but in reality proved nothing.[36]

Edwin B. Coddington, one of the most respected historians of the battle, was a bit more judicious than Stackpole, but he nevertheless concluded that Kilpatrick had made a fatal error:

As for Kilpatrick . . . his own men fought over ground too broken and rocky for operations by large bodies of cavalry. . . . When about 5:30 P.M. Kilpatrick received word of Union success in the center, he ordered an all-out effort by both brigades. . . . Although Farnsworth protested it was suicide, Kilpatrick insisted that he should charge with half his brigade against the center of Law's slender line . . . but the attack ended in a fiasco, including the death of Farnsworth. . . . Both Kilpatrick and Pleasanton in their reports exaggerated the impact of this attack on the enemy. . . . Kilpatrick had a point, however, when he observed that some Union infantry should have advanced on his right at the time he made his charge. . . . Nevertheless, Kilpatrick's complaint . . . does not excuse him from the charge of bad generalship.[37]

Then, in 1986, Edward G. Longacre published *The Cavalry at Gettysburg*. His criticism of Kilpatrick is scathing:

> Had Kilpatrick seriously threatened the other end of Law's refused right while Merritt made his push, he might have placed his foe in trouble. As it was, he wasted Merritt's diversion, making an ill-conceived assault against the Rebel center and then, when too late and with tragic results, committing a larger force against impregnable positions on Law's left. . . . Farnsworth's death capped a charge that had taken sixty-seven lives and a heavy toll in wounded and captured. It also marked the downturn of the career of the man who had ordered the attack. For utter recklessness, for self-indulgent folly, the doomed and senseless assault outshone the many other stains on Judson Kilpatrick's record.[38]

The criticism grew harsher as the years passed. Kilpatrick's biographer, Samuel J. Martin, has been the most severe of all. According to Martin,

> If Kilpatrick smashed into the flank of the panicked Confederates, he could win the battle for Meade and gain eternal glory for himself. Custer was still not there; Farnsworth would have to make the assault on his own. . . . The charge had been a fiasco. Kilpatrick had hoped to win glory (at Farnsworth's expense), but instead he gave the enemy "one little spot of silver lining" in the cloud that hung so darkly over the field of Gettysburg.[39]

Eric J. Wittenberg, who seems to have a firm grasp on what actually occurred on the southern portion of the Gettysburg battlefield on the afternoon of July 3, wrote, "Like the fabled charge of the Light Brigade, Farnsworth's Charge was brave, memorable and fruitless. . . . [T]heir attack was misdirected, unsupported, and led to no tangible gains. The primary result, it seems, was the death of Elon Farnsworth. A great opportunity was squandered that day, along with Farnsworth's life."[40] Finally, in *Gettysburg: Day Three,* historian Jeffry Wert wrote, "It was a senseless slaughter of good men," concluding simply, "Kilpatrick's aggressiveness and misjudgment had led the Vermonters into a bloody trap."[41]

Are the judgments of these historians fair? A reassessment proves otherwise. First, there are Kilpatrick's orders to take into account: *Attack the right and rear of the enemy.* This he accomplished beyond a shadow of a doubt. In a message to General in Chief Henry Halleck, sent at 8:35 P.M. on July 3, General Meade substantiated that Kilpatrick had followed orders. "After the repelling of the assault [i.e., Pickett's Charge]," Meade wrote, "indications leading to the belief that the enemy might be withdrawing, an armed reconnaissance was pushed forward from the left, and the enemy found to be in force."[42] Whether Kilpatrick actually accomplished anything is beside the point—he carried out the orders that were given to him. As far as the timing of the charge, it was launched at precisely the moment when the era's cavalry doctrine dictated it should have been.

Second, just how badly did Farnsworth's brigade suffer? It is difficult to justify the loss of a rising star like Elon Farnsworth, but what about the rest of his command? The number of cavalrymen who actually participated in the charge is hard to pinpoint. The 5th New York Cavalry did not play a role, as it was kept in support of Elder's Battery. Assuming that the attacking regiments made the assault with most or all of their men, then the 1st West Virginia made the charge with about 395 men, the 18th Pennsylvania attacked with some 509 soldiers, and the 1st Vermont rode off with about 600 troopers, for a total of 1,504.[43] These units suffered a total of 101 casualties during the assault, for a casualty rate of 6.7 percent.[44] One survivor from the 1st Vermont later claimed that only 312 men from his regiment participated in the charge.[45] If that number is substituted, the total number of cavalrymen making the charge would have been 1,216, and the casualty rate

8.3 percent. If the total number of each regiment that made the charge is reduced by half—which is highly unlikely—for an approximate total of 750 participants, the casualty rate still would have been a relatively low 13.4 percent.

How does the casualty rate for Farnsworth's Charge compare to similar cavalry assaults in other battles? At the Battle of Gaines's Mill on June 27, 1862, the 5th U.S. Cavalry charged headlong into Confederate infantry. The unit suffered a 22 percent casualty rate. During the Battle of Chancellorsville, the 8th Pennsylvania Cavalry also made a charge into a rebel infantry formation. Its casualty rate was 31 percent.[46] If these rates are compared to the casualty rate of Farnsworth's brigade, it becomes apparent the latter organization really did not take such a harsh beating after all.[47]

What did some of the men who served under Kilpatrick and participated in the assault think of their commander's generalship on that sultry July afternoon? And what did the Army of the Potomac's cavalry commander think? There is no indication that General Pleasonton was unhappy with Kilpatrick's decisions. "General Kilpatrick did valuable service with the First Brigade, under General Farnsworth, in charging the enemy's infantry," he wrote in his official report of the Gettysburg campaign, "and with the assistance of Merritt's brigade and the good execution of their united batteries, caused him to detach largely from his main attack on the left of our line."[48] (Coddington has suggested that Pleasonton overstated the case, since the Confederates had not planned to attack the Union left flank on July 3.[49] At the time, however, no one in the Union army knew exactly what the Confederates had planned.) General Meade, in his 8:30 P.M. dispatch to General Halleck, likewise seemed pleased: "My cavalry have been engaged all day on both flanks of the enemy harassing and vigorously attacking him with great success, notwithstanding they encountered superior numbers, both of cavalry and infantry."[50] One of Kilpatrick's subordinates, Col. Nathaniel Richmond of the 1st West Virginia, in temporary command of the brigade after Farnsworth was killed, wrote: "General Farnsworth was ordered to charge the enemy's right, which he at once did, making one of the most desperate, and at the same time one of the most successful charges it has ever been my lot to witness."[51] On the occasion of the dedication of the 18th Pennsylvania's memorial at Gettysburg twenty-six years after the battle, Capt. John W. Philips of that regiment's Company B said, "The whole object of the maneuver of General Kilpatrick on that day against the extreme right of the enemy's line was to divert his attention as to prevent a massing of his forces on General Meade's center. That it had its desired effect and that the 18th Pennsylvania Cavalry bore its full part in this strategic movement is well known to those who have studied the history of this battle."[52] Louis Boudrye, a veteran of the 5th New York Cavalry wrote in 1865, "Though this charge was not a success, its well directed blow prevented the flank movement, and thus the cavalry earned another dearly earned chaplet of honor, *dearly earned* because many of their bravest champions fell on that bloody field."[53] Captain Parsons, who led one of the 1st Vermont's charging columns, later wrote:

It is remarkable that the most deliberate and desperate cavalry charge made during the Civil War passed so nearly unnoticed that the attention of the country was first drawn to it by the reports of the enemy. The charge was directly ordered by General Meade and immediately after it was made he sent a congratulatory dispatch; and yet when the report went up that Farnsworth was killed and the regiment he led all but annihilated, the order was withheld from the Official Report. The friends of Farnsworth attacked Kilpatrick for having ordered a wanton waste of life and he remained silent. Farnsworth, who led the charge, was dead; . . . other officers, who might have given the story, were killed in a subsequent battle, and the men who survived, oppressed with grief over their losses, and resentment over their neglect, refused to come forward to claim credit for an action that they believed was well tuned, well directed and effective.[54]

The only critic of the charge who actually expressed his anger in writing at the time was Maj. Charles Capehart of the 1st West Virginia. Composing the regiment's official report in the absence of Colonel Richmond, Capehart stated:

> I cannot fail to refer you to the defensive position the enemy had availed themselves of, which is one that above all others is the worst for a cavalry charge—that is, behind stone fences so high as to preclude the possibility of gaining the opposite side without dismounting and throwing them down. The whole ground over which we charged was very adverse in every particular, being broken and uneven and covered with rock. Neither can I fail to bring to your notice that this regiment here charged upon infantry. . . . Any one not cognizant of the minutia of this charge upon infantry, under cover of heavy timber and stone fences, will fail to form a just conception of its magnitude.

As critical as he was of the decision to make a mounted charge over such rough terrain, Capehart nevertheless admitted, "Apparently our mission there had been filled, for we withdrew some 3 miles from where the engagement had taken place, and bivouacked in the open field."[55]

Judson Kilpatrick most certainly could have practiced better generalship. He ordered his units into battle in a piecemeal fashion, and he failed to coordinate the movements of Merritt and Farnsworth. He also ordered a cavalry charge across rugged terrain that was covered with rocks, fences, a stream bed, and patches of woods, to attack infantry well protected behind a stone wall. It will never be known whether Custer's presence would have made a difference. What is known is that a brand-new division commander was given a difficult task, and to accomplish this mission he had to rely on two equally new brigade commanders, one of whom was not even assigned to his own command. Perhaps if Custer had been in Merritt's place, Kilpatrick might have ordered that brigade to make the charge instead of Farnsworth, and the results might have been much different—or Custer may have been the victim of Confederate bullets instead of Sioux bullets. Kilpatrick also failed to coordinate with the infantry of the Fifth Corps on his right. Had the infantry supported him in his attack, as he claimed in his after-action report that it should have done, he just might have succeeded in rolling up the Confederate right flank.[56]

After the Battle of Gettysburg, Kilpatrick's division participated in the pursuit of the retreating Army of Northern Virginia. His command performed well at Monterey Pass on the rainy night of July 4, but he blundered at Smithsburg on July 5 by allowing an outnumbered Confederate cavalry force to escape. His generalship at Hagerstown on July 6 has been questioned, since he failed to hold the town, instead sending one of his brigades to support John Buford. On July 12 Kilpatrick and the infantry of the Sixth and Eleventh Corps seized Hagerstown, and on July 13 Kilpatrick ordered another mounted assault—again against infantry—with two companies of the 1st Vermont Cavalry, which suffered fourteen casualties. This time, General Meade gave Kilpatrick a written reprimand for the unnecessary loss of life.[57]

Kilpatrick had one last shot at the Confederates before they escaped back into Virginia. On July 14, he noticed the empty line of enemy rifle pits along the Potomac River below Hagerstown. Hoping to cut off Lee's rear guard, both Buford and Kilpatrick tried to swoop in and bag the divisions of Henry Heth and Johnston Pettigrew at Falling Waters before they too made it across the river. Again Kilpatrick ordered a charge with one of his units, this time Custer's 6th Michigan. Although General Pettigrew was mortally wounded, many Michigan troopers were cut from their saddles. For all intents and purposes, the Gettysburg campaign was over.[58]

Judson Kilpatrick's record during the Gettysburg campaign was uneven. Although new to division command, he seemed to make the same mistakes over and over. No one could ever accuse him of being timid, but he could be faulted for the way he recklessly sent men to their deaths. Cavalry leaders must be bold and daring, but they also must use good judgment. Perhaps this is why his subordinates gave him the unflattering nickname, "Kill-Cavalry."

Stung by the criticism heaped on him as a result of Farnsworth's Charge, Kilpatrick attempted in early 1864 to redeem his reputation with a plan to free the thousands of Union prisoners held in Richmond. Known as the Kilpatrick-Dahlgren Raid, the attempt failed, resulting in the death of Col. Ulric Dahlgren and another blow to Kilpatrick's already tarnished image. After the raid, Kilpatrick was transferred to William T. Sherman's army, where he commanded a cavalry division in the drive on Atlanta. Although he was wounded at Dalton, Georgia, he recuperated in time to participate in the March to the Sea and the drive through the Carolinas. When the war ended, Kilpatrick resigned his commission and accepted an appointment as minister to the Republic of Chile. In 1880 he ran for Congress but lost, then returned to his diplomatic post in Chile, where he died on December 4, 1881. He was a month shy of his forty-sixth birthday.[59]

Hugh Judson Kilpatrick will always be remembered as a vain, self-serving, and reckless officer. He made more than a few tactical blunders, and on several occasions he threw away the lives of men who served under him. When placed in the context of his entire military career, Farnsworth's Charge seems to be yet another example of Kill-Cavalry's quest for glory at the expense of his men. At Gettysburg, Kilpatrick was as inexperienced to division command as his subordinates were to brigade command, and his new command had only recently been organized. Then, Kilpatrick was given a difficult mission and was forced to accomplish it without one of his assigned brigades. He applied sound military doctrine, but he launched his mounted assault with the wrong part of his line. The casualties sustained during this charge, though high for a cavalry brigade, were lower than the casualty rates suffered in similar attacks. The major difference this time was that a promising young general officer was killed, one who also happened to be the nephew of a prominent congressman.

The purpose of this essay is not to vindicate Kilpatrick but to take an objective look at a controversial episode of the Battle of Gettysburg and in Kilpatrick's career. Most students of the Civil War still will find very little to like about Judson Kilpatrick, but at a time when the Union army was searching for offensively minded cavalry generals who were not afraid to tangle with their Confederate adversaries, he rose to the occasion. If Kilpatrick had been killed leading Farnsworth's brigade on July 3, 1863, the hard hand of history might not have struck him such a harsh blow, and he might have been remembered with the likes of John Reynolds or James Birdseye McPherson: Union generals slain while bravely leading their men into the fray.

6

Music Inspired by the
Battle of Gettysburg, 1863–1913

IT WAS THREE IN THE afternoon on July 3, 1863. A thick blanket of white smoke hung in the wide, shallow valley between Seminary and Cemetery Ridges. No sooner had the great bombardment of the Union position on Cemetery Ridge ended than the strains of a Confederate band could be heard in the distance. Some twelve thousand southern infantrymen were preparing to assault the center of the Army of the Potomac's defenses, and it was hoped that the bandsmen's martial airs would steel the gray- and butternut-clad soldiers for the onslaught. But no amount of musical inspiration could prepare the men from Virginia, North Carolina, South Carolina, Alabama, Mississippi, Tennessee, and Georgia for what lay ahead. More than five thousand Confederate soldiers would become casualties of the attack. Pickett's Charge, as it came to be called, was the grand finale of the dramatic overture known as the Battle of Gettysburg.[1]

Naturally, such a momentous event spawned countless volumes of history, some penned shortly after the battle, some before the end of the war, and thousands since 1865.[2] The battle also became the subject of poetry, paintings, novels, documentary films, board games, computer games, and of course, a feature-length Hollywood movie. It is little known, however, that the Battle of Gettysburg inspired composers and lyricists, some of whom wrote their music even before all of the fallen were properly buried. This essay will examine some of the musical compositions written during the fifty-year period between 1863 and 1913, the latter date marking the semicentennial of the battle and the year before the beginning of a much more terrible conflagration.

By November 1863, four months after the momentous battle, most of the Union dead had been collected and interred within a seventeen-acre plot of land adjacent to Gettysburg's civilian burial ground, Evergreen Cemetery. President Abraham Lincoln was asked to make some dedicatory remarks after Senator Edwin Everett of Massachusetts delivered the keynote address. It was a formal and solemn affair, with music provided by the U.S. Marine Band, Birgfield's Band, and the National Union Musical Association of Baltimore (popularly known as the Baltimore Glee Club). Tucked between Everett's two-hour oration and Lincoln's remarks, a hymn—which Benjamin B. French composed for the occasion—was performed by the Baltimore Glee Club. French, a longtime Washington bureaucrat, titled his work "The National Consecration Chant or Hymn." Wilson G. Horner, director of the Glee Club, set the words to music.[3]

When Horner rose to direct his vocalists, he held a small American flag, which he used as a conductor's baton.[4] "The National Consecration Chant" was written for bass, baritone, alto, and soprano voices. When the piece was later published, its cover inscription read, "The following beautiful lines were chanted at the dedication of the National Cemetery, Gettysburg, Pa., Nov. 19, 1863, by the National Union Musical Association of Baltimore, at the close of Mr. Everett's, and just before President Lincoln's Address. The deep pathos of the poetry—the words of which, being clearly enunciated, were distinctly heard by the assembled thousands—the occasion, and the surroundings, made it a solemn feature of the day, moving very many to tears."[5] Although the sheet

Benjamin B. French.
(Library of Congress)

music does not specify the tempo at which it is to be performed, the nature of the music and the solemnity of the occasion naturally dictate that the piece was to be sung slowly and deliberately. The verses emphasize the themes of sacrifice, freedom, the rule of law, and mourning:

1. 'Tis holy ground, This spot, where in their graves, We place our country's brave, Who fell in Freedom's Holy cause, Fighting for liberties and laws; Let tears abound.

2. Here let them rest, And summer's heat, and winter's cold, Shall glow and freeze above this mould, A thousand years shall pass away, A nation still shall mourn this clay, Which now is blest.

3. Here where they fell, Oft shall the widow's tear be shed, Oft shall fond parents mourn their dead, The orphan here shall kneel and weep, And maidens where their lovers sleep, Their woes shall tell.

4. Great God in Heaven! Shall all this sacred blood be shed, Shall we mourn our glorious dead? Oh, shall the end be wrath and woe, The knell of Freedom's overthrow, A country riven?

5. It will not be! We trust, O God! Thy gracious power To aid us in our darkest hour. This be our prayer: "O Father, says A people's Freedom from its grave; All praise to Thee!"

The sixteenth president of the United States next delivered his famous address, which was followed by another work written specifically for the occasion: "Dirge," a patriotic piece of four verses, written by James G. Percival with music by Alfred Delaney. The lyrics of the first, second, and fourth verses emphasize the nobleness of death for a righteous cause and the rewards that waited in heaven for those Union soldiers who died on the battlefield, but the third verse made an analogy to ancient Greece:

Not in Elysian Fields, by the oblivious river,
Not in the Isles of the Blest, over the blue rolling sea;
But on Olympian heights shall dwell the devoted forever;
There shall assemble the good, the wise, valiant, and free.

These lyrics were particularly appropriate to the location and the occasion, since the cemetery was designed in the Greek Revival style of landscape architecture then in vogue in the United States, and Edward Everett—who himself played an important role in America's Greek Revival—even pointed out in his oration that the Athenian dead at the Battle of Marathon, like the Union dead at Gettysburg, were buried on the battlefield where they fell. The dirge was musical evidence of the American idea that the United States was a second Athens.[6]

Delaney composed the music for several other Civil War songs, including another Gettysburg piece, appropriately titled "Gettysburg!" which was part of a collection of six "songs and odes" published in 1863 under the series name "Songs of the Loyal." The collection included "My Love Is on the Battlefield," "The Nation

Shall Not Die," "The Young Volunteer," "The Christian Commission," and "The Son Who Was His Mother's Pride." Robert Morris wrote the lyrics to "Gettysburg!" and the song was dedicated to Gen. George G. Meade, the victorious commander of the Army of the Potomac. Because the tune is performed at a lively pace, one can almost imagine the sounds of the galloping horses as Confederate cavalry came riding across the Mason-Dixon line, especially in the first verses: "The boldest and the bloodiest raid the Southern Legions ever made, / Was when their countless thousands strayed to Gettysburg! To Gettysburg! / Laden with spoils up-on each back, a wolf-like ferocious pack." The end of the first verse, however, informed the audience that the Rebels eventually paid the price for their invasion: "How few e're found the homeward track From Gettysburg! From Gettysburg! / How few e're found the homeward track From Gettysburg! From Gettysburg!"[7]

Several ballads written shortly after the battle touched the heartstrings of listeners by capitalizing on the great loss of life sustained by the two armies. One piece supposedly was based on a poignant episode about a dying Union soldier. According to the text on the cover of the sheet music, "On the battlefield at Gettysburg, among many of our wounded soldiers was a young man the only son of an aged mother. Hearing the surgeon tell his companions that he could not survive the ensuing night, he placed his hand upon his forehead, talking, continually of his mother and sister, and said to his comrades assembled around him, 'Break it gently to my mother.'" The words to "Break It Gently to My Mother" were written by Mary Griffith and the music by Frederick Buckley. Buckley was a popular violinist and a member of Buckley's Serenaders, the musical family who first performed this piece. Frederick died in October 1864, and thus did not live to see the end of the Civil War.[8]

An additional ballad featured as its subject another heretofore-unknown American who also made the supreme sacrifice but was *not* a soldier. On July 3, Virginia Wade was baking bread in her sister's home on the outskirts of Gettysburg when a bullet pierced the door and struck her, killing her instantly. "Jenny" Wade thus became the only civilian killed during the Battle of Gettysburg. Her musical tribute, "Jenny Wade: The Heroine of Gettysburg," was published in 1864, with lyrics by Albert Anderson and music by Rudolph Wittig. The song extolled the virtues of a "woman true" who was cut down by "traitors" while she was fulfilling her duty to the Republic. "She was making bread for our army during the battle, having refused to leave the house, which was in range of both armies," reads the narrative on the cover of the sheet music, "and she was shot through the heart." In reality, Jenny was just unlucky enough to get in the way of an errant bullet. Not surprisingly, the Confederates were described in harsh terms, while Jenny was portrayed almost as a goddess of liberty. Written for piano and voice, the song was to be performed at a moderately slow tempo. It contained four verses and a refrain. The third verse and refrain display the song's attitude about the Confederates and Jenny:

> When to the north wind rebels threw
> Their noisome traitor rag,
> The courage of a woman true
> Upheld our dear old flag.
> Wher-e're that starry flag shall wave,
> Mid clouds or on the plain,
> Remember'd be thy hallow'd grave,—
> For home and country slain.
>
> In the quiet church-yard sleeping,
> With the bravest fitly laid,
> Moans the wind through willows weeping
> O'er the grave of Jenny Wade.[9]

The refrain, however, used a good deal of poetic license. Jenny was not laid to rest in a "church-yard"—she was buried in Evergreen Cemetery—nor did willows grow over her grave.

Although the Battle of Gettysburg had caused the death of one young woman and thousands of young men, the passing of one particular Union soldier became a cause célèbre across the North. During the afternoon of July 1, two corps of the Army of the Potomac—the First and the Eleventh—were beginning to retreat under the weight of an overwhelming Confederate assault. Two divisions of the Eleventh Corps were heading back toward Cemetery Hill, where a third division already was digging defensive positions. Sensing that the rest of his corps needed help, the Union division commander on Cemetery Hill sent one of his brigades to the other side of Gettysburg to fight a delaying action while the rest of the corps escaped. This lone brigade quickly was overrun and soon was flying rearward to Cemetery Hill. One soldier from that brigade, a member of the 154th New York Infantry, was shot during the retreat and lay mortally wounded. Before he died, he pulled out a photograph of his children for one last look. When he was found several days later, his lifeless hands still clutched the photograph next to his heart. One recent historian has written: "He was only one of thousands of dead men strewn about Gettysburg's fields, but he was special. Of all the blackened, bloated, contorted corpses on the battleground, his death pose spoke of devotion. In the silence of death, he spoke of love."[10]

Unfortunately, the soldier bore no identification. The story was so touching that the children's image was reproduced all across the northern states, and newspaper editors published the moving account time and again. Wilson Horner, the director of the National Union Musical Association of Baltimore, composed the music for a song written by W. H. Hayward, titled "The Unknown Soldier Song (Who Is He?)." Published in 1864, it was dedicated to "the orphans of the brave soldiers who have fallen in defence of their country." Its six verses spoke of duty to country, love of flag and family, and the plight of the poor widow and children. Eventually, a woman living in western New York discovered that the celebrated photograph was the same one she had given her husband, Sgt. Amos Humiston. By the time Horner published "The Unknown Soldier," Humiston's identity already had been ascertained.[11]

The story of the nameless soldier touched everyone's heart, including a composer named James G. Clark, who had made a name for himself as a popular songwriter and performer during the antebellum period. Clark had entered a contest sponsored by the *American Presbyterian* newspaper to compose song lyrics concerning the Humiston incident. Announcing Clark as the winner, the paper proclaimed, "Out of several pieces sent to us on the death of Sergeant Humiston, we unhesitatingly give the preference to the following simple, sweet verses, very well adapted to music, which the author has already provided for them, and will soon publish." James Clark's "The Children of the Battle Field" was published in April 1864. Fine print on the sheet music announced, "The net proceeds of the sales of this music are reserved for the support and education of the Orphan Children."

The song was dedicated to Dr. J. Francis Bourns of Philadelphia, who took an early interest in identifying the soldier and later sold copies of the photograph—cartes de visite, or CDVs—to raise money for the orphans and widow. Notably, the Humiston family claimed they never received a penny from the sales of either the music or the CDVs. This is particularly ironic, especially considering the final line of each of the song's three verses: "O! Father, shield the soldier's wife, / And for his children care." The song became so popular that Clark made it part of his regular repertoire and published a second edition in October 1864.[12]

In addition to the pieces that focused on the battle's human-interest stories, several compositions were written to commemorate the victory itself. James Cox Beckel, a Philadelphia organist, was fifty-two years old at the time of the battle and was best known as a composer of sacred music and teacher of organ method. In his composition titled "Battle of Gettysburg," Beckel used his "artistic license" to alter the outcome of the battle: at one point, he imagined militiamen from New York and Pennsylvania assaulting the rear of the Army of Northern Virginia, culminating with a Union counterattack by the entire Army of the Potomac. Had this episode actually occurred—and Abraham Lincoln wished it had—the Civil War might have come to a close in 1863. Styled a "programmatic" composition, meaning that it described a particular story or historical event, it began with a section called "March of the Grand Army of the Potomac under Major Genl. George Gordon Meade into Pennsylvania July 1st 1863." The other episodes of the battle that Beckel featured in his composition were identified within the score, such as the "Rebels approaching under Gen. Lee," the death of Gen. John Reynolds, and the arrival of the Union Fifth and Sixth Corps, who "come up bravely to the tune of Yankee Doodle." The pianist was given clues about the "special effects" that the music was supposed to create, such as flying artillery shells, troops approaching from a distance, the sound of drums beating, "terrific cannonading," and even "Three Grand Hurrahs and a Tiger," indicating Union men cheering and growling in a victory celebration. The piece is typical for this genre, with dramatic changes in dynamics, meter, and tempo. Beckel's "Battle of Gettysburg" undoubtedly sparked the imaginations of many listeners.[13]

As the war continued, so too did more compositions about the Battle of Gettysburg but mostly from a northern perspective. Considering the outcome of the battle, it is not surprising that southern composers did not rush to publish songs about Gettysburg. John Prosinger, a professor at Hollins Institute in Virginia, wrote a piano piece titled "Picket's [sic] Charge March," which was published by B. Duncan & Company of Columbia, South Carolina. Prosinger dedicated the march to the Army of Northern Virginia—although the cover of the sheet music said it was "dedicated to the Northern Army of Virginia." Not only did he get the name of the army wrong, he also misspelled Gen. George Pickett's name.[14]

In 1864 T. C. Porter and J. B. Kevinsky published a piece for voice and piano, called "The Rocky Hills of Gettysburg." As with other northern songs about the battle, the Union soldiers were

heroic and selfless, while Confederate soldiers were haughty traitors, as evinced by the lyrics of the first and third verses:

> Oh dark the day, and dark the hour,
> When treason in her height of power,
> With all her gathered legions came,
> To waste the North with sword and flame!
> Right onward, swift exultant, proud,
> With burning wrath and curses loud,
> Up to yon chain of hills they crowd;
> The rocky hills of Gettysburg.
>
> In nameless graves the traitors sleep,
> Where none shall ever come to weep;
> But for her martyred sons, with tears,
> A monument the nation rears,
> And age to age shall pass it down,
> The story of their bright renown,
> And everlasting fame shall crown.
> The rocky hills of Gettysburg.[15]

Another song written in 1864 also paid tribute to the Union defenders of Gettysburg while it castigated the "traitor hoards" of
the Army of Northern Virginia. Titled "The Heroes of Gettysburg;
or, A Dirge for the Brave," it was dedicated "to the friends of the
heroes who fell in the Battle at Gettysburg." James A. Scott wrote
the music and Max J. Coble penned the lyrics. Coble was a Gettysburg native who in 1861 had enlisted in Cole's Maryland Cavalry
(recruited primarily from the Emmitsburg, Maryland, area, only
a few miles south of Gettysburg) and served as "First Bugler." The
song's seminal performance was by the Glee Club of Company C,
Cole's Maryland Cavalry. Coble sang lead and was accompanied
by his fellow troopers who sang the chorus and played guitar, vio-
lin, and flute. Sadly, Coble was captured before his music was pub-

lished, and he died from disease later that year as a result of his incarceration in Andersonville Prison.[16]

The song included six verses and two different choruses, and its tempo was marked "grave." The piece was sung softly at the beginning, increased in volume at the end of the verses, and was played and sung forcefully during the chorus:

1. From the bloody Rappahannock,
Where in myriads lie!
Those who perished for the nation,
That it might not die!
Came our glorious patriot army,
Here again to meet
Traitor hordes in shock of battle,
And their hopes defeat.
(First Chorus)
Up! shake off thy slumber,
Mighty nation, rise!
Marshal forth thy hearts for battle
Under Freedom's skies.

2. And they fought as those fight only
Who defend the right;
When the cause of truth and justice
Serves with double might;
'Till the foe, dismayed and beaten
Were compelled to yield,
With their broken columns flying
From the bloody field.
(First Chorus)

3. And the spot is now immortal
Where our heroes died,
'Mid the awful roar and carnage

Of the battle's tide.
Their dear memories in the nation
Never shall decay;
It shall bear in fond remembrance,
Gettysburg's proud day.
(Second Chorus)
Pause! The earth is holy
Where our heroes lie!
And the winds are ever wisp'ring
Of their victory.

The lyrics touched the old familiar theme that the Union defenders were heroes and martyrs, the Confederate invaders were traitors, and the field of battle was now a shrine to the fallen brave who wore the blue.

When the Civil War ended in the spring of 1865, the need for patriotic music diminished. The soldiers returned home and composers found other subjects upon which to base their titles and lyrics. In 1880, however, lyricist Irenaeus D. Foulon harkened back to memories of the battle to make a political point. That year, the presidential election pitted two former Union generals against each other. The Republican candidate, James Garfield, was a veteran of the Civil War's western theater and thus did not fight at Gettysburg. Winfield Scott Hancock was the Democratic contender. As the commander of the Army of the Potomac's Second Corps, Hancock had defended the center of the Union position on Cemetery Ridge on July 2 and 3. The postwar Republicans loved to wave the symbolic "bloody shirt" of fallen Union soldiers to reinforce the fact that the Democratic Party's antebellum stronghold was in the South. Even though Hancock was seriously wounded defending the Union at Gettysburg, the lyricist of the song titled, "The Veteran's Vote," opined that Hancock had become a turncoat: "Then he [Hancock] wore the Union blue / Now he's donned the Rebel gray." Charles Kunkel wrote the music of "The Veteran's Vote." Lyrics were even supplied in German so that the thousands of German immigrants who had served in the Union army could understand them. "The Veteran's Vote" (or *"Die Stimme des Veteranen"*) was part of The Boys in Blue series of Republican campaign songs for the election of 1880 and was "Respectfully dedicated to the Veterans of the War of the Rebellion."[17]

As the years passed and the physical and symbolic wounds healed, veterans of both sides began returning to the fields of strife. Northern veterans came in droves to Gettysburg, scene of their overwhelming victory in the eastern theater. They began erecting monuments and memorials to honor the sacrifices they made in 1863. In 1887, the first reunion of Union and Confederate veterans of Pickett's Charge occurred at Gettysburg. Perhaps opportunistically, two years earlier C. H. Burton had composed a guitar piece titled "Gettysburg," and in 1886 Septimus Winner, a well-known bandleader, composer, and music publisher, wrote "The Gettysburg March." Not to be outdone, Louis Conterno, another bandleader, wrote his own piece, also called "The Gettysburg March," in time for the twenty-fifth anniversary in 1888. Finally, James C. Beckel, now seventy-seven, published in 1888 another programmatic piece, with the ponderous title "The Battle of Gettysburg: Major General Geo. E. Pickett's Celebrated Charge at the Battle of Gettysburg, July 3, 1863." Unlike his first "Gettysburg" composition, this one was somewhat sympathetic to the southerners, especially now that Beckel's sheet music could be sold in the southern states. In this composition, Beckel once again stretched his artistic license, claiming that 3,500 men in Pickett's division had been killed, when in reality only 499 had been killed or mortally wounded.[18]

With the passing of the twenty-fifth anniversary, composers' interest in the battle waned. In 1913, the fiftieth anniversary of the battle was observed with a grand reunion of surviving Union and Confederate veterans. The U.S. government and the Commonwealth of Pennsylvania sponsored the event. More than fifty-three thousand veterans returned, and tens of thousands of spectators came to see them. President Woodrow Wilson gave a speech. Military bands played the old martial airs and, of course, songs were written especially for the occasion.[19]

The cover of one piece of sheet music proudly announced that it was written specifically for the "Gettysburg Semi-Centennial Reunion." Titled "Grand Old Gettysburg Boys," its lyrics were composed by Mrs. Findley Braden and the music by W. A. Webb. The words at the very top of the cover sheet claimed that it was the "National Peace Song." The lyrics themselves reflect the spirit of reconciliation and friendship that pervaded the anniversary celebration, as exemplified by the first verse:

They come today from far away,
To camp on once contested ground,
In blue and gray, long after fray,
Where only peace and rest are found.
And hand grasps hand, as oft they stand
Comparing notes about the past;
God in command a happy land,
And blest reunion now at last.[20]

Another reconciliation song was "Gettysburg," by James Wisler and Vivian Brooks. The song is a typical Tin-Pan Alley arrangement with a syrupy, ragtime accompaniment. The lyrics are absolutely dreadful:

Fifty long years all told,
On these green fields were formed,
Facing each other bold,
In battle lines we stormed.
Up from the South they came,
Down from the North we marched,
Clad in blue, musket true,
They in gray, with no delay.
(Chorus)
Never shall thy glory cease;

Gettysburg, Gettysburg,
Never more in days of peace.

The battle fierce did rage,
O'er meadow, valley, plain,
Round top big, Round Top small,
Join in the deadly combat.
Culp's Hill with shot and shell,
Man and tree alike now tell,
Broken branch, leaded tree,
Broken army and leaded limb.
(Chorus)

Now on these fields you see,
Many a Monument, Marker, tow'r
Culp's Hill off to the East,
Cemetery Hill near by.
Seminary Ridge West,
All tell of war in the past,
Thus shall they ever stand,
Emblems of peace, ended war.
(Chorus)[21]

The fiftieth anniversary of the battle came and went, and the next year the world was plunged into an even more terrible conflict. In 1917, the United States entered the World War, which soon had American composers and lyricists writing a whole new generation of war music with tunes such as "Over There," "K-K-K-Katy," and "Good-bye Broadway, Hello France." The Gettysburg Battlefield itself was turned into a large U.S. Army training camp. This war, like all those before it, proved not to be the "war to end all wars."

Music written in remembrance of—or about—the Battle of Gettysburg had evolved from compositions written immediately after the battle as a musical tribute to the fallen Union soldiers; to music that, thematically, told the story of the battle or one of its episodes from the viewpoint of one side or the other (normally the side of Union); to songs of reconciliation that were intended to heal the wounds and diminish the scars of the past. Although composers might return to the fields of Gettysburg for inspiration, it seems apparent that after the fiftieth anniversary in 1913, the Battle of Gettysburg had played its final cadence—with perhaps only a few widely scattered exceptions—as the subject of popular music.[22]

7

Cadet Gray, Khaki, and Camouflage

The U.S. Army and Gettysburg, Post-1863

UNITED STATES ARMY Field Manual 6–22 (formerly FM 22–100) is the standard guide for teaching leadership skills to the junior officers and noncommissioned officers of the modern army. It is used at West Point, in ROTC detachments, at the Officer Candidate School, and in all of the Warrior Leader Courses (formerly the primary leadership development courses) for junior noncommissioned officers (NCOs). Until it was replaced in June 2015 by a new edition, for more than thirty years the manual's second chapter included a case study of Col. Joshua Chamberlain's actions along the rock-strewn slope of Little Round Top. According to the manual,

> Colonel Chamberlain made sure that every man knew what was at stake when his unit prepared for battle at Gettysburg. Prior to the battle, he painstakingly developed his leaders and built his unit into a team with mutual trust between leaders and the subordinates. While teaching and training his Soldiers, he showed respect and compassion for his men and their diverse backgrounds, thus deepening the bond between the commander and his unit.

During the battle, he effectively communicated his intent and led by example, with courage and determination. His tactical abilities, intellect, and initiative helped him seize the opportunity and transition from defensive to offensive maneuver, achieving victory over his Confederate opponents. For his actions on 2 July 1863, Colonel Chamberlain received the Medal of Honor.[1]

The question arises: What is the relationship between a battle fought more than a century and a half ago and modern warfare? The answer is simple: although weapons and tactics change, the traits of a good leader remain the same, whether that leader fought at Gettysburg, in the Ardennes Forest, or Ia Drang. For several generations of Army leaders, including those who fought in the small wars of the 1980s, the Persian Gulf War, Afghanistan, and the Iraq War, the officers and NCOs who had studied this manual emulated Chamberlain's leadership. Although that particular historical episode is no longer included as a case study, modern soldiers return to the Gettysburg Battlefield on an ongoing basis to learn from the successes and mistakes of their predecessors, both Union and Confederate.

The relationship between the U.S. Army and the Gettysburg Battlefield is not a recent manifestation. In fact, it has been an intermittent affair since the initial days of July 1863. During the next century and more, American soldiers in blue, khaki, cadet-grey, olive-drab, and camouflage uniforms have descended upon these hallowed fields to study, train for other battles, and commemorate the deeds of those who went before them.

With the departure of the Army of Northern Virginia and the Army of the Potomac from the area surrounding the little town and its adjacent farms during the summer of 1863, the bond between the Army and Gettysburg began to dissipate. Winning the war and reconstructing the South would be more important to the Army than memorializing its heroes or learning from this great Civil War battlefield. Though invalid soldiers recuperating from battle wounds remained in Gettysburg and its environs through the end of 1863, there were few other troops in the area thereafter, except for units participating in the dedication of the National Cemetery in November 1863, and soldiers attending the 1865 dedication of the Soldiers' National Monument.[2] The surrender of the Confederacy in the spring of 1865 once again brought into focus the irregular warfare between soldiers on the frontier and the Native Americans they were trying to conquer. Subduing these formidable foes would keep military minds occupied for the next few decades.

The first time a large body of troops "invaded" Gettysburg after the war was when the Pennsylvania National Guard went into division camp at Gettysburg for seven days in 1884. What a sight these men from the Keystone State must have been as they arrived dressed in their Civil War–vintage uniforms, carrying the same muzzle-loading muskets used to such effect a generation before. Many of the officers had fought in the war, some even at Gettysburg, and surely there were guardsmen whose fathers had participated in the bloody struggle. Camped on the battlefield, the part-time soldiers were reviewed by Gen. Phil Sheridan, a Civil War legend in his own right, who in 1884 was the commanding general of the U.S. Army.[3]

The Pennsylvania National Guard, and sometimes Regular Army units assisting with various monument commemorations, would camp and train at Gettysburg on several more occasions during the rest of the nineteenth century and into the early years of the twentieth. Once in a while the presence of guard units had little to do with training. In 1889 a guard regiment from the Johnstown area went to Gettysburg to support the veterans' encampment of the Grand Army of the Republic. These guardsmen could not attend regular summer maneuvers with the rest of the state forces because they had lost most of their arms and equipment in the great Johnstown Flood.[4]

The first appearance of a large force of Regular units at Gettysburg was not until 1894, when elements of the active Army went into camp with the Pennsylvania National Guard. According to an early historian of the guard, "The Cavalry and artillery were encamped with Regular Army artillery on the east side of the Taneytown Road. General Headquarters and the rest of the troops were on Seminary Ridge on the same ground occupied by General Lee's forces during the Battle of Gettysburg."[5]

On February 11, 1895, Congress passed legislation establishing Gettysburg National Military Park. The Gettysburg Battlefield Memorial Association, founded less than a year after the battle, thereupon transferred to the park the six hundred acres it had acquired.[6] Daniel S. Lamont, Grover Cleveland's secretary of war, meanwhile had appointed a commission for "purchasing of land for avenues and marking the positions of troops, [supervising] . . . the construction and fencing of the avenues . . . and [the procurement of] . . . tablets . . . to mark the positions of troops." The three members of the commission and the park engineer, Lt. Col. E. B. Cope, formerly of the Corps of Engineers, were Civil War veterans. Lt. Col. John P. Nicholson, who fought at Gettysburg with the 28th Pennsylvania Infantry, served as chairman of the commission from its inception until his death in 1922.[7]

Under Nicholson's supervision, the Gettysburg Battlefield was transformed into one of the best known and most manicured historical sites in the country. When an officer from the Army Inspector General's Bureau examined the National Military Park in 1904, his report reflected the immense strides the commission had made. In the nine years since the Army assumed responsibility for the battlefield, avenues had been constructed, wood and steel fences erected, road gutters paved, and vegetation planted. Stone fences had been reconstructed where they had existed during the battle, 324 cannon and 462 tablets marking troop positions were erected, and five steel observation towers were built, a few of which still exist today. According to the inspector, "The character of the work done and the general conditions showed a very intelligent and thorough system as to construction, care, and maintenance." In a comment that would surprise anyone who has ever dealt with an "IG," the inspector wrote: "I have nothing to suggest in the way of improvements upon the methods and systems of the [Gettysburg National Military Park] Commission."[8]

About this time, around the turn of the century, cadets from the U.S. Military Academy began making the five-hundred-mile round trip to Gettysburg during the spring of their senior year. This "staff ride," as it was and still is called, made by the entire First Class of the Corps of Cadets, became an annual occurrence and lasted through 1916. During their excursion, cadets studied the lay of the land, analyzed the strategy of commanders, and evaluated unit tactics through the use of terrain walks and guided tours. For a bird's eye view of the field, they could ascend one of the new steel observation towers.[9]

Cadets who visited the park during these early years of the twentieth century included many future commanders of the world wars and the Korean War, such as Dwight D. Eisenhower, "Vinegar Joe" Stillwell, George S. Patton, and Omar Bradley. Some would pay the ultimate price of patriotism, just as their predecessors had done at Gettysburg only a few decades earlier. In 1905 one cadet wrote: "The [trips] have taught us many things which are not in the books and which some of us never would have learned otherwise."[10] Writing to his future wife from the Eagle Hotel in Gettysburg on May 11, 1909, Cadet Patton painted a mystical portrait of the battlefield:

There is to me strange fascination in looking at the scenes of the awful struggles which raged over this country. A fascination and a regret. I would like to have been there too.

This evening after supper I walked down to the scene of the last and greatest struggle on Cemetery Hill. To get in a proper frame of mind I wandered through the cemetery and let the spirits of the dead thousands laid there in ordered rows, sink deep into me. Then just as the son [sic] sank [behind] the South Mountains I walked down to the scene of Pickett's great charge and seated on a rock just where . . . two of my great uncles died I watched the wonder of the day go out.

The sunset painted a dull red the fields over which the terrible advance was made and I could almost see them coming growing fewer and fewer while around and behind me stood calmly the very cannon that had so punished them. There were some quail calling in the trees near by and it seemed strange that they could do it where man had known his greatest and last emotions. It was very wonderful and no one came to bother me. I drank it in until I was quite happy. A strange pleasure yet a very real one.

I think that it takes an evening like that to make one understand what men will do in battle. It was a wonderful yet foolish battle.[11]

Six years later, in the midst of what Americans then called the Great European War, Cadet Edwin Kelton, Class of 1915, shared his own impression of the battlefield. He reflected:

We had a glorious time at Gettysburg. The weather most of the time was ideal. Only when on top of the steel tower on Big Round Top did the mist get so thick that we could not see the battlefield. Monday morning we spent in driving over the field, reading tablets and trying to get an idea of how the fighting did take place. I can't say that we learned much in the way of tactics and how to lead troops, but at least we gained a wholesome respect for those boys and men who advanced in solid lines upon an infantry line that was hurling death at them, besides artillery sending out a steady stream of shrapnel. . . . No, I have not much desire to see this country go to war again, but if the Germans don't wake up pretty soon I shall be forced to become an Ally.[12]

In 1913, a year before the conflict broke out in the Europe, the U.S. Army assisted with the planning and administration of the fiftieth anniversary of the Battle of Gettysburg, also referred to as the "Peace Jubilee." As early as January 1912, War Department officials had met with representatives of the Pennsylvania Commission, Fiftieth Anniversary of the Battle of Gettysburg, and the

Joint Special Committee of the Congress to make provisions for the anniversary commemoration. An Act of Congress of August 26, 1912, authorized $150,000 to the War Department, matched by an equal amount from the Commonwealth of Pennsylvania.[13]

Soon after Congress gave the nod of approval, the Army set up a "joint headquarters" in Gettysburg with the Pennsylvania Commission. The bulk of administrative and logistical matters concerning the anniversary became the responsibility of the Quartermaster Department, which possessed expertise in transportation, supply, and food service for large numbers of men. The task would be monumental, with requirements to feed, shelter, and transport 53,000 elderly Union and Confederate veterans "whose average age was probably well over 70 years." An army physician who served during the celebration guessed that "never before in the world's history . . . [had] so great a number of men so advanced in years been assembled under field conditions." The Army sent nearly 1,500 soldiers to the "Great Camp," as the cantonment of the reunion would be called. The War Department deemed these soldiers "necessary for . . . proper administration of its many . . . details, and to police and protect the camp . . . [and] the avenues throughout the battlefield." When the reporters (155—invited as guests of the government) and the civilian cooks, bakers, and kitchen police (2,170) were added to the list, the total number of "campers" came to more than 57,000.[14]

To command the Great Camp, the Army detailed Brig. Gen. Hunter Liggett, who would become well known during World War I as commanding general of the American Expeditionary Force's First Army. Liggett's career would be remembered when the Army named a post in California after him, but two of his subordinates were destined to surpass him in the annals of American military history: lieutenants in 1913 were Simon Bolivar Buckner Jr. and George S. Patton Jr. The son of the Confederate general who surrendered Fort Donelson to Gen. U. S. Grant in 1862, Buckner rose to lieutenant general and became the ranking American soldier to die from enemy action during World War II when he was killed while commanding on Okinawa in 1945. In 1913 Patton accompanied the 1st Squadron, 15th Cavalry Regiment. This unit, along with two battalions of the 5th Infantry; Battery D, 3rd Artillery; Company C, 1st Engineers; and 288 officers and enlisted men of the Medical Department comprised the bulk of the Regulars at Gettysburg that year.[15] Remarkably, the usually long-winded Patton had little to note on this "visit" to Gettysburg. From his letters, he obviously was not enamored with his role as a "park policeman," as he called it. Commenting on the elderly veterans, he wrote: "They are a disgusting bunch, dirty and old, and of the people who 'God Loves.' One old hound has been beating a drum ever since he got here. Two others have a cannon which they fire as often as possible."[16]

From June 29 until July 6, the veterans took part in the commemoration honoring their deeds from fifty years before. Many of the addresses and official functions of the reunion took place in the "Great Tent," as it was called, that quartermaster troops had erected just east of the Emmitsburg Road. To truly appreciate the magnitude of the Army's responsibilities during the reunion, consider the following statistics: camp dimensions, 247 acres; tents erected, 6,592; mess kits issued, 54,000; meat consumed, 156,410 pounds; telephone wire laid, 90 miles; medical cases treated, 9,986.[17] Complicating matters was the heat, exceeding a hundred degrees on July 2. There was the confusion created by thousands of wandering tourists, and the frailty of the honored guests. Yet the celebration went off with nary a hitch.[18] It proved to be a dress rehearsal for a longer cantonment four years later, one that would prepare another generation of American soldiers for deadly combat.

On April 6, 1917, Congress declared war on Imperial Germany, President Wilson having addressed the lawmakers for this purpose four days earlier, on April 2. Gettysburg's leading citizens seized the opportunity to establish a training camp on the battlefield, which would bring an economic stimulus to the town. A report in the *Gettysburg Times*, one of several local newspapers, stated, "It was apparent to many of our people that the Gettysburg National Military Park would offer a site of great value to the government for the mobilization and training of troops. About two weeks ago it was decided by a number of our business men to get busy and push the claims of Gettysburg. . . . The officers training camps had been designated, so a mobilization camp was asked for." A select committee even had been designated to visit Washington to plead Gettysburg's case, but Andrew R. Brodbeck (D), representing the Twentieth Congressional District, of which Gettysburg was a part, pulled the right strings and GNMP was designated a military cantonment.[19] The people of Gettysburg got their mobilization camp, which the *Times* earlier had reported was more desirable than an officers' school "because it would bring a larger number of men and they likely would stay a longer period of time."[20] The presence of the camp obviously had more to do with the influx of capital than it did the patriotic fervor of Gettysburg's leading citizens.

On May 14, 1917, the townsfolk of Gettysburg received good news, headlined on the first page of the *Times:* "GETTYSBURG WILL GET LARGE CAMP FOR NEW TROOPS. War Department Selects National Park Ground for Mobilization Point." It reported, "The regiments to be mobilized and trained at Gettysburg will be the Fifty Eighth, Fifty Ninth, Sixtieth, and Sixty First Regular Infantry. Each regiment will have as its nucleus a number of trained Regular Army men. In most cases one regiment of already trained Regulars will be used as the basis for the formation of two regiments of recruits." The story also enumerated the volume of troops that possibly could be assigned: "This will mean a camp of between 7500 and 8000 men. The war strength of a regiment is 1942 men which includes a machine gun company of 74, a headquarters company of 58, and a supply company of 10." Finally, the reporter noted that the Quartermaster Department immediately received orders to assemble the necessary shelter materials for shipment to Gettysburg, as troops were expected to arrive within a week and a half.[21] No doubt, town merchants and souvenir dealers stocked their shelves and reordered merchandise to prepare for the onslaught, but they pledged, in writing, not to arbitrarily raise prices just to take advantage of the economics of supply and demand. Hotel owners promised the same.[22]

The town government and local law enforcement officials also had to plan ahead, but the experiences of the fiftieth anniversary commemoration surely gave them the confidence to handle such a large flood of people. Back then, however, the visitors had been only temporary guests, and more than fifty thousand were elderly veterans. Four years later, in 1917, the guests would be staying for a still undetermined amount of time, and they would be energetic, virile, youthful men, many away from home for the first times in their lives. Luckily for the ordinary citizen of Gettysburg but to the dismay of the town's saloonkeepers, the Prohibition era was about to dawn, and the U.S. Army, not afraid to experiment with new social ideas on its captive, regulated audience, would ensure that no American soldiers would be authorized to imbibe alcoholic spirits of any kind, at least not while they were in uniform.

Lieutenant Colonel Nicholson, chairman of the GNMP Commission, received the same news from the War Department, although somewhat belatedly. Desiring to know what regiments would be posted on the park, Nicholson fired off a letter to the assistant secretary of war on May 21. Two days later the local papers announced the designated regiments, and about a week after that Nicholson got the same information from Washington.[23] Now it was official: his beloved shrine was in peril of being abused and maltreated, the same way the Chickamauga Battlefield (Chickamauga and Chattanooga National Military Park was created in 1890) had been damaged in 1898, when it served as a mobilization camp for volunteers destined for Cuba. (Chickamauga was getting another go-round in this war, too.[24])

As expected, when Gettysburg was selected as a mobilization and training camp, businesses and merchants eagerly expected to profit from the arrival of thousands of new customers. According to a May 17 report in the *Adams County News*, a weekly news organ,

Gettysburg will be brought more prominently into the limelight. To its prominence as a battlefield town, there will be added the distinction of a military center. It should mean a new era of prosperity for Gettysburg and this section of the state. Its value as a tourists' resort will be greatly enhanced. That Gettysburg should experience an immediate real estate boom and a general business revival was the opinion of certain of its citizens when they were informed last night of the action of the War Department.

Another section of the article laid out the reasons why Gettysburg National Military Park was a good site for a mobilization camp: pure, existing wells initially dug for the fiftieth anniversary commemoration, adequate railroad facilities for off-loading supplies, and gently rolling ground expansive enough for a large cantonment, as had been proven during the Peace Jubilee of 1913 and the various National Guard encampments and maneuvers. Continuing, the story noted:

> Included in the many things about which there is conjecture is the attitude of the government regarding the distance the camp must be from a hotel. It has generally been published that no mobilization camp be located within two miles of a licensed saloon. If this is followed out here, one of three things may happen: the camp may be put out of the two mile limit and proprietors instructed not to sell to men in uniform, or the town may be put under martial orders and the licensed places closed by Army orders.[25]

Obviously, owners of establishments selling alcohol in town would not be happy to hear this bit of news. Rowdy, inebriated soldiers might somewhat benefit the saloon owners, but their presence would contribute to public drunkenness, vice, crime, and the spread of sexually transmitted diseases. Not to be forgotten was that temperance advocates were pushing hard to nationally outlaw, through a constitutional amendment, the manufacture and sale of all liquor/

alcohol products, and Woodrow Wilson's Progressive followers in Gettysburg certainly could not find fault with the Army's policy. One such organization, the Adams County Dry Federation, within a month of the soldiers' arrival, expressed its apprehension: "The war has not only made the liquor situation most serious on account of the grain it consumes, but it has made the local situation acute by establishing a training camp here." Of immediate concern was the report "that the soldiers are getting liquor somehow and it is one of the aims of the Federation to put a stop to this."[26] The local temperance advocates would get some special help from their Uncle Sam.

To ensure that business owners complied with the rules and that communities near training camps enforced the federal policies, the Commission on Training Camp Activities (CTCA), a consortium of civilian benevolent organizations and public services like the YMCA, Salvation Army, Knights of Columbus, and similar groups, was created and overseen by the War Department. According to a report in the *Gettysburg Times,* "The war department means to spare no effort in the vicinity of big training camps where hundreds of thousands of American boys will be taught soldiering." Raymond J. Fosdick, a lawyer, Wilson confidant, and trustee of two Rockefeller philanthropies, was placed in charge of the CTCA at the national level. His, and the CTCA's, mission, was to promote athletics and other wholesome activities and divert the doughboys from drinking, gambling, prostitution, and vice in general. The CTCA also became responsible for the Army's anti–venereal disease campaign. The *Times* article carried the warning that communities that failed to comply with army policy risked having the camps moved elsewhere, but in cases where that option proved impossible, "the government could place the districts immediately surrounding the training camps or even large portions of the city under military law, the threat of which alone would probably be sufficient to bring about a change."[27] If its citizens were not yet aware of this policy by the summer of 1917, the town of Gettysburg and its surrounding townships thus had been placed on notice.

The local citizens who had not been around for the 1863 battle, though accustomed to seeing soldiers in town for training exercises and ceremonies in more recent years, had never witnessed so many troops at one time, not even during the 1913 Peace Jubilee or the Pennsylvania National Guard encampments. The first two regiments to arrive, the Fourth and Seventh Infantries, had been posted on the Mexican border and made the long train ride from there to Gettysburg. They would comprise the nucleus of the four newly created regiments. On Sunday, June 10, soon after the doughboys' appearance but before the onslaught of new recruits arrived in town, hundreds of civilians gawked at the veterans of the Mexican Punitive Expedition as they prepared for the flood of new trainees. Lost in the rush to set up camp was the fact that the ground being occupied had once been a bloody battlefield and now was an important national historic site. One newspaper article observed, "[Every] day sees many machines occupying that portion of the battlefield, and the [town] occupants watching the operations of construction, the drilling of the troops, and the many other camp activities."[28] Army trucks and motorcycles plied borough streets, county roads, GNMP avenues, and the newly laid company streets in the camp. Horses and mules continued to arrive by the hundreds in July, requiring thousands of tons of fodder and forage, while depositing an almost equal amount of manure.

Certainly the historic significance of where they were camped was not lost on the soldiers. Joseph J. Stone, a private in Company L, 59th U.S. Infantry, kept a detailed journal of his time in service. He was very literate and had a "historic-mindedness" that is apparent in his entries. Stone noted that "the men who formed the nucleus of the organization came from Co. 'L' 4th Inf. Grant's old regiment. They were mostly N.C.O.s, all of the old army school and hardened into the service through years of experience in the old Regular Army." After describing their arrival in Gettysburg and his initial experiences with the other new recruits, Stone wrote: "Drill now began in earnest. The old battle field of Gettysburg became alive with men seeking to master the art that made the name of Gettysburg historic." Then, he philosophized on the exploits of other American soldiers a half-century before and the historical importance of the land on which he and his comrades were living and training:

> The place, too, was ideal for the purpose and aided much in keep-
> ing and developing the martial spirit in the company. Who could
> drill or march on the ground made famous by Lee's charge and
> not feel in his bones the martial influence of that veteran hero of
> the Southland? And who could stand on the same ground made
> sacred by so many of our fathers and not feel, as Lincoln did, that
> these brave dead have died for things and principles that we ought
> to live for and die for as they have done before us. It was a patri-
> otic atmosphere that Company L was surrounded with and the
> boys who made the company became full of the spirit and devo-
> tion that made sacred the place on which they drilled. [29]

In late summer laborers found tangible evidence of the grim toll of that battle when they uncovered the remains of a Rebel soldier who had been killed-in-action more than a half century earlier. An article in the *Harrisburg Telegraph* revealed,

> Workmen digging in the camp of the Sixty-first Regiment un-
> earthed part of what is thought to be the remains of a Confeder-
> ate soldier killed during the battle. It is probable the man was
> one of Pickett's men, for it was over the ground where the find
> was made that the Virginia division marched to attack the center
> of the Union line. A portion of the skull and some of the hair and
> two teeth, one of them a gold one, were found, and with them
> were eighty-three Confederate bullets, part of the cartridge box,
> one minie ball [probably the one that killed him], a part of the
> soldier's woolen blanket and part of his gum poncho or coat. [30]

The laborers made the discovery while deepening the camp's water-supply line trenches to ensure that the water pipes were beneath the frost line. The *Gettysburg Times* reported that the doughboys "took a great interest in the news of the discovery and that many of them joined in the hunt for more bullets" which, they declared, they would take with them to France as souvenirs of the earlier war. The very next day, workmen uncovered the remains of a Union soldier, identifiable by the vestiges of his uniform and equipment, who then was reburied in the National Cemetery.[31]

Gettysburg National Military Park was suffering a severe environmental impact, and its cultural resources were endangered. Excavation of the historic landscape for structural foundations, latrines, and sewage lines and the grading of the land itself for building sites and camp roads changed the topography of the battlefield where the Confederate onslaughts of July 2 and 3, 1863, took place. The detritus of the modern camp would mingle in the earth with Civil War relics for generations to come, possibly frustrating future archaeological studies. Parts of the battlefield were closed to visitors for security purposes. Hundreds of board and batten structures, including office buildings, stables, mess halls, latrines and bath houses occupied the battlefield. Monuments and memorials were surrounded by the hustle and bustle of a modern army training area and cantonment, and thus susceptible to damage from vehicular accidents and vandalism from bored doughboys. Capt. Stuart A. Howard, of the West Point Class of 1903, in temporary command of the newly activated 61st Infantry, sent a note to GNMP Commission chairman John Nicholson in early summer to allay his fears about damage to the park:

> You may be sure that every effort will be made by myself to see that enlisted men of the 61st Infantry do not molest in any way the monuments, trees, shrubbery, woods, etc. of the Gettysburg National Park. I personally hold this park to be sacred, and through the battalion and company commanders to see that this nuisance is abated. This regiment already has four noncommissioned officers on duty in the park to assist the park police in regulating the conduct of the soldiers.[32]

Military discipline was a sure way to keep bored soldiers under control. Providing for their welfare and off-duty entertainment was another. To keep the doughboys occupied and out of trouble, local government, businesses, the Red Cross, YMCA, YWCA, YMHA, Knights of Columbus, and civic-minded citizens, all under the auspices of the CTCA, sprang to action. By the third week of June plans were being formulated to manage the situation. The local Red Cross chapter agreed to provide rest and reading rooms for the troops, complete with government-furnished phonographs; that a swimming area would be built; and that the town playground would be made accessible to the soldiers during certain daytime hours. An *Adams County News* story reported,

> Other things suggested . . . were the erection of a bandstand in Centre Square where band concerts and programs by the chorale society, and other like organizations, could be given during the summer; the holding of socials for the soldiers, the entertainment of one or two in each home of town, and the enlargement of the commercial activities looking toward the soldiers' entertainment. This would include the moving picture shows, bowling alleys, pool rooms, and so on. Already several of the churches have offered their lecture rooms to be used as centers for the soldiers, and others will follow.

Since there were about four hundred soldiers of the Jewish faith in camp, a representative of the Young Men's Hebrew Association attended the meeting, as did an employee of the YMCA. "The few Jewish families in Gettysburg have consented to open their homes to the soldiers of their faith," noted the reporter. [33] As of June 18, there was only one Christian chaplain assigned to the camp, "and there is a specially heavy burden of caring for the idle moments of the young men." The local churches were well-attended by the troops, and as more uniformed clergy arrived, sometimes the camp's chaplains taught Sunday school for the town's various congregations. A report in the *Star and Sentinel* recounted that, at

St. James Lutheran on June 10, "the church was crowded with the boys in khaki. . . . when the Rev. Baker called for converts . . . about seventy of the men arose in their places."[34] Even Pennsylvania's "Free State Library Commission" lent a hand by sending books and magazines to Gettysburg and other military activities in the Commonwealth. By the middle of July, the Red Cross had established a reading room on Chambersburg Street and a poolroom on the town square. St. James Lutheran Church set up a reading room, and Father W. F. Boyle of St. Francis Xavier Church arranged several club rooms "with piano, writing tables, magazines, dance floor, and stage for minstrel shows and vaudeville shows." The Presbyterian Church on Baltimore Street and Trinity Reformed Church on High Street likewise established reading and recreation rooms for the soldiers.[35] Try as the various agencies and churches might, the soldiers nonetheless would find ways to get into trouble, despite that liquor had been outlawed for men in uniform.

It did not take the doughboys very long to find their much-desired spirits. Only two weeks after the soldiers' arrival, the U.S. District Attorney issued warrants on June 20 for the arrest of two Gettysburg saloonkeepers for selling liquor to the troops and one Philadelphia man for buying alcoholic drinks for uniformed soldiers. According to a newspaper report, "All three are liable to a year in jail or $100 fine, or both, if convicted."[36] Problems associated with bootlegging, drunken soldiers, and prostitution plagued Gettysburg throughout their stay. Then, on October 2, 1917, U.S. Attorney Rogers L. Burnett issued orders to the federal marshal to close all saloons within a five-mile radius of the camp. A report in the *Gettysburg Times* the next day specified, "The execution of the order will put Gettysburg in the 'dry' column, as all of the saloons . . . and at least one wholesale house are within the prescribed zone."[37]

With all of the social problems that transpired with the deluge of thousands of young men into what had been a rural yet well-traveled town, it was easy to forget the primary reasons that the soldiers were there in the first place. The dual purposes of the camp were to organize four new regiments and train their men to fight. A typical day included drill and ceremonies, physical exercise, bayonet training, weapons familiarization and maintenance, small-unit tactics, chemical-warfare training, signaling, and map reading. With no suitable firing ranges in the vicinity of the camp, plans were made to transport the soldiers to the Pennsylvania National Guard training facility at Mount Gretna, some forty miles distant, for marksmanship training.[38] There are no extant records to specify that trench warfare was taught at the Gettysburg camp, but archeological evidence exists indicating that at least some trenches were dug and barbed wire was strung.[39] Troops also received training in the prevention of venereal disease, under the guidance of the CTCA.[40]

One new recruit at the Gettysburg camp was destined to be unique in the entire U.S. Army during the war as its youngest combat soldier. Ernest L. Wrentmore had stowed away on an eastbound freight train from his home in West Farmington, Ohio, and landed in Altoona, Pennsylvania, where he found a recruiting station and enlisted in the Regular Army. A half-century later he recalled, "The day I stepped into an Army recruiting office to tell a tough-looking individual my desire to enlist, I was twelve years old. The date was September 29, 1917." Smart, large in frame and mature for his age, Wrentmore indeed was not even a teenager yet and had convinced the recruiter that he was eighteen years old. He signed an alias on his enlistment form: "Henry E. Monroe." His ruse worked, and soon he was on another train, this time as a legitimate passenger, destination Gettysburg. Wrentmore wrote in his memoirs, "The campsite was situated on the memorable battlefield, Gettysburg! Our eyes were met with an endless sea of tents and low buildings. It was a thrilling site, never to be forgotten." He subsequently was assigned to Company I, 60th Infantry. Now going by the name "Henry," he described the training regimen of an infantryman:

> The training began, an endless routine of learning to become a
> combat team—individually and collectively—in learning how to

save our necks in hand-to-hand fighting. Perpetual drill—miles of hiking—utter exhaustion. It seemed that the drive of the officers and non-coms would never cease. Following a few weeks of this training, I discovered that I was putting on weight—good, hard muscle. I found that I was having no trouble staying right in there with the rest of them. I liked bayonet drill, and I hit the dummy with as hard an impact as any of the boys. I was fast becoming a good combat soldier. [41]

The recently adopted .30 caliber Browning machine gun and the Browning Automatic Rifle had not even gone into production when the infantry camp was established at Gettysburg, so recruits like Pvt. Henry Monroe trained on the Lewis-Savage light machine gun and the Hotchkiss M1909 Benét–Mercié machine gun that had been brought with the 4th and 7th Regiments from the Mexican Border campaign. Their rifle was the caliber .30–06 (or "ought-six" as the soldiers called it) U.S. Springfield that they also had used against Pancho Villa's bandits, and the recruits were issued the same rifle. Officers, noncommissioned officers, and soldiers in non-infantry specialties, such as bandsmen, usually carried the M1911 .45 caliber Colt semiautomatic pistol. When the Gettysburg doughboys finally arrived in France in May 1918, they exchanged their rifles for the newer U.S. Enfield Model of 1917, the same caliber as the Springfield and to an untrained eye very similar in appearance. They also received their individual gas masks after disembarking in France.[42] There is no record of the troops being issued their steel helmets while they were encamped at Gettysburg.

As summer faded into autumn, and with no winter barracks at the Gettysburg camp, the War Department decided to relocate the six regiments to warmer climes in North Carolina. The *Gettysburg Times* publicized the impending transfer on Thursday, October 25: "All six regiments of the United States Regulars are to be moved from the Gettysburg Camp as soon as the railroads can provide the necessary facilities. This announcement came on Wednesday evening, and regimental officers were advised to be in readiness for breaking camp on short notice." The writer expressed surprise that the move was announced so suddenly, but he allayed the fears of the townsfolk by informing them that it could take several weeks to transport all of the soldiers to North Carolina: "The railroads are now taxed to their utmost to provide facilities for the movement of troops and conscripts and it is predicted that it will take the better part of a month to get 12,000 or 15,000 men out of here." The article concluded with encouraging news that it was likely that another camp would be established in Gettysburg in the spring, as "several new storage houses have been rented [by the Army] in Gettysburg within the last few days, and all things point to the opening of the camp very early."[43]

The onset of colder weather was not the only reason that the "Camp of the United States Troops, Gettysburg, Pa." was disestablished. The *Times* announced in bold letters on the front page of its November 2 edition, "CAMP NEXT YEAR IS ENDANGERED . . . Intoxication and Certain Diseases Will Not Be Permitted, and Question is up to Communities." The U.S. Army would flex its muscle and not allow another camp at Gettysburg in the spring if the local authorities and businesses did not clean up their act. According to the report,

That the liquor and evil social conditions in Gettysburg and surrounding towns were in part responsible for the removal of the troops to the South earlier than had been anticipated, was the statement of an Army officer at a conference Thursday afternoon, attended by representatives from Gettysburg, Hanover, and Emmitsburg. That these same conditions, if not remedied, will prevent the reestablishment of the camp in the spring was brought clearly to the attention of those in attendance. . . . Attention to conditions surrounding the town . . . was directed by the September medical report which showed an increase in cases of intoxication of 100 percent over that of August, while the number of cases of diseases resulting from vice was more than 100 percent. . . . The

War Department is determined that an army of strong young men shall be sent abroad, and that this army dare not be menaced by the ravages of liquor and vice. *If Gettysburg, and the towns in this neighborhood, do not take the necessary steps to safeguard the soldiers during the remainder of their time here, and make necessary arrangements for them next spring their return in 1918 will be out of the question.* The number of men here is small compared to other places and accommodations can readily be found for them.

The message was fairly straightforward: the responsibility for stamping out vice and liquor lay with the community, not with the Army. If the citizens of Gettysburg and the surrounding area wanted to continue to profit from the soldiers' presence, they must take the appropriate measures or risk losing next year's camp to another locale.[44] Gettysburg civilians were indignant about the accusations that the Army leveled and believed the Army itself was partly to blame for allowing the soldiers to travel to other towns to get booze and solicit prostitutes. Yet, wrote a *Times* reporter, "the situation largely resolves itself into a necessity for better conditions in towns and cities near Gettysburg, that this place gets a minor share of the blame but that it also has something to do in order to protect the soldiers."[45] The town leaders would have about four months to come up with a plan for improvement.

One man who undoubtedly hoped that the soldiers *would not* return was GNMP Commission chairman Nicholson. In September, he received a letter from his friend and fellow Union veteran, Col. Henry S. Huidekoper. "I hope you are quite well," he remarked, "and as happy as one can be with 12,000 soldiers injuring your beautiful park." Huidekoper snidely concluded, "They had better have gone elsewhere, even to honoring another southern general by naming the camp after him. My mind reverts to the sentiments of fifty years ago." Despite the passage of time, the efforts at reconciliation characterized by the 1913 Peace Jubilee and a common enemy in "Kaiser Bill," old grievances and hard feelings persisted more than a half-century later. In early November

Chairman Nicholson sent a note to U.S. district attorney Rogers L. Burnett asking him to "not let up on the liquor business with the hotels and rum houses at Gettysburg." Nicholson suggested that the military police were not doing their job; if they had been, "there would have been much less liquor there, and less confusion and vandalism. Our Guards in one day collected more liquor by holding up automobiles on Hancock Avenue than was gathered by the military police during their whole service here."[46] For Nicholson, the soldiers' relocation to North Carolina could not come soon enough.

The Army's transportation officers were able to move the soldiers, their equipment, and the horses much faster than anticipated. By the end of the second week of November only a rear guard remained in the town.[47] The six regiments that had been posted at Gettysburg in 1917 would comprise one brigade each in the 3rd, 4th, and 5th Divisions of the American Expeditionary Forces. These three divisions would participate in the horrific, bloody campaigns of the summer and fall of 1918, including Chateau Thierry, Second Battle of the Marne, Soissons, St. Mihiel, and the Meuse-Argonne Offensive. Undoubtedly, many of Gettysburg's Army brides who had been married in the summer and fall of 1917 would become new widows by the end of 1918.

Rumors flew through the streets of Gettysburg during the winter of 1917–18 concerning the prospects of another Army camp. The *Gettysburg Times* printed an article on February 18 titled, "RUMORS ON CAMP MOST NUMEROUS." In it, the reporter chronicled the speculations of the townsfolk regarding the reopening of the camp. The writer concluded, "All . . . is street rumor for the truth of which The Times does not vouch, but several of the stories are apparently well founded."[48] The wild tales came to an abrupt halt on March 8. "A telephone message from Congressman Brodbeck this morning told that all doubt about the opening of the Gettysburg camp had been removed," wrote a *Times* correspondent, verifying "that it would be prepared for troops and that a regiment of engineers would be stationed here within a short time. This confirms the accounts published in this paper from time to time over the past few weeks." The newspaper reiterated that earlier rumors had been hogwash, especially one that had alarmed white citizens about black soldiers being stationed in Gettysburg: "The old story of 10,000 negro troops being ordered to Gettysburg, and many other reports were stated, none of which were given credence by those in touch with the situation."[49] So now it was official. Gettysburg would get another camp for white soldiers in 1918.

In 1918 the camp would become the first training ground for the fledgling Tank Corps, and command went to Capt. Dwight D. Eisenhower, an infantry officer who yearned to see combat in France before the war was over. Eisenhower; his wife, Mamie; and their new baby arrived in the spring. As Mamie tried to make a home out of the residence the Eisenhowers had rented, Captain Eisenhower and his staff attended to the administration and logistics of running an army training camp. He assumed command on March 29, 1918. The new cantonment, unlike the infantry camp of a year earlier, actually received an official name, designated "Camp Colt," in memory of Samuel Colt (1814–1862), the man who invented and mass-produced the revolving-cylinder, six-shot pistol used by both sides during the Civil War.[50] Camp Colt occupied the same ground as the previous year's infantry camp, but more structures were authorized, and a target range was situated some two miles south of camp, near Big Round Top. Additional hospital accommodations, the conversion of the old stables and warehouses into personnel quarters, and the procurement of heating plants for the troops' bathing facilities were required, all to the tune of more than $17,000.[51]

During the first months of his command, the camp grew from an initial contingent of 500 men to a population, by the end of July, of more than 6,400 soldiers. Tents and more temporary buildings sprang up on both sides of the Emmitsburg Road. Hoping to avoid the problems of the previous year, Eisenhower soon issued orders to saloons and bars in town not to sell liquor to his troops. He was authorized to close all such establishments within five miles but opted to keep them open and have his provost marshal "keep an eye on them." According to Eisenhower, "Things seemed to be working out until I got a report that a man who owned a sizable hotel with a bar had been surreptitiously serving liquor to men in uniform." Eisenhower thus had a decision to make: he could close the hotel and run the risk of angering the local politicians, or he could ensure that his soldiers could not sneak in for drinks. Ike chose the latter course, posting guards at the front of the hotel to prevent any soldiers from entering. The owner complained to his congressman. Eisenhower would not lift the guard. The owner wrote to the War Department; Ike received a letter from the assistant secretary of war, commending him. The owner relented, and even apologized to Eisenhower. Threatening to shut him down if anything happened again, Ike removed the guards.[52]

Tanks were not available in the spring of 1918, so Eisenhower's ordnance personnel fabricated a sheet-metal, dynamic mockup, dubbed the "Battling Lizzie." Because it was modeled on the Mark V heavy tank, Ike's soldiers at least could get a feel for being inside one of the steel monsters. If nothing else, "Battling Lizzie" made a great backdrop for group photographs.[53] No heavy tanks ever were delivered to Camp Colt, but on June 6, 1918, a lone FT-17 Renault light tank arrived at the Western Maryland depot in Gettysburg. "With the cheerful cynicism of soldiers," Eisenhower recollected, "we had not expected to see one until we reached Europe."[54] A *Times* reporter wrote, "The long expected tank is here. Camp Colt's officers and men are as happy as a playground full of children with a new toy. This morning one of the small French tanks was received by freight from an automobile factory 'Somewhere in America.' It was soon unloaded and driven through town while scores of people watched it with the greatest interest." The tank had been built in France but delivered to an American manufacturer for study, most likely the Maxwell Motor Company (forerunner of Chrysler) of Dayton, Ohio, which had received a contract, along with several smaller companies, to supply the Army with 4,400 tanks of the Renault design.[55]

Before the tank arrived, however, Ike drilled his men by practicing with machine guns and a small-caliber naval cannon, the former mounted on truck beds. Years later, the man who became the thirty-fourth president reminisced about those days: "The only satisfactory place for firing was Big Round Top, a terrain feature that has a prominent place in the history of the Battle of Gettysburg. Its base made a perfect backstop. Soon, soldiers were shooting from moving trucks at all kinds of targets there and the firing might have been heavier than during the great battle fifty-five years earlier."[56]

Eisenhower's biggest problem would come in the early autumn, and it had nothing to do with tanks or trench warfare. Instead, Ike and his men would face an invisible killer known as the Spanish influenza. In September 1918, Camp Colt received a group of drafted men from Camp Devens, Massachusetts, an area already wracked with the dreaded influenza. Eisenhower reported that soon after, some of the men were "registering high fevers and were obviously very ill. The camp surgeon immediately took countermeasures. Before noon, 'Spanish Flu' was recognized." As in 1863, the town's churches were again converted to makeshift hospitals, and army doctors treated soldiers and civilians alike. Before the crisis abated, approximately 160 of Eisenhower's soldiers were dead.[57] From the camp, the flu spread to the town and outlying areas, killing more than 150 civilians.[58]

Gradually, the camp returned to normal, and by the autumn of 1918 Ike had ascended to the rank of brevet lieutenant colonel. The Army was planning on transferring his troops to North Carolina before colder weather, as there still were no suitable winter quarters at Camp Colt. Before the move could occur, however, November 11 arrived, and the war was over. Tank training was discontinued on November 18—one day before the fifty-fifth anniversary of the Gettysburg Address. The camp was abandoned on August 15, 1919.[59] However, the Eisenhowers could not totally

Captain Dwight D. Eisenhower at Camp Meade, Maryland, with a Renault FT-17 light tank, 1919. (Dwight D. Eisenhower Presidential Library and Museum)

abandon Gettysburg. Ike and Mamie would return years later to purchase a farm and pass their remaining years in the solitude of the old battlefield.

The end of World War I and departure of the doughboys from Camp Colt did not end relations between the U.S. Army and Gettysburg. The War Department administered the National Military Park until 1933, when it was transferred to the National Park Service. Throughout the interwar years and beyond, Army, National Guard, and Marine Corps units camped and trained on the battlefield, but only for short periods. In 1938 the Army returned, this time as part of the seventy-fifth anniversary celebration of the battle, as it had during the fiftieth anniversary in 1913.

The Park Service had taken over the administration of Gettysburg National Military Park five years earlier, so the Army's responsibility during the 1938 battle anniversary was far less than it had been in 1913. In fact, the presence of the soldiers was more theatrical than practical. According to the official report, "a large, active United States Army representation . . . would do much to indelibly impress upon the minds of all that Americanism is the only form of 'ism' patriotically sanctioned in this country."[60] During an era racked by fears of Communism, Nazism, and Fascism, with the country still in the grips of the worst depression in its history, the presence of the Army at the anniversary of the battle, more than anything else, was symbolic of a strong central government.

Infantry, artillery, cavalry, armor, and coast artillery conducted maneuvers, to the delight of the old warriors and hundreds of thousands of spectators. An equipment exhibit was set up, and the

Air Corps staged a flyover. Construction and administration of the veterans' camp was accomplished by the 28th Division, Pennsylvania National Guard. But there were only a few old veterans this time. Their attendance was 1,800, with an average age of ninety-one.[61] The torch was being passed to a newer generation of heroes.

During World War II, Gettysburg was not heard from much, and it nearly slipped from public notice. Few people had time or gasoline to visit, and the Army had better things about which to worry than teaching officers the problems of Lee and Meade. The Eternal Light Peace Memorial, lit by President Franklin D. Roosevelt during the seventy-fifth anniversary, had to be extinguished during evening hours, lest it be seen by an enemy aircraft.[62] More realistically, the natural gas it consumed needed to be conserved for the war effort. Then, on November 9, 1943, Gettysburg National Military Park again welcomed American soldiers. They would be housed in what had served as a Civilian Conservation Corps camp during the Great Depression, located in McMillan Woods on Seminary Ridge. Many of these soldiers—mostly Jews who had fled Germany and Nazi-occupied countries—were not yet American citizens, and some spoke with foreign accents. They comprised four "mobile radio-broadcasting" units and were trained at Gettysburg for psychological warfare and propaganda dissemination. Named "Camp Sharpe" in honor of the intelligence chief of the Army of the Potomac, the camp was a sub-installation of the U.S. Army Military Intelligence Training Center at Fort Ritchie, Maryland, about eighteen miles southwest of Gettysburg. Once trained, they would broadcast Allied propaganda to the German army and German citizens to erode their will to resist. They also crafted propaganda leaflets and interrogated prisoners of war. Their stay was brief, and they departed for the European theater of operations in July 1944.[63]

Just before the departure of the Camp Sharpe soldiers, a prisoner-of-war (POW) camp was established on the battlefield to detain German prisoners, who provided agricultural labor for Adams County's many farms, orchards, and food processing plants.

Housed first in the National Guard Armory on Seminary Ridge and then relocated to a tent camp in the fields adjacent to a tourist motel along Long Lane, the camp housed up to 500 POWs and 65 guards. Once Camp Sharpe closed, the guards were housed in those barracks. But when the demand for labor diminished as winter approached, the prisoners were moved, and the tent camp was closed in January 1945, although the last POWs did not leave the area until April 1946.[64]

In 1951, in the midst of the Korean War, the Army War College moved to Carlisle Barracks, only twenty-eight miles from Gettysburg. Ever since, the senior officers who attend the school have made annual battlefield tours.[65] The late Jay Luvaas and retired brigadier general Hal Nelson, two historians who authored *The U.S. Army War College Guide to the Battle of Gettysburg* in 1986, in essence a staff-ride manual, commented in their preface what modern-day officers strive to learn. A staff ride "seeks to enable the professional soldier to learn more about his trade through the study and analysis of an old battlefield in areas involving leadership, battle intelligence, the use of terrain, unit cohesion, tactics, the psychology of man in combat, or any other aspect of the military art that will always be applicable."[66] But senior officers are not the only students who still learn from Gettysburg. Beginning in 1986, cadets of the U.S. Military Academy once again began making the annual Gettysburg visit. Since then, cadets enrolled in "History of the Military Art" have been offered staff rides to enhance classroom instruction. The week before each trip, they receive a classroom introduction to the battle and prepare with read-ahead assignments. Upon arrival at the park, the cadets set out for the field in small groups, employing maps and firsthand accounts of the fighting to get an understanding of what it might have been like to wage combat during those three terrible days in July so long ago.

During a staff ride in the late 1980s, one cadet group was told to make its way up the rocky front slope of Little Round Top. As the cadets struggled over the boulders and through the brush, they were reminded that Confederate soldiers who attempted the same climb in 1863 were carrying muskets and equipment, were wearing wool uniforms in ninety-degree heat, and probably were hungry, thirsty, and scared out of their wits; thousands of lead balls were whizzing past—with some finding their marks—artillery shells cracked overhead, the smoke and noise numbed their senses, and comrades lay dead and wounded all around them. Afterward, when questioned how a young officer might have inspired his men under those circumstances, one cadet said, "Sir, I've seen pictures of this place and read about it before, and if I was asked that question in class I probably would have given a textbook response." Pausing for a moment, he reflected, "But out here, actually climbing up the hill and imagining what those guys went through . . . well, I just don't know. We had a tough time getting to the top with nobody shooting at us." Another cadet just shook his head and remarked, "Those men sure had guts." Perhaps the real lesson of the staff ride was pointed out by another cadet on a trip two years later; she said, "Looking back now I realize that the most important thing that I learned was how it must feel to stand on a piece of terrain and make a decision that will affect the lives of soldiers and their families."[67] Many of those cadets, some long since retired after successful Army careers, fought in the Persian Gulf War in 1991 as junior officers and then, as senior leaders, commanded battalions, brigades, and divisions in Afghanistan and Iraq.

In the last three decades, especially since the Ken Burns series of the early 1990s and Ted Turner's 1993 movie about the battle, the American people have gained a renewed interest in Gettysburg. Gone, however, are the vestiges of Camp Colt, although a housing development and city park occupy part of the site and bear the camp's name. Ike Eisenhower still is remembered though, as droves of sightseers board buses that take them to his farm, now known as Eisenhower National Historic Site. They gaze at his bed and remark on the color of Mamie's drapes, but few know, or even care, that the thirty-fourth president first came to Gettysburg both as a cadet and a young officer, long before D-Day or the White House.

In the many years since the end of the Battle of Gettysburg, the U.S. Army has changed dramatically. M-1 tanks, Apache Attack Helicopters, Patriot Missiles, automatic weapons and attack drones have replaced horses and muzzle-loading weapons; artillerymen no longer have to see their targets to hit them; and battlefield computers are commonplace. Yet there are still lessons to be learned from places like Devil's Den, the Peach Orchard, and Culp's Hill. A very recent (August 2015) group of West Point cadets conducted a staff ride on the battlefield, returned to the academy and reported on their website, "The Cadet Leadership embarked on a journey to Gettysburg, Pennsylvania in late August to build cohesive command teams by focusing on honorable living and winning culture. The Cadet Chain of Command reflects upon the historical lessons learned and applies them to their own experience leading others. Cadets return from this staff ride ready to inspire and lead the Corps of Cadets."[68] The description of their experience helps to explain why the current and future leaders of the U.S. Army continue to return to this hallowed ground, like Antaeus of Greek mythology, to touch the earth and renew their strength.

8

The History of Civil War Reenacting

A Personal Recollection

THEY STOOD IN THEIR woolen uniforms, perspiring from the humidity and the hot July sun. They were out of shape and too old to look like Civil War soldiers. Many of them had too much to drink the night before, and now they were dehydrated as well. They were a pathetic sight: gray-haired, pot-bellied men pretending to be soldiers. Sound like a typical Civil War reenactment? The date was July 3, 1913, and the reenactors were Civil War veterans who had just restaged Pickett's Charge on the actual site where it had occurred fifty years earlier. The veterans were not toting weapons, but some were attired in their Grand Army of the Republic or United Confederate Veterans uniforms, and several old soldiers carried the colors of their regiments. These men were the forerunners of Civil War reenacting.

"Historical reenactment" is a hobby or activity in which costumed participants reconstruct a particular event, such as Washington's Crossing of the Delaware; a specific period, like Jacksonian America; or, more generally defined, an entire era, such as the Renaissance. Participants in "living history" try to bring history to life, either for spectators or for themselves. "Living historians" usually assume the role of a real person in a specific time period, such as Frederick Douglass in 1859, or a fictitious character involved in a certain event, like a Confederate soldier at the Battle of Shiloh. Individuals who particpate in living history may, like actors, stay in character and talk in "first person," as if they actually are caught in a time warp, or they might give presentations in present-day terms by explaining the cultural, social, economic, and political trends and issues of a particular event or era by using their clothing and other props as instructional aids. This essay will lay out the historical roots of "reenacting" and "living history" and then assess the merits, demerits, and controversies associated with these forms of historical interpretation.

Reenactments and living history are not recent manifestations. The ancient Romans reenacted their victories to cheering crowds in the Coliseum, and during the English Civil War the Roundheads restaged one of their battles with the Royalists even while the war still was being waged. During the nineteenth century, survivors of the 7th U.S. Cavalry returned to the scene of Custer's Last Stand to restage the battle for photographers, and Buffalo Bill's Wild West Show featured mock battles between costumed actors portraying cowboys, soldiers, and real-life Native Americans. In 1895 in Great Britain, members of the Gloucestershire Engineer Volunteers restaged the 1879 Battle of Rorke's Drift in order to raise money for a new drill hall.[1]

What was probably the first bona fide Civil War reenactment occurred in New Jersey in 1878 on the farm of ex-Union cavalry commander Maj. Gen. Judson Kilpatrick. In a three-day Grand Army of the Republic encampment, Kilpatrick organized a sham battle between Union veterans and the New Jersey National Guard, which Governor George B. McClellan, former commander of the Army of the Potomac, had authorized to participate. The first day of the encampment saw the arrival of the veterans and the guardsmen, who were fed and entertained and drank some of the ten thousand kegs of beer that Kilpatrick had delivered to his farm.

Day 2 was filled with political speeches, musical serenades, and fireworks. On day 3, some thirty thousand spectators witnessed the sham battle, fought by more than fifteen hundred "combatants." Ironically, the Union veterans portrayed Confederates while the national guardsmen took on the roles of the Yankees. Just as the battle was nearing its climax, a mounted Judson Kilpatrick rode to the middle of the "battlefield" and gave a speech to thunderous applause from the veterans, guardsmen, and onlookers.[2]

In 1903 and again in 1905, Confederate veterans from Maj. Gen. William Mahone's Brigade restaged their counterattack at the Petersburg Crater, minus, of course, the slaughter of the U.S. Colored Troops. A decade later, during the Fiftiethth Anniversary of the Battle of Gettysburg, Union veterans from Alexander Webb's brigade—now aging members of the "Philadelphia Brigade Association"—awaited the mock attack by Confederate veterans of "Pickett's Division Association." On July 3, 1913, at 3:15 P.M., the two sides lined up on opposite sides of the stone wall at the so-called Angle on Cemetery Ridge. With thousands of spectators watching, standard bearers for each side moved up to the stone wall and crossed flags, followed by another man with the U.S. flag, who held it high above the crossed staffs. Finally, the former enemies whooped and hollered and approached the stone wall and clasped each other in handshakes and hugs while the crowd erupted in applause.[3] The average age of the veterans was seventy-two, which meant that their reenactment antics were coming to an end. If reenactments were to be staged in future years, younger men would have to undertake them, and, initially, those men were from federal and state military forces.

The use of old battlefields by soldiers and national guardsmen for training actually began soon after the Civil War. Starting in the 1880s, the Pennsylvania National Guard began using portions of the Gettysburg Battlefield to stage their summer maneuvers. Although they did not recreate the battle, they were dressed in uniforms very similar to those worn by Union soldiers more than a decade earlier, and their weapons and equipment were not much different, either. Later, units of the Regular Army also participated in maneuvers at Gettysburg, even after the battlefield became one of the early national military parks.[4] But Chickamauga, not Gettysburg, was the first battlefield to attain national military park status, and it was that park that saw tens of thousands of blue-clad soldiers prepare for yet another war in 1898.[5] Fifteen years later, in 1913, during the fiftiethth anniversary of the Battle of Chickamauga, soldiers from the 7th U.S. Infantry Regiment staged a reenactment on the actual battlefield for thousands of returning veterans and spectators. During the First World War, the Chickamauga Battlefield again was used for military training, as was Gettysburg National Military Park.[6]

In September 1904, far to the north of Chickamauga and almost a decade earlier, on the battlefields of Manassas and nearby Thoroughfare Gap, the U.S. Army leased more than 65,000 acres and trained National Guard units from eighteen states alongside Regular Army units. All told, some 26,000 full- and part-time soldiers—from the North and South, both black and white—trained together in large-scale maneuver units and in operational scenarios. The inclusion of African American guardsmen caused racial tensions with white guardsmen from the southern states, so the black soldiers' camps were relocated to a remote area to prevent further friction.[7]

The maneuvers and semipermanent training areas at places like Chickamauga and Gettysburg were precedent-setting events in the history of Civil War reenacting. After World War I, the U.S. Marine Corps also got into the act, staging maneuvers and a so-called sham battle at Chancellorsville in 1921 and recreating Pickett's Charge at Gettysburg in 1922, but this time the "Confederates" had air support. Tragically, Capt. George W. Hamilton, a Marine aviator who had fought in World War I, was killed in a crash during the Gettysburg maneuvers.[8] North Carolina National Guardsmen used the remaining earthworks at Bentonville, North Carolina, to reenact one of the final battles of the Civil War when a battle monument was erected there in 1927. At Petersburg, Virginia, reenactments continued to be staged to commemorate the Battle of the Crater, one in 1932 and another in 1937. At the 1937 event, the 5th Regiment of Marines, the Virginia Military Institute Corps of Cadets, and Virginia National Guard units participated in front of 45,000 spectators. The highlight of the event was the explosion of 150 pounds of black powder in the original crater where 8,000 pounds had been touched off some seventy-three years earlier, while young Billy Mahone, the great-grandson of General Mahone, romped around the battlefield as a Confederate courier.[9] Soon, the United States would be involved in another world war, and reenactments would be sidelined while real battles were fought by American youth all over the world.

With the end of the Second World War and the approach of the Civil War centennial, Americans once again turned to reenacting as a way of commemorating the sectional conflict, but in a way that would greatly differ from earlier reenactments. It was during the centennial that modern reenacting was born, but its roots can be traced back to the 1950s, with the genesis of the North-South Skirmish Association, more commonly known by its initials, the "N-SSA." The stirrings of the N-SSA began in 1950 when a group of black-powder enthusiasts put on a shooting match, pairing the Berwyn (Maryland) Bluebellies against the Norfolk (Virginia) Gray Backs. As news of the match spread, other shooting groups formed, and in 1956 they banded together to organize the N-SSA, which was incorporated in 1958, just in time for the centennial. Although the organization was focused on competitive shooting using original Civil War weapons and reproductions, members of the N-SSA were—and still are—required to dress in reproduction Civil War uniforms. According to its official website, the organization's purpose is "to conduct company and individual target competition (skirmishes) in . . . traditional form; to promote black-powder shooting through the use of Civil War weapons fired in the original manner and to encourage the preservation and display of Civil War material; and to commemorate the heroism of the men of both sides who fought in the Civil War, 1861–1865 as a reminder of our national heritage." It fell on the N-SSA, as one of the first organized groups of living-history practitioners, to form the nucleus of the Civil War reenacting community as the Civil War centennial approached.[10]

One of the seminal centennial reenactments occurred in West Virginia at the little town of Philippi, site of the first land skirmish of the Civil War. Although there were not as many reenactors as there had been real combatants, the reenactment lasted longer than the actual battle, and there were more spectators lining the streets of Philippi in June 1961 than there had been citizens of the little town a century earlier.[11] The first truly significant centennial reenactment was the First Battle of Manassas, which was sanctioned by the National Civil War Centennial Commission and the National Park Service. One of the participants was sixteen-year-old Harry Roach, who portrayed a Union soldier. His reminiscences of that reenactment appeared in the *Camp Chase Gazette,* a journal for and about Civil War reenactors. According to Roach,

The 1961 event was held on the actual battlefield—the National Park Service had not yet closed its doors to battle reenactments. The equestrian statue of Stonewall was covered with camouflage netting to hide it from the cameras. Stuffed dummies were scattered around the hill as "casualties." And about 2,500 troops were ready to do battle. Some were . . . [VMI] cadets. Some were Virginia National Guardsmen wearing gray work clothes and carrying M-1 rifles. But the majority came from the ranks of the North-South Skirmish Association. . . . 99.99% of the participants at the 1961 Bull Run [reenactment] would be considered "farbs" by today's standards. The uniforms looked good only from a distance. I was in the N-SSA's 150th Pennsylvania Infantry, and we considered ourselves hot stuff because we actually had blue wool coats. They were original five-button blouses from the Indian War period, but they looked better than the work shirts most units seemed to have. For trousers we wore light blue Sears work pants. Any shoes were OK as long as they were black: combat boots, engineers, Wellingtons, oxfords, you name it. The only outfit that was genuinely authentic was the 2nd North Carolina, led by the late George Gorman. They had hand-made wool trousers and jackets, and no two uniforms looked alike, which we thought was pretty bizarre. About that time, George started using the term "farbie" to describe inauthentic garb. When asked what the word meant, George responded: "Far be it from me to criticize inauthentic uniforms!" . . . If our uniforms were awful, our weapons and accouterments were authentic. They had to be, because they were originals. Nobody was retailing repro[duction] gear back then. In 1960 I bought an original M1864 Springfield for $85. A mint-condition cartridge box was $20. And there was plenty of that stuff around. We carried it into battle and generally banged it up. Nobody gave it a second thought. We did not camp authentically. The only canvas tents to be seen were WW2 surplus. Our camp was away from the battlefield, out of sight of the spectators. And there were spectators—50,000 came to see the battle. A few of them died, from heat stroke and heart attacks and bee stings. It was hot! The reenactment was scripted and it followed fairly closely to the original fight for the Union batteries on Henry House Hill. On Friday we had a walkthrough rehearsal. On Saturday and again on Sunday the battle was fought. We did no complicated maneuvering, because nobody knew Civil War drill. Before coming out of the woods we formed a line of battle and stayed that way through the whole fight, only moving forward and back. . . . Through the haze I see a National Guardsman, zigzagging like a running back, firing his M-1 from the hip as fast as he can pull the trigger. Yes, it was a farb fest, but it was great.[12]

Roach's memories of First Manassas illuminate the state of reenacting more than a half century ago. The term "farb" refers to reenactors who are not authentically dressed or armed; obviously, uniform and tactical accuracy was not very important at that reenactment. Entertaining huge crowds—more than fifty thousand spectators watched—while at the same time exposing them to a bit of Civil War history were the primary reasons for such a monumental reenactment. But safety issues, heat casualties, damage to cultural resources, and excessive costs were enough to convince the director of the National Park Service not to sponsor any more such events. There were other issues as well. There seemed to be something irreverent about grown men (and teenage boys) pretending to slaughter and maim each other on the actual field where real killing had occurred a hundred years earlier. The well-known popular historian Bruce Catton remarked that reenactments "require us to reproduce, for the enjoyment of attendant spectators, a thin-shadow picture of something which involved death and agony for the original participants."[13] The executive director of the Civil War Centennial Commission, a young historian named Bud Robertson, commented that "reenactments possess too much celebrative spirit and too little commemorative reverence. This soldier playing mocks the dead."[14] Historian Allan Nevins, the head of the Centennial Commission, announced that it would not sanction any more reenactments. This policy, however, did not last long. After meeting with President Kennedy at the White House to discuss the work of the Centennial Commission, the *New York Times* reported the conversation between the president and Nevins:

"When are you going to put on another sham-battle?" President Kennedy asked.

The Chairman said none were planned.

"That's a pity." Mr. Kennedy mused. "I like sham-battles."

Thereafter, reenactments continued, even if the Centennial Commission or the Park Service did not "officially" sanction them.[15] The reenactment for the Battle of Antietam focused on the Union assault on the Sunken Road and was staged on September 15 and September 16, 1962. It took place on the Roulette Farm, then in private hands but within the legislative boundary of Antietam National Battlefield. The reenactment, however, was sponsored by the Antietam–South Mountain Centennial Association, not the NPS. It was scripted, and two professional announcers provided narration.[16]

As the centennial continued, more reenactments were scheduled, usually coinciding with the anniversary of a battle. At Gettysburg during the summer of 1963, Pickett's Charge was restaged on the actual ground where it had occurred a hundred years earlier. It was far from authentic, however, with lots of overweight, middle-aged men in gray or blue work uniforms decorated with an overabundance of gold, red, or light blue stripes and piping. One of the park rangers remembered that the woman in charge of the reenactment followed behind the advancing Confederate line in a jeep with a flashing red light affixed.[17] Nonetheless, at least one presidential hopeful was on hand at the Gettysburg event: Governor George Wallace, who only a few weeks earlier, on June 11, 1963, had vowed to keep the University of Alabama segregated.[18]

The end of the Civil War centennial in 1965 coincided with the escalation of the Vietnam War. Interest in battle reenactments waned as a result, although a few diehards kept the hobby going into the 1970s. By then, President Kennedy was long dead, and the National Park Service had outlawed reenactments on its sites. In addition, units of the North-South Skirmish Association returned to competitive shooting and put battle reenacting aside. With the end of the Vietnam War and a surging enthusiasm for American history with the coming of the nation's bicentennial, a renewed interest in reenacting took hold, first with the War for Independence and to a lesser extent with the Civil War. The "Rev-War" reenactors, as they called themselves, for the most part took great pains in uniform and weapon authenticity, which carried over to the Civil War reenacting community, many of whose members reenacted both periods of history.[19]

It was during the mid-1970s that I personally became involved in Civil War reenacting. I was an avid Civil War buff even though I had not majored in history as an undergraduate. Having just served a two-year hitch in the U.S. Army and about to enroll in

Army ROTC at York College of Pennsylvania, I knew somewhat what it was like to be a real soldier, unlike some of the reenactors whom I would come to know. I contacted a fellow student who was in charge of a local Civil War reenactment unit, the 87th Pennsylvania Volunteer Infantry, and signed up. I joined for a number of reasons, but most importantly I wanted to experience what it might have been like to have been a Yankee soldier—minus the killing, of course—and to be around others of my ilk who enjoyed studying and talking about Civil War history. Unfortunately, not everyone in the hobby felt the same as me.

My unit had what we thought were high standards of authenticity. We required wool uniforms using patterns based on original uniforms. Historically accurate leather accoutrements were required. I personally carried an original Civil War musket and an original canteen. Correct footwear was a problem; most of us wore ankle length "desert boots" that were dyed black, but they were a far cry from the rough-side-out brogans that had been worn by Union soldiers. Headwear also proved to be a challenge. Slouch hats were easy to procure, but authentic-looking forage caps were difficult to make unless you knew someone who had a sewing machine that could penetrate the leather brim to affix it to the wool cap.

The first reenactment in which I ever participated took place in north-central Pennsylvania. The encampment was located within a state park, but the "battle" was fought on a high-school football field, complete with cheering spectators, a narrator, and loud speakers. It was, by any standard, a true "farb fest," but it was my first reenactment and I was hooked. I remember that some of the old salts who had been reenactors during the centennial gave us a few good-natured jabs for staying at a motel. They were "roughing" it in their pop-up campers or Coleman tents, complete with electrical hook-ups. A few weeks later, my unit took part in an "authentics only" reenactment. What a difference! Real camping with company streets, open fires, and pit latrines. Limited spectator interaction. Safety inspections *and* uniform and equipment inspections. Most importantly, the majority of the reenactors were

The 5th New York Infantry, Duryee's Zouaves reenactment unit, Remembrance Day, Gettysburg, 1982. The author is in the rear row, seventh from
right. (Author's collection)

young enough and thin enough to actually look like Civil War
soldiers, including a few women in the Iron Brigade who had cut
their hair, dirtied their faces, and passed as teenaged boys. I continued to reenact through the rest of my college days, but took a
break after graduation when I was stationed in Germany.

When I returned to the United States and was posted in the
northeast, I joined a Maryland artillery battery but soon left that
unit and joined the 5th New York Infantry, commonly known as
Duryee's Zouaves. It was then that I met the late Brian Pohanka,
one of the giants in the field of living history and reenacting who,
as a well-known popular historian, brought a bit of professional-
ism to the hobby. Brian's penchant for historical accuracy was leg-
endary, and he later was hired as a consultant for the films *Glory*,
Gettysburg, and *Gods and Generals*. He also appeared regularly as a
"talking head" on The History Channel's *Civil War Journal* and was
an editor for the Time-Life multivolume Civil War series.

Two years later, my army career took me away once again, this
time to Georgia. I tried my hand at being a Confederate, but my
heart was not in it. As it turned out, there were quite a few trans-
planted Yankees in Georgia, so we founded the 21st Ohio Infantry,

a unit whose real heritage included Stones River, Chickamauga, Chattanooga, the Atlanta campaign, the March to the Sea, and the Carolinas. Since we were located in the Deep South and based in Atlanta where there were very few Union reenactment units, we quickly became well known and in high demand. The 21st Ohio is still an active reenactment organization, and it marched in George Bush's second inaugural parade in 2005. It turns out that former vice president Dick Cheney's great-grandfather was the ranking officer remaining in the 21st Ohio after the Battle of Bentonville.[20]

Marriage, two young sons, and a demanding army career put an end to my reenacting days. So, I hung up my uniform and accoutrements for the last time, even though the 125th anniversary of the Civil War was approaching, which strengthened the hobby of reenacting and spurred a renewed interest in the subject. Then, in 1990, Ken Burns released his PBS documentary, and three years later the movie *Gettysburg* appeared in theaters, and millions of Americans again became enamored with Civil War history, just in time to ensure that the 130th, 135th, 140th, 145th, and 150th anniversaries of the war would have thousands of reenactors and tens of thousands of spectators to attend the commemorative reenactments. Today, a conservative estimate places the number of Civil War reenactors in the United States at thirty thousand although some sources put the number at close to a hundred thousand and not all are Americans, as the British, Germans, Canadians, and French also have Civil War reenactment units.[21]

Some of these reenactors were instrumental in the making of several Hollywood films, all of which made Americans even more aware of the bloody fratricide while at the same time attracting more recruits to the ranks of the reenacting legions. One of my former students watched *Gettysburg* when he was a child and decided that he wanted to be a reenactor like the extras in the movie.[22] The 1989 Academy Award–winning film *Glory* gave momentum to the organization and recruitment of African Americans into U.S. Colored Troops reenactment units, but at least one such group predates the film and took an active role in its production. The recreated Company B, 54th Massachusetts Colored Volunteers is a nonprofit organization of professional and amateur historians formed in 1988 as a National Park Service "Volunteers in Parks" unit.[23]

Nonetheless, compared to white participation in Civil War reenacting, black participation is miniscule, less than 1 percent (0.8 percent) of total reenactors according to a survey taken in the summer of 1999 of nearly a thousand reenactors, prepared and compiled by Mark L. Sheets for a scholarly audience. What side do they portray? The percentage of reenactors who wear blue or gray is nearly equal. Approximately 25 percent of the respondents portrayed both Union and Confederate soldiers. When it comes to their educational level, 50 percent have taken college courses in history (although not all in this category graduated from college), while 19 percent only studied history at the high-school level, and 12 percent said that they were "self taught" or never studied history. Only 11 percent of those surveyed possessed a bachelor's degree in history, while 7 percent held an MA or PhD.[24]

More than half of those surveyed were over the age of forty. (The average age of a Civil War soldier was twenty-three by the mid-point of the war, so it should be readily apparent that there are too many middle-aged men involved in Civil War reenacting, something that greatly detracts from the historical accuracy that so many in the hobby are trying to achieve.) Two-thirds of those who took the survey portrayed infantrymen. There are several reasons for this. First, an infantryman's uniform and equipment is relatively easy to obtain and costs much less than a cavalry impression, even if the horse is not included, since a dismounted cavalryman is still required to own a uniform, cavalry boots, a carbine, a pistol, and a saber. An artillery impression obviously requires someone in the unit to own a cannon and limber, and since these items are very expensive—a Model 1857 Napoleon reproduction barrel, carriage, limber, ammunition chest, and implements will cost approximately $25,000—it limits the number of reenactors portraying this branch of the service. According to the

survey, there were more people portraying Civil War–era civilians than artillerymen or cavalry troopers, perhaps because those
impressions require less of an outlay of cash, and age and weight
are irrelevant. The high cost associated with military reenacting
might also explain why so many middle-aged men—men who are
financially comfortable—are involved in the hobby, compared to
younger men.[25]

Additionally, there is a large gap between the number of male
and female reenactors.[26] Many women who participate in reenacting portray civilians, nurses, or camp followers, but some depict
soldiers, something that has become very controversial in the reenacting community and has brought at least one lawsuit against
the National Park Service. In 1991, a reenactor named Lauren
Cook Burgess filed a civil suit after Antietam National Battlefield
officials barred her from portraying an infantryman. Burgess took
her grievance all the way to the U.S. Supreme Court and won on
sexual-discrimination grounds. However, the ruling applies only
on NPS-administered sites.[27] On private ground, however, "authentics only" events have been staged where women have been
barred altogether. Some see this practice as hypocritical. A female
reporter from the *Baltimore Sun* wrote: "In other words, men who
are probably too old and far too well-fed to play the part of young,
starving Confederate soldiers with historical accuracy don't want
women who look too much like women to play the part of Confederate soldiers because it would not be historically accurate.
Wow. Is this a stupid argument, or what?"[28]

The practice of Civil War living history also has its own tradition dating back to the centennial, thanks to the National Park
Service. Although the NPS dabbled in living history at a few sites
as early as the 1930s, in 1961 historic firearms demonstrations,
which would play a major part in the service's living-history programs, were begun at Antietam National Battlefield as well as
Chickamauga and Chattanooga National Military Park. The firearms demonstrations soon spread to other military-related parks,
and in 1965 Fort Davis National Historic Site in Texas became the

first to dress interpreters in period uniforms.[29] The National Park Service was not the only organization to promote living history during the Centennial; in 1964, a private museum in Gettysburg started an outdoor living history area known as "Hardtack and Coffee," named after the well-known memoirs of Union soldier John Billings. Ross Kimmel, a longtime reenactor, recalled his time volunteering there:

> The idea was to establish an outdoor museum of the Civil War soldier in the Gettysburg environs. By the late spring of '64, it was happening, and very impressive it was. Located behind and next to the large brick museum and relic venue of the Marinos family on the Baltimore Pike . . . it offered the visitor a tour through Civil War soldier micro-environments. There was a section of trenches and bombproofs, a la Vicksburg/Petersburg; a sample of Civil War road surfaces, including a corduroy road; encampments with tents (Sibley, A-frame, dog tents), complete with camp detritus, including stacked muskets (which had to be taken down each night); a signal tower; a pontoon bridge unit; wagons and stables, with draft animals; a full-scale replica of Professor Lowe's balloon *Intrepid;* an embalmer's field operation, complete with life-like (or "death-like") corpse; a field hospital, complete with a barrel of severed limbs; an amphitheater for special programs; the whole thing festooned with all the Union corps flags. They hired summer help to wear uniforms and interpret the place to the public. . . . Withal, a very forward looking attempt to interpret Civil War soldier life in a way no museum had ever attempted. Unfortunately, what the . . . [owners] had in historical expertise and enthusiasm, they lacked in capital and business sense, and after limping through one or two summers, the effort collapsed. But, while it existed, boy, what a playground![30]

Unlike the "Hardtack and Coffee" Museum, the National Park Service continued its living-history programs at Civil War–related parks and other historic sites, demonstrating not just martial skills but also farming methods, manufacturing techniques, and craft making. By 1968, 41 parks included living-history programs as part of their historical interpretation, and six years later, 114 national parks had some sort of living-history program.[31] These programs were not without their own unique set of problems, however. One critic was the respected NPS historian Robert Utley, who in 1974 wrote,

> I fear that we have let the public's enthusiasm for living history push us from interpretation of the park's features and values into productions that, however entertaining, do not directly support the central park themes. . . . Inappropriate living history, more-over, is not merely harmless diversion. The more "living" it is, the more likely it is to give the visitor his strongest impression, and memory, of his park experience. Thus a program that is not unusually supportive of key interpretive objectives may be corre-spondingly distractive if not actually subversive. We are obsessed with showing what everyday life was like in the past. . . . But most of our historic places are not preserved because of the everyday life that occurred there. The visitor whose fascination with "liv-ing" portrayals of everyday activity inhibits his understanding and appreciation of the momentous significance of Lee's surren-der to Grant, or the progress and consequences of the Battle of Saratoga, has not been well served by our interpretive program, no matter how well conceived and presented.[32]

Despite such reservations, the National Park Service has con-tinued its living-history programs and even has invited reenac-tors to help them with these expensive and labor-intensive con-structions of public history. On any given weekend during the summer, the national parks at Gettysburg, Vicksburg, Antietam, Chickamauga, and other sites host reenactors who demonstrate drill, tactics, camp life, and musketry, all under the watchful eyes of National Park Service employees who have been designated to enforce historical accuracy and safety. Unfortunately, the accuracy is limited to the uniforms, equipment, and historical interpretation, not to the age, weight, and gender of the reenactors. Nonetheless, those who participate in living history, whether as actors or spectators, immerse themselves in the historical context of the Civil War in order to have some semblance of appreciation for those who lived during that dark period of American history.

Just outside of Petersburg, Virginia, is Pamplin Historical Park, a privately owned historic site that includes original earthworks, historic farms, state-of-the-art museums, and battlefield land. Funded by the Pamplin Foundation and proceeds from admission fees and other revenue sources, Pamplin Park employs a staff of living-history professionals that portrays soldier life, historic farming, civilian life in wartime, and even slavery. The park also utilizes living-history volunteers on selected weekends. Where Gettysburg's "Hardtack and Coffee" museum failed—with lack of vision and money—Pamplin Park succeeds. Coincidentally, the restaurant located at the park is called the "Hardtack and Coffee Café."

Some scholars, both inside and outside of academia, have cast disparaging looks at those who use living history to teach the past. If it is properly employed, living history is an effective way to convey some types of information and knowledge. For example, one semester I asked reenactors/students enrolled in my Civil War course if they would like to earn some extra credit. These young men were proud to call themselves "hard-core authentics"—they were lean, authentically outfitted, and rugged looking. One of them even went so far as to soak his brass buttons in a jar of urine to give them the patina of well-worn military buttons. (There's a slang term for guys like him in the reenacting ranks—they're called "button pissers.") I asked these students if they would re-create the September 14, 1862, eleven-mile march that the Army of the Potomac's 6th Corps made prior to the Battle of Crampton's Gap, a hike that took the actual soldiers about six hours to accomplish. There is some debate concerning the amount of time the 6th Corps spent in the village of Jefferson, Maryland, as they awaited the arrival of a division from the 4th Corps. I have always contended that the 6th Corps probably spent about an hour in Jefferson, but there is no written record of the exact length of the halt.

Early one November morning, the intrepid students began their trek at first light and made it to the edge of Burkittsville, at the base of Crampton's Gap, in about four and a half hours. Included in that interval was a one-hour rest in Jefferson. So, incorporating that break, our twenty-first-century living historians cut about an hour and a half off of the original time it took the 6th Corps to make the same march. How could the reenactors do it so much faster, I asked them? First, they speculated that perhaps the 6th Corps spent longer than an hour in Jefferson. Then, they theorized that they themselves were bigger and stronger than the Union soldiers of 1862 and could march faster, especially since they were not carrying weapons and ammunition like the men of the 6th Corps. Finally, they guessed that ten thousand men and their accompanying artillery and wagons might move quite a bit slower than just three men who could march at their own pace and were not worried about the whereabouts of the enemy. Our academic experiment in living history thus provided no conclusive results, but it gave my students—including those who did not make the march but were briefed about it in class—a unique way of experiencing history and testing historical theory.

On the surface, it would seem that the practice of living history, if done properly, can cross the divide between battle reenactment and the more traditional construction of Civil War military history. More than half of the reenactors surveyed in 1999 participated in living history "regularly," while 19 percent "always" did living history instead of reenacting and 24 percent occasionally did living history. A combined 3 percent of those surveyed rarely or never did living history, and 1 percent did not even know what it was.[33] So what does this reveal about reenactors in general? It seems that the majority are as interested in using their historical impression to educate the general public as they are about just experiencing what it might have been like to live back during the Civil War era. It also tells us that a small minority only wants to dress up and play soldier, even though they probably would not admit it. A sociologist who studied Civil War reenactors has made the following observation:

> Re-enacting is not a predetermined effect of some historical or social situation. It is a pleasure structure, a voluntary creation shared by those who for whatever reason feel a resonance with any of the significances re-enacting might have—resonances with their personalities, personal histories, identities. For some it is a political statement, for others an affirmation of cultural identity, a complex and intriguing game, an opportunity to go camping and get drunk with friends, an alternative to a dreary existence, a "thing to do" in a social set, or a fascinating window on a world they know from books and photographs but have never participated in as an experienced reality.[34]

When reenactors escort the remains of a Union or Confederate soldier who has been missing in action for the past 150 years, or when they form an honor guard at the unveiling of a new memorial sculpture, or when they march in a Memorial Day parade, they are participating in the commemoration of a historical event or paying tribute to a long-dead contestant in that epoch. They help bring the past to life for laymen who normally would have no concept of a Civil War soldier's uniform, equipment, mannerisms, or drill. For the reenactors themselves, these types of activities can be extremely emotional, especially when they take place on a historic site, such as the "Remembrance Day" ceremonies at Gettysburg National Military Park held on the Saturday closest to the anniversary of the Gettysburg Address every November. I personally have witnessed reenactors crying during Remembrance Day ceremonies; however, some reenactors come to Remembrance Day because it is the last "event" of the year, an opportunity to dress up, show off, and "party with their pards" one last time before winter sets in.

Regardless of one's opinion of reenactors, reenacting, or living history, this cultural phenomenon has a long history in its own right and has become an important way for some Americans to remember the Civil War. Although I no longer participate, this activity got me started on the slow and arduous trail toward my second career, and for that I am grateful.

Epilogue

Casinos and Other Entertainments

The following essay, other than a few minor stylistic changes, appeared as a guest post for Kevin Levin's *Civil War Memory* blog (http://cwmemory.com/2010/09/12/gettysburg-and-battlefield-preservation-another-perspective/) in response to a post by Larry Cebula of Eastern Washington University. Cebula attacked a film by the Civil War Preservation Trust (CWPT—now called the Civil War Trust) that stood against a plan to build a casino on the edge of Gettysburg National Military Park. Although Cebula's posting was a criticism of what he saw as a propaganda film, he also seemingly defended the developers' right to build the casino. Kevin asked me to respond, as he knew that I lived only a few miles from the proposed gambling complex. In April 2011, the Pennsylvania Gaming Commission voted down the bid to open the casino. Note: the image in this chapter did not appear in the original blog posting.

I will not attempt to debate Professor Cebula, nor try to address most of his points. This debate actually can be traced back to 1863—how much of the battlefield should be set aside to honor the

The relic remains of Fort Defiance. (Courtesy of Karl Stelly)

men who fought, bled and died there—and it has been going on ever since. Anyone interested in that history, should read *Gettysburg: Memory, Market, and American Shrine,* by the late Jim Weeks.[1]

Let's get right to the crux of the matter: Is the site of the proposed casino—the Eisenhower Inn and Conference Center, its adjacent sports complex and Devonshire Village condominiums—a place where Union and Confederate soldiers met in combat? The answer is no. We do know, however, that it was a staging area for Wesley Merritt's cavalry brigade prior to its fight against the right flank of the Army of Northern Virginia on the afternoon of July 3, 1863. Is that, in itself, worth saving? The question and its answer are irrelevant, since the area has been developed for more than four decades.

Directly across the Emmitsburg Road (U.S. Business Route 15) from the proposed casino are the relic remains of a failed commercial venture known as Slippy Slide, a water park that incorporated a blockhouse from "Fort Defiance," another extinct tourist trap that formerly sat on the Taneytown Road near Fantasyland, itself a 1950s-era theme park where the current Park Service Visitor Center now sits. All of these commercial enterprises, and many more, were built in Cumberland Township with the explicit approval of the township's supervisors, the political predecessors of the ones who recently approved the proposed casino.

For the record, I am not morally offended by a casino that could be located about a mile and a half from my farm. My libertarian views tell me that if people want to gamble their money away, so be it. But again, part of me wants to say, "Hey, Atlantic City! How are those casinos working out for you now?" The real issue here is not the casino itself, but the ancillary commercial development that, based on the Cumberland Township supervisors' past record, is sure to blossom along the Emmitsburg Road. Many years ago, I was a member of the Cumberland Township Planning Commission. I eventually resigned because I believed that the supervisors seemed all too eager to yield to development pressure at the expense of historic preservation, the historic landscape, and the historic view-shed.

The area in the immediate vicinity of the proposed casino is zoned "mixed use," which, according to the Cumberland Township Zoning Ordinance, would include motels (a few older one- and two-star establishments already exist there), restaurants/bars, gas stations, convenience stores, automobile/motorcycle dealers, and the like. Any number of national and regional franchises could easily install a ready-made business in a very short period of time in order to take advantage of the casino's clientele. Based on past trends of commercial development that had been approved by the township supervisors, I am deeply concerned that this tendency will continue, this time within a half mile of the South Cavalry battlefield, part of Gettysburg National Military Park. Will the presumed tax revenues—at the expense of the historic view-shed so close to the battlefield—offset the longer-term costs to local government? Ask the good people of Atlantic City, New Jersey, how it has worked out for them. And don't forget to factor the increased bus and car traffic along the already congested Emmitsburg Road. Will that require widening of the road and perhaps traffic lights?

My main worry, as a taxpayer within Cumberland Township and Adams County, is not with rising taxes. I have witnessed rapid commercial development in the past twenty years, yet my property and school taxes have continued to rise, despite promises that business development would lower my taxes. My greatest concern—the reason that I chose to move to Gettysburg after retiring from the U.S. Army—is the maintenance of the rural and historical environment of the area. Anyone who has visited Harpers Ferry National Historical Park can attest to the burgeoning commercial development between there and Charles Town after a casino was added to Charles Town Races. The landscape along U.S. Route 340 between those two towns only recently—in the past two decades— had been pastoral and rural, too. It no longer looks that way.

To Americans who understand the battle, Gettysburg also is defined by the roads leading there—the military "avenues of approach" that are as much a part of the battlefield landscape as the area currently protected by Gettysburg National Military Park. But those roads, laid out in the eighteenth and nineteenth centuries, are fast losing their rural character, as anyone traveling along U.S. Route 30 east or west of the town will see. Can we afford to continue that trend?

One last thing needs to be addressed, which was the starting point for Professor Cebula's guest blog-posting. It's obvious that he did not like the Civil War Preservation Trust film.[2] I found the film, for the most part, moving and heartfelt, but it is understandable why Dr. Cebula would question the use of "talking heads" such as Stephen Lang, Ken Burns, Matthew Broderick, Sam Waterston, and Susan Eisenhower. They are not Civil War historians. They do, however, have a passionate interest in the era and Gettysburg: several have portrayed Civil War personalities on film, another produced an award-winning documentary on the subject, and another spent her childhood weekends in Gettysburg. All donated their services to the Trust. All are recognizable by the American public. If CWPT just filmed eggheaded historians like Cebula and me—or even David Blight—who would want to watch it, and what impact would it have?

Will Gettysburg's legacy be a landscape littered with crass development, or will we try to restore it to a place of national historic significance, including the areas that buffer the park? President Dwight David Eisenhower (grandfather of Susan) loved this area so much that he bought a historic farm adjacent to the battlefield and retired there. Thinking about his own "Gettysburg address," he wrote, "I shall leave this place better than I found it." That's my goal, too.

Notes

PREFACE AND ACKNOWLEDGMENTS

1. William Faulkner, *Intruder in the Dust* (New York: Random House, 1948), 195.

2. Allan Ballard, "Demons of Gettysburg," Op-Ed, *New York Times*, May 30, 1999.

1. MY GETTYSBURG ADDRESS

1. Casualty figures for the 1st Provisional Tank Brigade are from Dale E. Wilson, *Treat 'Em Rough: The Birth of American Armor, 1917–1920* (Novato, CA: Presidio, 1990), 173. Dale and I served as captains and then majors in the USMA history department during the late 1980s, and our families lived on Machin Place in the old Stony Lonesome housing area, just above Michie Stadium, home of Army football. Ike mistakenly recalled that 175 succumbed to the Spanish flu, but actually, the number was nearly 160.

2. Mark Nesbitt, *Ghosts of Gettysburg III: Spirits, Apparitions, and Haunted Places of the Battlefield* (Gettysburg: Thomas Publications, 1995), 18.

3. Before the war, Cromer lost a twenty-year old daughter, Sarah Elizabeth, to a farm accident in 1858. She allegedly was kicked by a horse in the barn's paddock.

4. Thanks to researcher—and neighbor—Kendra Debany, for sharing her extensive knowledge about my farm's history and providing the documentation to back it up.

5. Dwight D. Eisenhower, *At Ease: Stories I Tell to Friends* (Garden City, NY: Doubleday, 1967), 193–94.

6. Rock Creek Chapel was the forerunner of Mount Joy Lutheran Church. Cromer gained permission to demolish the chapel after it was abandoned (1852) and used the large stones with which it was built to stabilize the stream (a tributary of Rock Creek) behind his house. I recovered those stones and recycled them into a patio on the far side of that same stream.

7. George Eliot, *Daniel Deronda* (London: Blackwood, 1876), chap. 3.

2. EAST OF GETTYSBURG

1. Georg R. Sheets, *To the Setting of the Sun: The Story of York* (York, PA: Windsor, 1981), 13–16, 21, 45–50.

2. Although York was not the first capital of the rebellious thirteen colonies, the town took advantage of the wording in the Articles of Confederation, which for the first time used the term "United States." Thus, York became the "First Capital of the United States."

3. U.S. Census Office, *Population of the United States in 1860*, for York County, PA, original unpublished returns. The county's townships in 1860 were Carroll, Chanceford, Codorus, Conewago, Dover, Fairview, Fawn, Franklin, Heidelberg, Hellam, Hopewell, Jackson, Lower Chanceford, Lower Windsor, Manchester, Manheim, Monaghan, Newberry, North Codorus, Paradise, Peach Bottom, Shrewsbury, Springfield, Spring Garden, Warrington, Washington, West Manchester, West Manheim, Windsor, and York Township. The boroughs and villages included Dillsburg, Dover, Franklintown, Glen Rock, Goldsborough, Hanover, Lewisberry, Loganville, Shrewsbury, Stewartstown, Wrightsville, and York.

A tabulation of the county's population statistics also appears in George R. Prowell, *The History of York County*, 2 vols. (Chicago: J. H. Beers, 1907), 1:30; and John Gibson, *The History of York County* (Chicago: F. A. Battey, 1886), 588.

4. Sheets, *Setting of the Sun*, 82.

5. Charles Denig, *The York Gazetteer and Business Directory for 1856* (York: Eagle Press, 1856), 10–15.

6. Ibid.; Tabular Statement for York County. Of the 293 teachers employed at the public schools, 258 were male and 38 were female. The average monthly salary was $23 for the men, but the women received an average salary of only $16 a month.

7. Ibid., 8–9, 48, 98. Oddly enough, there were no women's charitable, voluntary, or temperance societies listed in this directory. A search of the county newspapers and existing church records for the 1850s also failed to produce any evidence that might shed light on any women's associations in York County during the antebellum period. Although Quakers had separate prayer meetings for women, there is no evidence that any York County Quaker women used these as a basis for associations to further political or social reforms. Quaker women were active in the Underground Railroad, but their actions in support of this organization were in collabo-

ration with men, not separate from them. In *Cradle of the Middle Class: The Family in Oneida County, New York, 1860–1865* (Cambridge: Cambridge Univ. Press, 1981), Mary Ryan attributes the growth of women's associations in that particular county to the evangelistic crusades that swept that area of the country in the 1830s and '40s (83–144). South-central Pennsylvania was largely unaffected by these crusades; perhaps this can help to explain the virtual absence of female associations in York County before the war.

8. Denig, *York Gazetteer*, 35, 17–30.

9. Ibid., 7–8.

10. *York Democratic Press*, Mar. 20, 1861.

11. Prowell, *History of York County*, 610–12. According to Prowell, after the line was completed to Wrightsville, "for several years transportation across the Susquehanna was by means of boats until the track was laid in the covered bridge which spanned the river at that place." On the other side of the river at Columbia, the cargo could be reloaded on a train and shipped on the line running from there to Philadelphia. Consequently, convenient trade links with Philadelphia were not established until at least five years after they were with Baltimore. The inconvenience of off-loading the train at Wrightsville and reloading it at Columbia, coupled with the fact that more convenient trade links had previously been established with Baltimore may help to explain York's strong sense of economic bonding to the South.

12. Ibid.

13. G. A. Mellander and Carl E. Hatch, *York County's Presidential Elections* (York: Strine, 1972), 2. In 1812, 1816, and 1824, county residents gave the majority of the vote to the candidates of the Jeffersonian Democratic Party, which is considered to be of Democratic Party lineage. There were no statistics kept for the 1820 election.

14. Ibid., 3.

15. Ibid. Although the exact number of immigrants who settled in York County during the antebellum period is not known (and is beyond the scope of this study), a perusal of the 1860 census reveals a large number of foreign-born people living in the county at that time, with the Germans as the most predominant nationality. The Republican ties to nativism in the 1850s is a possible explanation for why the Democrats reigned supreme in the county during that time period.

16. *Democratic Press*, Feb. 5, 1861. ("Parson Beecher" was a sly reference to the radical abolitionist Rev. Henry Ward Beecher.)

17. Ibid.

18. Sheets, *Setting of the Sun*, 83–84; Prowell, *History of York County*, 592–98.

19. *York Gazette*, Nov. 13, 1860. The results of this election were also tabulated in Mellander and Hatch, *York County's Presidential Elections*, 6. A breakdown of the Democratic votes in the county had Douglas receiving 562, with the rest (5,497) going to the "Reading Ticket," which listed both Douglas and Breckinridge. Although the strong Democratic tradition in

the county before, during, and after the Civil War might indicate that voters were not necessarily interpreting their votes as a secession referendum, and that they would have voted Democratic regardless of the election issues, there is enough evidence from the local newspapers that the point of contention receiving the most attention during the presidential election campaign was secession.

20. Arnold Shankman, *The Pennsylvania Antiwar Movement* (Rutherford, NJ: Fairleigh Dickinson Univ. Press, 1980), 32–34. It is estimated that at least twenty Wide Awake organizations existed in the county during the 1860 election campaign (Gibson, *History of York County*, 385–86).

21. *York Democratic Press*, Feb. 19, 1861. The Guthrie and Crittenden Compromises were attempts to appease the South by granting various concessions regarding slave laws and promises that the government would not interfere with slavery in states or territories where it already existed. Other conciliatory measures were proposed by committees not only in York but in a few other Pennsylvania counties. One such meeting in York called upon the state legislature to rescind the commonwealth's personal-liberty law, which made it illegal to kidnap a freedman and transport him over the state line for the purpose of reenslavement. Likewise, the same law forbade any Pennsylvania justice of the peace from taking cognizance of any fugitive slave case (Shankman, *Pennsylvania Antiwar Movement*, 44).

22. *York Gazette*, Jan. 16, 1861. The minutes of this meeting were also included as an appendix in *My Little War Experience* (York: York Daily Publishing, 1904): 154–55, by Edward R. Spangler. The author of this war reminiscence was a private in Company K, 130th Pennsylvania Volunteer Infantry and felt very strongly about the "righteousness" of the war. It is interesting that Spangler left out the Union meeting's resolution to approve and accept the Crittenden Compromise.

23. *York Democratic Press*, Feb. 19, 1861.

24. *York Democratic Press*, Feb. 26, 1861.

25. *York Gazette*, July 18, 1862. A list of donations and the names of the contributors usually followed a request for aid.

26. Private David W. Mattern to his family, Aug. 20, 1862, in "A Pennsylvania Dutch Yankee: The Civil War Letters of Private David William Mattern (1862–1863)," ed. Carolyn J. Mattern, *Pennsylvania Folklife* 36, no. 1 (1986): 4.

27. *York Gazette*, Sept. 2, 16, 1862.

28. P. A. & S. Small, *Reminiscences of One Hundred Years—1809–1909* (York: York Printing, 1909), 6. This was a promotional pamphlet celebrating the company's hundredth birthday.

29. The 1862 emergency organizations included three companies of the "Stillinger Guards," four companies of the "Auth Infantry," "Ness's Independent Cavalry Company," "Pollack's Independent Artillery Battery," and Company K, 5th Regiment ("The Wrightsville Guards"). This information was furnished through the courtesy of the Pennsylvania Capitol Preserva-

tion Committee of Harrisburg, which conducted extensive research on every Pennsylvania military organization that served during the Civil War.

30. Prowell, *History of York County*, 405. The Confederate troops were members of Col. E. V. White's 35th Virginia Battalion. They entered Hanover via the Adams County hamlet of McSherrystown, which straddled the western border of Hanover.

31. Ibid. The June 27 issue of the Lancaster *Daily Evening Express* reported that civilians from the west bank of the Susquehanna were seeking refuge in Lancaster County and that "an almost continuous stream of horses and cattle are passing over the Columbia bridge [connecting York and Lancaster Counties]" (quoted in Gerald A. Robinson Jr., "Confederate Operations in York County, 1864" [MA thesis, Millersville State College, 1965], 40).

32. Joseph H. Trundle, *Gettysburg Described in Two Letters from a Maryland Confederate* (Montgomery County, MD: Montgomery County Historical Society, 1959), 211–12, quoted in Scott L. Mingus Sr., and James McClure, *Civil War Voices from York County, Pa.: Remembering the Rebellion and Gettysburg Campaign* (Ortanna, PA: Colecraft, 2011), 55.

33. The most thorough account of the organization and actions of the Department of the Susquehanna is found in Glenn E. Billet, "The Department of the Susquehanna," *Journal of the Lancaster County Historical Society* 66 (1962): 1–64. The Department comprised units organized under the national call for six-months' volunteers, units organized into national service for the duration of the emergency, units organized into the state service for ninety-days, and a smattering of units detached from the Army of the Potomac and other organizations (14).

34. James W. Latimer to Bartow Latimer, June 15, 1863, typescript, file 3577, York County Heritage Trust, York, PA (hereafter cited as YCHT). The town burgess called the meeting to which Latimer referred to discuss preparations for the expected invasion. A "Committee of Safety" was formed which met the next day and "issued a call in obedience to the governor's proclamation, for the formation of military companies to be sent to Harrisburg for the defence of the State." One company was organized, and the committee eventually succeeded in convincing the town council to appropriate enough money to pay a $25 bounty to each volunteer from the borough (*York Gazette*, July 14, 1863).

35. *York Gazette*, June 18, 1863.

36. The military events surrounding the Battle of Hanover and the destruction of the Wrightsville Bridge have been recounted in numerous books, articles, and monographs, and it is not my intent to retell the story here. For thorough and accurate portrayals of these engagements, see Edwin V. Coddington, *The Gettysburg Campaign: A Study in Command* (New York: Scribner's, 1968); Coddington, "Pennsylvania Prepares for Invasion," *Pennsylvania History* 31, no. 2 (1964): 157–75; Billet, "The Department of the Susquehanna," and Scott L. Mingus Sr., *Flames beyond Gettysburg: The Gordon Expedition, June 1863* (Columbus, OH: Ironclad, 2009).

37. One study of the Confederate invasion and occupation of York during the Gettysburg Campaign is Robinson, "Confederate Operations in York County, 1863." The most recent study is Mingus, *Flames beyond Gettysburg*.

38. James Latimer to Bartow Latimer, June 24, 1863, typescript, file 3577, YCHT (emphasis in original).

39. "The Crisis—An Appeal: A few practical reasons why the People of the Border Counties of Pennsylvania should respond to the last call of the President for Volunteers," *York Gazette*, June 23, 1863. A manuscript version in Franklin's handwriting is in the W. B. Franklin Papers, YCHT.

40. General Orders No. 72, *The War of the Rebellion: A Compilation of the Official Records of the Union and Confederate Armies*, 128 vols. (Washington, DC: GPO, 1880–1901), ser. 1, vol. 47, 3:912–13 (hereafter cited as *OR*; all references are to ser. 1). These orders did allow provisions to be secured by payment (with Confederate money), and confiscation was allowed if the owners refused to accept payment or when requisitions remained un-filled. Additionally, if a person was found to be concealing supplies from the Confederates, anything owned by that person that was of value to the army could be seized without payment being rendered.

41. General Orders No. 73, *OR*, vol. 47, 3:942–43.

42. *York Gazette*, June 30, 1863.

43. *The Civil War Memoirs of Captain William J. Seymour: Reminiscences of a Louisiana Tiger*, ed. Terry L. Jones (Baton Rouge: Louisiana State Univ. Press, 1997), 66.

44. James Latimer to Bartow Latimer, July 8, 1863, file 737, YCHT.

45. Cassandra Small to Lissie Latimer, June 30, 1863, in Cassandra A. Small, *Letters of '63* (Detroit: Stair, Jordan & Baker, 1930), 14–16. Gordon also remembers this incident in his *Reminiscences*: "Halting on the main street, where the sidewalks were densely packed, I rode a few rods in advance of my troops, in order to speak to the people from my horse. As I checked him and turned my full dust-begrimed face upon a bevy of young ladies very near me, a cry of alarm came from their midst; but after a few words of as-surance from me, quiet and apparent confidence were restored."

After commenting on the chivalrous behavior of his troops in almost the same terms that Miss Small described, Gordon concluded "by pledg-ing to York the head of any soldier under my command who destroyed pri-vate property, disturbed the repose of a single home, or insulted a woman" (John B. Gordon, *Reminiscences of the Civil War* [New York: Charles Scrib-ner's Sons, 1904], 142–43).

46. James Latimer to Bartow Latimer, July 8, 1863. General Early was also confused by the people he met along his line of march who would come out of their homes and make strange signs at him. As it turned out, he learned that some enterprising shysters had passed ahead of his army and convinced the civilians that if they flashed certain "signs" at the rebels their property would go unmolested. To learn the signs, however, they would first have to

pay these crafty individuals. When the signs failed to deter the Confederates from "requisitioning" supplies, the chagrined citizens realized they had been taken (Jubal A. Early, *Autobiographical Sketch and Narrative of the War Between the States* [Philadelphia: J. B. Lippincott, 1912], 265).

47. Cassandra Small to Lissie Latimer, June 30, 1863, 17.

48. *York Gazette*, June 30, 1863.

49. James Latimer to Bartow Latimer, July 8, 1863. The Confederate money that was used to pay for Small's supplies "was subsequently sent to York soldiers [confined] in Libby prison at Richmond, Virginia" (P. A. & S. Small, *Reminiscences of One Hundred Years*).

50. *York Gazette*, June 30, 1863; James Latimer to Bartow Latimer, July 8, 1863. Latimer said $28,600 was collected, mostly from the banks, but collections were also solicited from the citizens: "When the Committee came to our house Mr. P. A. Small was with them & represented that they had given all the money they had, that other people were doing the same, that it would be repaid, & that they wanted all the money we had in the house. We had nearly two hundred dollars in the house, and very foolishly gave them one hundred dollars. I found out afterwards that many other people had not given nearly so much in proportion & that some had refused entirely."

51. *York Gazette*, June 30, 1863.

52. Cassandra Small to Lissie Latimer, July 8, 1863, in *Letters of '63*, 25.

53. James Latimer to Bartow Latimer, July 3, 1863, file 737, YCHT.

54. Prowell, *History of York County*, 421.

55. *Hanover Spectator*, July 10, 1863.

56. Cassandra Small to Lissie Latimer, July 8, 1863, 32.

57. Mingus and McClure, *Civil War Voices from York County*, 95.

58. Quoted in ibid., 61.

3. UNION LIFELINE

1. Quoted in Martin Van Creveld, *Supplying War: Logistics from Wallenstein to Patton* (Cambridge: Cambridge Univ. Press, 1977), 1.

2. Discussions of theater-level logistics can be found in Herman Hattaway and Archer Jones, *How the North Won: A Military History of the Civil War* (Urbana: Univ. of Illinois Press, 1983); Edward Hagerman, *The American Civil War and the Evolution of Modern Warfare: Ideas, Organization, and Field Command* (Bloomington: Indiana Univ. Press, 1988); and several studies of Civil War railroads. (Hagerman discusses logistics—and their impact on tactical doctrine—during the Gettysburg campaign in moderate detail, but mostly from the perspective of Rufus Ingalls, quartermaster general of the Army of the Potomac.) The role of northern and southern industry in manufacturing weapons and supplies, as well as the role of agriculture in feeding the armies has received scholarly attention, but not nearly the consideration it deserves. In *The Gettysburg Campaign: A Study in Command*,

Edwin Coddington devotes a chapter to the discussion of arms, equipment, and organization of the two armies, but his concentration was not a detailed analysis of logistical operations. See the chapter "Arms and Men" in *The Gettysburg Campaign: A Study in Command* (New York: Charles Scribner's Sons, 1968), 242–59. The best overall treatment of military logistics is Martin Van Creveld's *Supplying War*, but, unfortunately, the author focused on European wars and failed to even mention the impact of the American Civil War on the evolution of military logistics. The one study of tactical logistics during the Civil War is William J. Miller's "'Scarcely Any Parallel in History': Logistics, Friction, and McClellan's Strategy for the Peninsula Campaign" in *The Peninsula Campaign of 1862: Yorktown to the Seven Days*, vol. 2 of 2, ed. William J. Miller (Campbell, CA: Savas Woodbury, 1995), 129–88. A brief, yet well-written discussion of Civil War field logistics can be found in Charles R. Shrader, "Appendix 1: Field Logistics in the Civil War," *The U.S. Army War College Guide to the Battle of Antietam: The Maryland Campaign of 1862*, ed. Jay Luvaas and Harold Nelson (Carlisle, PA: South Mountain, 1987), 255–84.

3. Erna Risch, *Quartermaster Support of the Army: A History of the Corps, 1775–1939*, 2d ed. (Washington, DC: Center of Military History, U.S. Army, 1989), 136, 334.

4. Ibid., 202, 382–83.

5. Carl L. Davis, *Arming the Union: Small Arms in the Civil War* (Port Washington, NY: National Univ. Publications, 1973), 14.

6. Risch, *Quartermaster Support*, 397.

7. Stephen W. Sears, *To the Gates of Richmond: The Peninsula Campaign* (New York: Ticknor & Fields, 1992), 263.

8. Hagerman, *American Civil War and the Origins of Modern Warfare*, 51.

9. Meigs's life is chronicled in Russell B. Weigley's *Quartermaster General of the Union Army: A Biography of Montgomery C. Meigs* (New York: Columbia Univ. Press, 1959).

10. Ibid., 382–85. For a discussion of European methods of subsisting the troops, from the early Napoleonic campaigns through 1866, see Van Creveld, *Supplying War*, 40–82.

11. Davis, *Arming the Union*, 12–14, 76. Davis provides a revisionist interpretation of the role of the Ordnance Department. He convincingly argues that the officers of the department were extraordinary in their untiring efforts to place first-rate rifled arms in the hands of the troops.

12. For a listing of small-arms calibers and types by unit, see Dean Thomas, *Ready, Aim, Fire: Small Arms Ammunition in the Battle of Gettysburg* (Gettysburg: Thomas Publications, 1991), 52–59. The three types of cannon predominantly employed by the Army of the Potomac at Gettysburg were the Model 1857, 12-lb. bronze smooth-bore gun howitzers, known as "Napoleons"; the 3-inch ordnance rifles; and the 10-lb. Parrot rifles. The 3-inch rifles and Parrots were the same caliber, but the Parrot, with its reinforced breech, fired a larger powder charge, thus propelling the projectile with greater range.

13. Patricia L. Faust, ed., *Historical Times Illustrated Encyclopedia of t Civil War* (New York: Harper & Row, 1986), 383.

14. Miller, "Scarcely Any Parallel in History," 184.

15. Ibid., 180.

16. Dabney H. Maury, *Recollections of a Virginian in the Mexican, Indian, and Civil Wars* (New York: Charles Scribner's Sons, 1894), 53–54.

17. Miller, "Scarcely Any Parallel in History," 184–85.

18. George W. Cullum, *Biographical Register of Officers and Graduates of the United States Military Academy at West Point, New York, from Its Establishment in 1802 to 1890*, 3 vols. 3rd ed., rev. and extended (Boston: Houghton Mifflin, 1891), 2:814. "General Orders No. 185, Headquarters Army of the Potomac, Nov. 21, 1862," *War of the Rebellion: The Official Records of the Union and Confederate Armies*, 128 vols. (Washington, DC: GPO, 1880–1901), ser. 1, 21:785 (hereafter cited as *OR;* all references are to ser. 1).

19. Shrader, "Field Logistics," in Luvaas and Nelson, *U.S. Army War College Guide to the Battle of Antietam*, 260–61. The personnel authorizations apply to volunteer units. Generally, fewer logistical personnel were authorized for Regular Army units.

20. Thomas Weber, *The Northern Railroads in the Civil War, 1861–1865* (1952; repr., Westport CT: Greenwood, 1970), 162.

21. Risch, *Quartermaster Support*, 439.

22. Ingalls to Meigs, Sept. 29, 1863, *OR*, vol. 27, 1:21.

23. Weber, *Northern Railroads*, 138–41.

24. S.O. No. 286, HQ of the Army, Adjutant General's Office, Washington, DC, June 27, 1863, *OR*, vol. 27, 3:367–68.

25. "Estimated Numbers of Wagons and Horses, Gettysburg Battlefield Vicinity, June–July 1863," U.S. National Park Service Report (July 1993), Gettysburg National Military Park Library.

26. Cited in Hagerman, *American Civil War and the Origins of Modern Warfare*, 73. The figure of 93,500 is used as the strength of the Army of the Potomac for the Battle of Gettysburg (Coddington, *Gettysburg Campaign*, 249). Thus, 93,500 troops divided by 3,652 wagons equals 25.6 troops per wagon; 1000 troops divided by 25.6 wagons equals 39.06 troops per wagon. These figures do not include ambulances.

27. Blake A. Magner, *Traveller and Company: The Horses of Gettysburg* (Gettysburg: Farnsworth House Military Impressions, 1995), 47.

28. Ingalls to Pleasonton, June 26, 1863, *OR*, vol. 27, 3:338.

29. Meigs to Ingalls, June 28, 1863, *OR*, vol. 27, 3:378.

30. Ingalls to Meigs, June 28, 1863, *OR*, vol. 27, 3:379.

31. Sawtelle to Meigs, June 28, 1863, *OR*, vol. 27, 3:379.

32. Ingalls to Meigs, June 28, 1863, *OR*, vol. 27, 3:379.

33. Meigs to Ingalls, June 28, 1863, *OR*, vol. 27, 3:380.

34. Ingalls to Meigs, Aug. 28, 1864, *OR*, vol. 27, 1:221–22.

35. Clarke to Taylor, June 30, 1863, Records of the Commissary General of Subsistence, General Correspondence, Letters Received, 1828–86, box 145, National Archives, Washington, DC.

36. Clarke to Taylor, July 1, 1863, Records of the Commissary General of Subsistence, General Correspondence, Letters Received, 1828–86, box 146. Marching rations consisted of hard bread, salt pork, and coffee.

37. Cited in Thomas, *Ready, Aim, Fire*, 60.

38. Flagler to Brig. Gen. James W. Ripley, July 1, 1863, Record Group 156, Records of the Office of the Chief of Ordnance, General Records, Letters Received, 1812–94, box 276.

39. Weber, *Northern Railroads*, 164–65.

40. Ingalls to Meigs, Aug. 28, 1864, 222.

41. Ingalls to Meigs, July 3, 1863, *OR*, vol. 27, 3:502–3.

42. A file on Butterfield in the Robert L. Brake Collection, USAMHI, has a note that states that a tag was attached to a relic shell fragment. The tag reads: "While Generals Meade, Ingalls, and Butterfield were conversing at the battle of Gettysburg, July 3, 1863, this piece of shell from a Confederate gun knocked down and severely wounded Major General Butterfield, Chief of Staff of the Army of the Potomac."

43. 7th Wisconsin Infantry File, Gettysburg National Military Park Library.

44. Lt. Col. George Woods to Maj. Gen. David Birney, July 3, 1863, George H. Woods Papers, USAMHI.

45. Sgt. Austin C. Stearns, *Three Years with Company K*, ed. Arthur A. Kent (Rutherford, NJ: Fairleigh Dickinson Univ. Press, 1976), 203–4. Stearns was in the 13th Massachusetts Infantry.

46. Weigley, *Quartermaster General of the Union Army*, 280–82.

47. Circular, *OR*, vol. 27, 3:542.

48. "Report of Brig. Gen. Henry J. Hunt, U.S. Army, Chief of Artillery, Army of the Potomac," *OR*, vol. 27, 1:241.

49. Flagler to Ripley, July 6, 11, 1863, Office of the Chief of Ordnance, Letters Received, 1812–94, box 276.

50. "Report of John R. Edie, Acting Chief Ordnance Officer of the Army of the Potomac," *OR*, vol. 27, 1:225–26.

51. Gregory A. Coco, *A Strange and Blighted Land: Gettysburg: The Aftermath of a Battle* (Gettysburg: Thomas Publications, 1995), 318–25.

52. Ingalls to Meigs, Aug. 28, 1864, 222.

53. Report of Surgeon Jonathan Letterman, U.S. Army Medical Director, Army of the Potomac, *OR*, vol. 27, 1:197.

54. Ingalls to Meigs, Aug. 28, 1864, 222.

55. Ibid., 223–24.

56. Hagerman, *American Civil War and the Origins of Modern Warfare*, 76. By the end of July, some two weeks after the campaign had ended, the supply system seemed back on track. In one command, however, a few officers went to bed hungry, necessitating the following circular order: "Many officers have complained of their inability to procure proper food for their own use, when the troops of their commands have been fully supplied owing to the neglect of the Brigade Commissaries in furnishing supplies for

their use at the same time they issued rations to the men. *Officers are human as well as enlisted men* and have natural wants and the duty of Brigade Commissaries attends to supplying officers as well as men." Circular of the 2d Division, III Corps, dated July 29, 1863, George H. Woods Papers, USAMHI (emphasis added).

57. Hagerman, *American Civil War and the Origins of Modern Warfare*, 77. The breakdown was six wagons for baggage, seven for subsistence and quartermaster supplies, five for ordnance, and two for medical supplies.

58. William J. Miller, "Scarcely Any Parallel in History," 185; Francis B. Heitman, *Historical Register and Dictionary of the United States Army, from Its Organization, September 29, 1789, to March 2, 1903*, 2 vols. (1903; repr., Urbana: Univ. of Illinois Press, 1965), 1:307.

59. Heitman, *Historical Register*, 424; Ordnance Hall of Fame file, U.S. Army Ordnance Museum, U.S. Army Ordnance Center & School, Aberdeen Proving Ground, Maryland; Cullum, *Register of Graduates*, 2:814.

60. Heitman, *Historical Register*, 562; Miller, "Scarcely Any Parallel in History," 180.

4. (West) Virginians in the Gettysburg Campaign

1. Opinion on the admission of West Virginia into the Union, Dec. 31, 1862, *The Collected Works of Abraham Lincoln*, ed. Roy P. Basler, ed., 8 vols. (New Brunswick, NJ: Rutgers University Press, 1953), 6:26–28.

2. "Willey Amendment," *A State of Convenience: The Creation of West Virginia*, Web site of the West Virginia Division of Culture and History, 2015, accessed Mar. 23, 2016, http://www.wvculture.org/history/statehood/willeyamendment.html.

3. Most of the earlier studies about West Virginia and the Civil War underestimate the total number of Confederate troops recruited from the counties of what would become the state of West Virginia. The *Third Biennial Report of Archives and History of the State of West Virginia* (1909–11) places the number ("a conservative estimate") at approximately seven thousand Confederate soldiers (224). Boyd Stutler, in *West Virginia in the Civil War* (Charleston, WV: Education Foundation, 1966), estimates there were between eight thousand and ten thousand Confederates. In 1985, Otis K. Rice raised that number to somewhere between ten thousand and twelve thousand West Virginia Confederate troops in *West Virginia: A History* (Lexington: Univ. Press of Kentucky, 1985), 125. More recent scholarship, particularly James Carter Linger in *Confederate Military Units of West Virginia* (N.p.: privately published, 1989) and Jack L. Dickinson, *Tattered Uniforms and Bright Bayonets: West Virginia's Confederate Soldiers* (Huntington, WV: Marshall Univ. Library Association, 1995), places the number at more than 20,000. The George Tyler Moore Center for the Study of the Civil War at Shepherd University also is compiling, on a database, the service records of all soldiers assigned to West Virginia Union military organizations and Confederate military organizations

that were recruited wholly or partly in West Virginia counties. Once this multiyear project is complete, the actual number of Union and Confederate soldiers from West Virginia will finally be ascertained.

4. Mark A. Snell, *West Virginia and the Civil War: Mountaineers Are Always Free* (Charleston, SC: History Press, 2011), 28–29.

5. A complete listing of military organizations partly or wholly comprising West Virginians can be found on the interactive compact disc produced by the George Tyler Moore Center for the Study of the Civil War titled *Mountaineers of the Blue and Gray: The Civil War and West Virginia* (Shepherdstown, WV: Shepherd Univ., 2008).

6. Ibid. During the battle, two Union regiments and part of a third, the 1st West Virginia Cavalry, the 7th West Virginia Infantry, and the 3d West Virginia Cavalry as well as Battery C, 1st West Virginia Light Artillery, were in the thick of the fighting. They were opposed by Confederate units raised wholly or partly from West Virginia counties, including several regiments of the famed Stonewall Brigade (the 2d, 27th, and 33d Virginia Infantry); the 25th and 31st Virginia Infantry, the 1st, 7th, 9th, 11th, 12th Virginia Cavalry; Albert Gallatin Jenkins's entire cavalry brigade; and Battery B, 1st Virginia Artillery.

7. Stephen W. Sears, *Gettysburg* (Boston: Houghton Mifflin, 2003), 62–64.

8. Eric J. Wittenberg, *The Battle of Brandy Station: North America's Largest Cavalry Battle* (Charleston, SC: History Press, 2010), 74–78.

9. "Reports of Brig. Gen. W. E. Jones, C. S. Army, commanding brigade," June 11, 1863, *War of the Rebellion: The Official Records of the Union and Confederate Armies*, 128 vols. (Washington, DC: GPO, 1880–1901), ser. 1, vol. 27, 2:748 (hereafter cited as *OR*; all references are to ser. 1).

10. "7th, 11th and 12th Virginia Cavalry," *Mountaineers of the Blue and Gray.*

11. Wittenberg, *Battle of Brandy Station*, 88.

12. Ibid., 93–103.

13. "Return of Casualties in the Union Forces at Brandy Station (Fleetwood), Beverly Ford, and Stevensburg, Va., June 9, 1863," *OR*, vol. 27, 1:168.

14. Patrick Bowmaster, ed., "A Confederate Cavalryman at War: The Diary of Sergeant Jasper Hawes of the 14th Regiment Virginia Militia, the 17th Virginia Cavalry Battalion, and the 11th Virginia Cavalry," 29, manuscript, Special Collections, Newman Library, Virginia Polytechnic Institute and State Univ., Blacksburg.

15. Sears, *Gettysburg*, 74.

16. "Return of Union Casualties in the Union forces at Winchester, Va., June 13–15, 1863," *OR*, vol. 27, 2:53.

17. Sears, *Gettysburg*, 78–81.

18. "Report of Capt. John Carlin, Battery D, First West Virginia Light Artillery, of operations June 13–15," *OR*, vol. 27, 2:74–75.

19. *Daily Intelligencer*, June 25, 1863, in *Carlin's Wheeling Battery: A History of Battery D, First West Virginia Light Artillery*, comp. and ed. Linda Cunningham Fluharty and Edward Phillips (Baton Rouge: Linda Fluharty, 2005), 33.

20. William Frassanito, *Early Photography at Gettysburg* (Gettysburg: Thomas Publications, 1995), 124–28.

21. John R. King, *My Experience in the Confederate Army and in Northern Prisons, Written from Memory* (Clarksburg, WV: Stonewall Jackson Chapter No. 1333, United Daughters of the Confederacy, 1917), 4–5.

22. Roger P. Chew, *Military Operations in Jefferson County Virginia (Now West Virginia), 1861–1865*, ed. James Holland (Shepherdstown, WV: James Holland, 2004), 13.

23. Quoted in Edward H. Phillips, *The Lower Shenandoah Valley in the Civil War: The Impact of War upon the Civilian Population and upon Civil Institutions* (Lynchburg, VA: H. E. Howard, 1993), 117.

24. Henry Kyd Douglas, *I Rode with Stonewall: The War Experiences of the Youngest Member of Jackson's Staff* (1940; repr., Chapel Hill: Univ. of North Carolina Press, 1968), 234.

25. Sears, *Gettysburg*, 96; General Orders No. 73, *The Wartime Papers of R. E. Lee*, ed. Clifford Dowdey (New York: Bramhall House, 1961), 533–34.

26. John O. Casler, *Four Years in the Stonewall Brigade* (1906; repr., Dayton, OH: Morningside, 1971), 168.

27. Sears, *Gettysburg*, 97–101.

28. *Daily Intelligencer*, June 20, 1863 (emphasis added).

29. Edward G. Longacre, *The Cavalry at Gettysburg: A Tactical Study of the Mounted Operations during the Civil War's Pivotal Campaign, 9 June–14 July 1863* (Lincoln: Univ. of Nebraska Press, 1986), 172–81; Compiled Service Records of Collins and Selby, National Archives and Records Administration; "9th Virginia Cavalry," *Mountaineers of the Blue and Gray*.

30. "Report of Col. Thomas C. Devin, Sixth New York Cavalry, Commanding Second Brigade. Hdqrs. Second Brigade, First Cavalry Division, August 6, 1863," *OR*, vol. 27, 1:942–43.

31. King, *My Experience in the Confederate Army and in Northern Prisons, Written from Memory*, 6.

32. "Report of Lieut. Col. Jonathan H. Lockwood, Seventh West Virginia Infantry. Camp Near Gettysburg, Pa., July 5, 1863," *OR*, vol. 27, 1:463–64.

33. Casler, *Four Years in the Stonewall Brigade*, 174.

34. Sears, *Gettysburg*, 246; Douglas, *I Rode with Stonewall*, 242–43.

35. Sears, *Gettysburg*, 346–47, 357–60, 375, 383.

36. "Battery C, 1st West Virginia Light Artillery," *Mountaineers of the Blue and Gray*.

37. "Report of Capt. Wallace Hill, Battery C, First West Virginia Light Artillery, Berlin Heights, Md., July 17, 1863," *OR*, vol. 27, 1:895.

38. Compiled Military Service Record of Charles Lacy, National Archives and Records Administration.

39. "7th Virginia Infantry and 24th Virginia Infantry," *Mountaineers of the Blue and Gray*.

40. "1st Virginia Cavalry, 5th Virginia Cavalry, 10th Virginia Cavalry, 14th Virginia Cavalry, 16th Virginia Cavalry, 17th Virginia Cavalry, 34th

Virginia Battalion, 36th Virginia Battalion," *Mountaineers of the Blue and Gray.*

41. "Chew's Battery, 7th Virginia Cavalry, 11th Virginia Cavalry," *Mountaineers of the Blue and Gray;* Eric J. Wittenberg, *Gettysburg's Forgotten Cavalry Actions* (Gettysburg: Thomas Publications, 1998), 68–91.

42. John Blue, *Hanging Rock Rebel: Lt. John Blue's War in West Virginia and the Shenandoah Valley,* ed. Dan Oates (Shippensburg, PA: Burd Street, 1994), 203.

43. Steve Cunningham and Beth White, "'The Ground Trembled as They Came': The 1st West Virginia Cavalry in the Gettysburg Campaign," in *Gettysburg: Regimental Leadership and Command,* ed. Mark A. Snell, special issue of *Civil War Regiments: A Journal of the American Civil War* 6, no. 3 (1999): 69–71.

44. Cunningham and White, "Ground Trembled," 71–72, 76; "Report of Maj. Charles E. Capehart, First West Virginia Cavalry, Headquarters, First West Virginia Cavalry. Near Hardwood Church, Va., August 17, 1862," *OR,* vol. 27, 1:1019.

45. Longacre, *Cavalry at Gettysburg,* 246–48.

46. Quoted in Cunningham and White, "Ground Trembled," 76.

47. "Report of Maj. Charles E. Capehart," 1019.

48. Casler, *Four Years in the Stonewall Brigade,* 178.

49. Theodore Lang, *Loyal West Virginia: From 1861 to 1865* (Baltimore: Deutsch Publishing, 1895), 169.

50. Diary of George W. Morehead (May 1, 1863–June 10, 1864), Morehead file, Civil War Artificial Collection, West Virginia Archives, Charleston, West Virginia. Morehead was referring to Fort Loudon, Pennsylvania, about fifteen miles west of Chambersburg.

51. "Report of Maj. Charles E. Capehart," 1020.

52. Longacre, *Cavalry at Gettysburg,* 252–69.

53. Steve Cunningham and Beth White, *Their Deeds Are Their Monuments: Celebrating the Centennial Anniversary of the Dedication of the West Virginia Monuments at Gettysburg, 1898–1998* (Charleston: West Virginia Book, 1998), 8.

54. Ibid., 8–18

5. "A HELL OF A DAMNED FOOL"

1. See, for example, Edward Longacre, *The Cavalry at Gettysburg: A Tactical Study of Mounted Operations during the Civil War's Pivotal Campaign, 9 June–14 July 1863* (Lincoln: Univ. of Nebraska Press, 1986), 244; Edward Stackpole, *They Met at Gettysburg* (Harrisburg, PA: Stackpole, 1956), 275; Samuel Martin, *Kill-Cavalry: The Life of Union General Hugh Judson Kilpatrick* (Mechanicsburg, PA: Stackpole, 2000), 117.

2. Edwin Coddington, *The Gettysburg Campaign: A Study in Command* (New York: Charles Scribner's Sons, 1968), 525.

3. Longacre, *Cavalry at Gettysburg*, 244; Martin, *Kill-Cavalry*, 116.

4. In *They Met at Gettysburg*, Edward Stackpole described the assault as "a hell-for-leather mounted attack which reminds one of the Charge of the Light Brigade at Balaclava in the Crimean War" (274–75).

5. Coddington, *Gettysburg Campaign*, 525; Jeffry Wert, *Gettysburg: Day Three* (New York: Simon & Schuster, 2001), 280.

6. Longacre, *Cavalry at Gettysburg*, 244.

7. Martin, *Kill-Cavalry*, 2.

8. James H. Wilson, *Under the Old Flag: Recollections of Military Operations in the War for the Union, the Spanish War, the Boxer Rebellion, etc.* 2 vols. (New York: D. Appleton & Co., 1912), 2:13.

9. Ezra Warner, *Generals in Blue* (Baton Rouge: Louisiana State Univ. Press, 1964), 266.

10. Ibid.

11. Martin, *Kill-Cavalry*, 57.

12. *The War of the Rebellion: A Compilation of the Official Records of the Union and Confederate Armies, 128 vols.* (Washington, DC: GPO, 1880–1901), ser. 1, vol. 25, 2:71–72 (hereafter cited as *OR;* all references are to ser. 1).

13. Martin, *Kill-Cavalry*, 66.

14. Stephen Sears, *Chancellorsville* (New York: Ticknor & Fields, 1996), 368.

15. Longacre, *Cavalry at Gettysburg*, 80, 109; James Moore, *Kilpatrick and Our Cavalry* (New York: W. J. Widdleton, 1865), 63.

16. Longacre, *Cavalry at Gettysburg*, 128, 129.

17. Ibid., 166–67.

18. Mark A. Snell, "The Battle of Hanover," in *Encyclopedia of the American Civil War: A Political, Social, and Military History*, ed. David Heidler and Jeanne Heidler, 5 vols. (Santa Barbara, CA: ABC Clio, 2000), 2:924–25.

19. Longacre, *Cavalry at Gettysburg*, 200–201.

20. Kilpatrick's report, *OR*, vol. 27, 1:992.

21. Longacre, *Cavalry at Gettysburg*, 223.

22. Kilpatrick's report, 992–93.

23. Ibid.; Pleasonton's and Merritt's reports also can be found in *OR*, vol. 27, 1:914, 943.

24. Dennis Hart Mahan, *An Elementary Treatise of Advanced, Out-Post, and Detachment Service of Troops* (New York: John Wiley, 1861), 58.

25. Brigade personnel strengths are from John W. Busey and David G. Martin, *Regimental Strengths at Gettysburg* (Baltimore: Gateway, 1982), 103, 107. The strength of Merritt's brigade does not include the 6th U.S. Cavalry.

26. Longacre, *Cavalry at Gettysburg*, 241.

27. H. C. Parsons, Co. L, 1st Vermont Cavalry, typescript recollections of "Farnsworth's Charge and Death," 3, 1st Vermont Cavalry File, Gettysburg National Military Park. A version of this was published in the "Battles and Leaders" series in *Century Magazine*. See Parsons, "Farnsworth's Charge and Death," in *Battles and Leaders of the Civil War*, ed. Robert Johnson and Clarence Buell, 4 vols. (1888; repr., Edison, NJ: Castle Books, 1995), 3:393–96.

28. Parson, "Farnsworth's Charge and Death," typescript, 4.

29. Recollections of Capt. Henry Clay Potter, 18th Pennsylvania Cavalry, 18th Penn. Cavalry File, Gettysburg National Military Park.

30. Steven A. Cunningham and Beth A. White, "'The Ground Trembled As They Came': The First West Virginia Cavalry in the Gettysburg Campaign" in *Gettysburg: Regimental Leadership and Command*, ed. Mark A. Snell, special issue of *Civil War Regiments: A Journal of the American Civil War* 6, no. 3 (1999): 71–72. The quotation is from Pvt. James Dean, who wrote a description of the charge for his hometown newspaper, the *Daily Intelligencer* (quoted in Cunningham and White).

31. Recollections of H. C. Potter, Gettysburg National Military Park. In his *Century Magazine* article, Capt. Henry Parsons stated that Farnsworth protested the order to charge, Kilpatrick offered to lead it if Farnsworth was afraid, and Farnsworth yelled at Kilpatrick to "take that back." According to Parsons, Kilpatrick said he did not mean it, and then Farnsworth led the charge after Kilpatrick took full responsibility for ordering it.

32. Recollections of H. C. Potter. Potter mistakenly remembered the 5th New York also participating in the charge, but that regiment remained as support for Elder's battery.

33. Parsons, "Farnsworth's Charge and Death," 6–7.

34. Letters from Thomas Cheney and Dr. P. O. Edson, former members of the 1st Vermont Cavalry, to the editor of the *Gettysburg Compiler*, November 7, 1899. Farnsworth's body was found with five gunshot wounds— four in the chest and abdomen and one on the upper thigh. Apparently, another 1st Vermont officer, Captain Cushman of Company E, suffered a terrible gunshot wound to the face (although it was not mortal). He was left on the field for dead, and some of the Confederates who saw the body assumed it was Farnsworth and that he had shot himself in the head. (Letters to the editor transcribed by John Heiser, Elon J. Farnsworth file, Gettysburg National Military Park.)

35. A. T. Cowell, *Tactics at Gettysburg: As Described by Participants in the Battle* (Gettysburg: Gettysburg Compiler Print, 1910), 80.

36. Stackpole, *They Met at Gettysburg*, 274–75.

37. Coddington, *Gettysburg Campaign*, 524–35.

38. Longacre, *Cavalry at Gettysburg*, 242, 244.

39. Martin, *Kill-Cavalry*, 113–17. Unfortunately, Martin's biography is not based on Kilpatrick's personal papers, which had been destroyed in a fire.

40. Eric J. Wittenberg, *Gettysburg's Forgotten Cavalry Actions* (Gettysburg: Thomas Publications, 1998), 44.

41. Wert, *Gettysburg*, 280.

42. Meade to Halleck, July 3, 1863, *OR*, vol. 27, 1:75.

43. Busey and Martin, *Regimental Strengths at Gettysburg*, 107.

44. "Report of Casualties in the First Brigade, Third Division, Cavalry Corps, from June 29 to July 9, 1863," *OR*, vol. 27, 1:1008. The casualties are broken down by type and by engagement. There were 14 casualties in the

18th Pennsylvania (1 killed, 5 wounded, 8 missing); 18 in the 1st West Virginia (4 killed, 8 wounded, 6 missing); 68 in the 1st Vermont (13 killed, 19 wounded, 36 missing); and General Farnsworth, KIA. The total killed was 19, including the general.

45. Joe Allen, *The Anthology of Another Town*, photocopy excerpt in the 1st Vermont Cavalry File, Gettysburg National Military Park, 174.

46. The 5th U.S. Cavalry sustained 55 casualties out of 250 men (22 percent). See Stephen Sears, *To the Gates of Richmond: The Peninsula Campaign* (New York: Ticknor & Fields, 1992), 245–46. The 8th Pennsylvania Cavalry lost 109 men of its approximately 350 troopers (31 percent). See Sears, *Chancellorsville*, 288; John Bigelow, *Chancellorsville* (New York: Smithmark, 1995), 194.

47. Even if we use only the 1st Vermont's casualty rate, and even by using Joe Allen's figure of 312 men who made the charge, the casualty rate still remains lower (21.8 percent) than that of the 5th U.S. at Gaines's Mill and the 8th Pennsylvania at Chancellorsville.

48. "Reports of Maj. Gen. Alfred Pleasonton, U.S. Army, commanding Cavalry Corps," *OR*, vol. 27, 1:916.

49. Coddington, *Gettysburg Campaign*, 524–25.

50. Meade to Halleck, July 3, 1863, 75.

51. "Report of Col. Nathaniel P. Richmond, First West Virginia Cavalry, commanding First Brigade, 3rd Division," *OR*, vol. 27, 1:1005.

52. Address of Capt. John W. Philips at the dedication of the 18th Pennsylvania Cavalry monument, typescript in the 18th Pennsylvania Cavalry File, Gettysburg National Military Park.

53. From "Historic Records of 5 NY Cav" (1865), typescript copy in 5th New York Cavalry File, Gettysburg National Military Park (emphasis in original).

54. Parsons, "Farnsworth's Charge and Death," 1.

55. Report of Maj. Charles. E. Capehart, First West Virginia Cavalry," *OR*, vol. 27, 1:1018–19.

56. Kilpatrick's report, 993.

57. Longacre, *Cavalry at Gettysburg*, 248–250; 253–54; 256–58; 260–62; 265–67.

58. Ibid., 268–69.

59. Warner, *Generals in Blue*, 266.

6. Music Inspired by the Battle of Gettysburg

1. Edwin B. Coddington, *The Gettysburg Campaign: A Study in Command* (New York: Charles Scribner's Sons, 1968), 503; U.S. National Park Service, *Gettysburg: Official Map and Guide* (Washington, DC: GPO, 2000).

2. Richard B. Sauers's *The Gettysburg Campaign, June 3–August 1, 1863: A Comprehensive, Selectively Annotated Bibliography* (Westport, CT: Greenwood, 1982) lists 2,757 articles, books, and monographs written about this

campaign. In the decades since Sauers's bibliography was compiled, hundreds, if not thousands more have been published.

3. *Washington Morning Chronicle*, Nov. 21, 1863, quoted in John B. Horner, *Lincoln's Songbird: Wilson G. Horner, a Brief Life of Melody and Harmony* (Gettysburg: Horner Enterprises, 1998), vi.

4. Ibid.

5. B. B. French and W. G. Horner, "National Consecration Chant or Hymn" (Baltimore: Henry McCaffrey, 1864).

6. Alfred Delaney, "Dirge Sung at the Consecration of the Soldiers' Cemetery at Gettysburg" (Philadelphia: Lee & Walker, 1863). The piece was written in C major, in common time, and for four voices. Delaney dedicated his composition to Pennsylvania's wartime governor, Andrew Curtin. Everett's role in America's Greek revival is discussed in Garry Wills, *Lincoln at Gettysburg: The Words That Remade America* (New York: Touchstone / Simon & Schuster, 1992), 41–62.

7. Alfred Delaney and Robert Morris, "Gettysburg!" Songs for the Loyal series (Philadelphia: Lee & Walker, 1863).

8. Mary Griffith and Frederick Buckley, "Break It Gently to My Mother" (Boston: Henry Tolman, 1863); *The New Grove Dictionary of American Music* (1986 ed.), s.v. "Buckley," by Robert B. Winans.

9. Albert Anderson and Rudolph Wittig, "Jenny Wade: The Heroine of Gettysburg" (Philadelphia: William R. Smith, 1864). The song was dedicated to George G. Meade.

10. W. H. Hayward and Wilson Horner, "The Unknown Soldier—Who Is He?" (New York: William A. Pond, 1864); Mark H. Dunkleman, *Gettysburg's Unknown Soldier: The Life, Death, and Celebrity of Amos Hummiston* (Westport, CT: Praeger, 1999), xi.

11. Dunkleman, *Gettysburg's Unknown Soldier*, 169; James G. Clark, "The Children of the Battle Field" (Philadelphia: Lee & Walker, 1864).

12. Dunkleman, *Gettysburg's Unknown Soldier*, 171–73.

13. F. O. Jones, ed., *A Handbook of American Music and Musicians* (1886; reprint, New York: Da Capo, 1971), s.v. "Beckel, James C."; James C. Beckel, "Battle of Gettysburg" (Philadelphia: Winner, 1863).

14. John Prosinger, "Picket's Charge March" (Columbia, SC: B. Duncan, [ca. 1864]). This march was the only southern composition I could find that even touched on the Battle of Gettysburg.

15. J. B. Kevinsky and T. C. Porter, "The Rocky Hills of Gettysburg" (Philadelphia: Lee & Walker, 1864). The song was dedicated to "the Officers and Soldiers of the Army of the Potomac."

16. Max J. Coble and James A. Scott, "The Heroes of Gettysburg; or, A Dirge for the Brave" (Philadelphia: Lee & Walker, 1864). The cover of the sheet music included the dedication and the makeup of Company C's glee club. On Coble, see C. Armour Newcomer, *Cole's Cavalry: Or, Three Years in the Shenandoah Valley* (1895; repr., Freeport, NY: Books for Libraries Press, 1970), 15. The Adams County Historical Society in Gettysburg has a photo-

graph of Coble and Thaddeus Welty just before they enlisted. It is part of the J. Howard Wert Collection. Wert was a young Gettysburg schoolteacher at the time of the battle; he later joined the Union army and was wounded at the Battle of Petersburg. On the back of the photo, Wert wrote, "Here is a photo of two young men of Gettysburg taken at the time they enlisted in the Union Army, April 1861. The one on the left is my cousin, Thaddeus Welty, the other Max J. Coble, a talented young musician, who wrote the music to James A. Scott's 'Heroes of Gettysburg,' and who was so starved in the foul prison of Andersonville that he died a few days after his exchange whilst on a steamer that was conveying him to Annapolis."

17. Irenaeus D. Foulon and Charles Kunkel, "The Veteran's Vote" (St. Louis: Kunkel Brothers, 1880).

18. C. H. McD. Burton, "Gettysburg," in *The Compositions of C. H. McD. Burton for the Guitar* (Philadelphia: William H. Bonner, 1885); Septimus Winner, "The Gettysburg March" (Philadelphia: Sep. Winner & Son, 1886). For more on Winner, best known as the composer of "Listen to the Mocking Bird," see *The New Grove Dictionary of American Music* (1986 ed.), s.v. "Winner, Septimus," by Nicholas E. Tawa; Louis Conterno, "Gettysburg March" (Brooklyn: Joseph Mocs, 1887); James C. Beckel, "The Battle of Gettysburg . . ." (Chicago: National Music, 1888). Casualty figures were found in Jeffry Wert, *Gettysburg: Day Three* (New York: Simon & Schuster, 2001).

19. For a detailed description of the reunion, see Commonwealth of Pennsylvania, *Fiftieth Anniversary of the Battle of Gettysburg: Report of the Pennsylvania Commission* (Harrisburg, PA: Wm. Stanley Ray, State Printer, 1914), and Stan Cohen, *Hands across the Wall: The 50th and 75th Reunions of the Gettysburg Battle* (Charleston, WV: Pictorial Histories, 1997). Also, see chapter 7 of this anthology.

20. Mrs. Findley Braden and W. A. Webb, "Grand Old Gettysburg Boys" (Doylestown, PA: Braden, 1913).

21. James Wisler and Vivian Brooks, "Gettysburg" (Washington, DC: H. Kirkus Dugdale, 1913).

22. A search of several sheet music databases, including Peabody Institute's "Lester S. Levy Collection of Sheet Music," yielded only one "Gettysburg" composition written after 1913. Published in 1917, E. T. Paull's "Battle of Gettysburg" was labeled a "Descriptive March." It was similar in structure to James C. Beckel's programmatic pieces. See E. T. Paull, "Battle of Gettysburg" (New York: E. T. Paull Music, 1917).

7. Cadet Gray, Khaki, and Camouflage

1. Field Manual No. 6–22, *Army Leadership: Competent, Confident, Agile* (Washington, DC: Headquarters, Dept. of the Army, 2006), 2-6-2-7. The Chamberlain case study was first included in 1983.

2. William A. Frassanito, *Gettysburg: A Journey in Time* (New York: Charles A. Scribner, 1975), 123.

3. Charles M. Clement, ed., *Pennsylvania in the World War*, vol. 1 of 2 (Pittsburgh: States Publication Society, 1921), 101.

4. Ibid., 102. This was the 12th Regiment.

5. Ibid., 104.

6. Frederick Tilberg, *Gettysburg*, rev. ed. (Washington, DC: GPO, 1962), 46–47.

7. U.S. War Department, *Annual Reports of the Gettysburg National Military Park Commission to the Secretary of War, 1893–1904* (Washington, DC: GPO, 1905), 7–10.

8. Ibid., 103–7.

9. Richard Rowe, "Gettysburg 'Staff Ride,'" *Assembly* 45, no. 2 (Sept. 1986): 32–33, 56, 30–31.

10. Quoted in ibid.

11. George Patton to Beatrice Ayer, May 11, 1909, *The Patton Papers, 1885–1940*, ed. Martin Blumenson, 2 vols. (New York: Houghton Mifflin, 1972), 1:191–92.

12. Cadet Edwin C. Kelton to Florence Hatton, May 5, 1915, Kelton Papers, USMA Special Collections, USMA Library, West Point, NY.

13. Commonwealth of Pennsylvania, *Fiftieth Anniversary of the Battle of Gettysburg: Report of the Pennsylvania Commission* (Harrisburg: William S. Ray, State Printer, 1914), 11–14. The total amount allocated by the various state governments and veterans' organizations for the anniversary came to over $1,175,000 (37).

14. Ibid., 14, 60, 40. In addition to soldiers of the Regular Army, officers and men of the Pennsylvania National Guard as well as the Pennsylvania State Police helped to administer the anniversary commemoration.

15. Ibid., 42–45.

16. George S. Patton Jr. to Beatrice Ayer, *Patton Papers*, 1:280.

17. *Fiftieth Anniversary of the Battle of Gettysburg*, 40–42, 64.

18. Ibid., 55, 232–34. Nine of the old veterans died during the celebration or on their way to or from Gettysburg, but considering the advanced age of participants and the problems associated with the heat and general excitement, the mortality rate was quite low.

19. *Gettysburg Compiler*, May 19, 1917.

20. *Gettysburg Times*, May 10, 1917.

21. *Gettysburg Times*, May 14, 1917. As deployed to the American Expeditionary Forces, each infantry regiment would have an authorized strength of 112 officers and 3,720 men assigned to three battalions and a machine-gun company. The battalion comprised four companies with 6 officers and 250 men each.

22. *Gettysburg Times*, May 23, 1917.

23. Assistant Secretary of War William Ingraham to Chairman, Gettysburg National Park Commission, May 26, 1917, General Correspondence, 1916–17, Gettysburg National Military Park (GNMP) Archives.

24. Bradley S. Keefer, *Conflicting Memories on the "River of Death": The*

Chickamauga Battlefield and the Spanish-American War, 1863–1933 (Kent, OH: Kent State Univ. Press, 2013), 272–73.

25. *Adams County News*, May 17, 1917. The new Selective Service Law had a clause that prohibited the sale of alcohol to uniformed servicemen.

26. *Gettysburg Compiler*, June 23, 1917.

27. *Gettysburg Times*, July 9, 1917; Kennedy, *Over Here*, 186. For an in-depth look at the CTCA's work at Gettysburg, see Peter Miele, "Men, Morality, and Misbehavior: A Social Study of the World War I Camps at Gettysburg and the Town That Surrounded Them, 1917–1918," in *Duty Calls at Home: Central Pennsylvania Responds to the Great War, 1914–1918*, ed. Steven Burg et al. (Shippensburg, PA: Shippensburg Univ. Center for Applied History, 2014), 45–76.

28. *Adams County News*, June 16, 1917.

29. Joseph J. Stone journal, World War I Veterans Questionnaires, 59th U.S. Infantry, 4th Division, U.S. Army Heritage and Education Center (AHEC), Carlisle, PA.

30. *Harrisburg Telegraph*, Sept. 13, 1917.

31. *Gettysburg Times*, Sept. 11, 12, 1917.

32. Howard to Nicholson, July 10, 1917, General Correspondence, 1916–17, GNMP Archives. (Also in the archives are the blueprints of every structure that the Army built on the Park in 1917.)

33. *Adams County News*, June 23, 1917.

34. *Star and Sentinel*, June 16, 1917.

35. *Gettysburg Compiler*, July 14, 1917.

36. *Gettysburg Compiler*, June 20, 1917.

37. *Gettysburg Times*, Oct. 3, 1917. Burnett had attended West Point but was dismissed in 1878, during his senior year, and never graduated. (*Official Register of the Officers and Cadets of the U.S. Military Academy* [June 1879], 31.)

38. *Harrisburg Telegraph*, Sept. 14, 1917.

39. Mr. Don Hinks, owner of Gettysburg Electronics (a purveyor of metal detectors), excavated an artifact known as a screw picket, or "pig tail" (from the French term *queue de cochon*), which was used to secure barbed-wire entanglements in front of trench systems. It was found in the vicinity of modern-day Colt Park Recreational Complex, which in 1917 was part of the U.S. camp.

40. Allen M. Brandt, *No Magic Bullet: A Social History of Venereal Disease in the United States Since 1880* (New York: Oxford Univ. Press, 1987), 61–70.

41. Ernest Wrentmore, *In Spite of Hell: A Factual Story of Incidents That Occurred during World War I, as Experienced by the Youngest Soldier to Have Seen Combat Duty with the American Expeditionary Forces as a Member of the Famous Company I, 60th Infantry, Fifth (Red Diamond) Division* (New York: Greenwich, 1958), 11, 28–29.

42. Joseph Stone journal.

43. *Gettysburg Times*, Oct. 25, 1917.

44. *Gettysburg Times*, Nov. 2, 1917 (emphasis added).

45. *Gettysburg Times*, Nov. 3, 1917.

46. Huidekoper to Nicholson, Sept. 14, 1917, Nicholson to Burnett, Nov. 6, 1917, both in General Correspondence, GNMP Commission, 1916–17, GNMP Library.

47. *Gettysburg Times*, Nov. 5, 1917.

48. *Gettysburg Times*, Feb. 17, 1918.

49. *Gettysburg Times*, Mar. 8, 1918.

50. General Orders No. 7, Mar. 29, 1918, Records of United States Army Continental Commands, 1821–1920, National Archives Record Group 393, Camp Colt, General Orders (hereafter cited as RG 393, Camp Colt).

51. Director of the Tank Corps to the Adjutant General of the Army, Apr. 18, 1918, Records of the Adjutant General's Office, RG 407, NARA.

52. Dwight D. Eisenhower, *At Ease: Stories I Tell to Friends* (Garden City, NY: Doubleday, 1967), 140, 144–45.

53. Photographs of "Battling Lizzie" can be found in the Pennsylvania State Archives, RG 19 (Records of the Department of Military and Veterans' Affairs War History Commission [World War I]) GENERAL FILE, 1915–1920, 1928, [13–1311, carton 4]).

54. Eisenhower, *At Ease*, 146.

55. *Gettysburg Times*, June 6, 1918; Dale E. Wilson, *"Treat 'em Rough": The Birth of American Armor, 1917–1920* (Novato, CA: Presidio, 1990), 76.

56. Eisenhower, *At Ease*, 144–45, 147.

57. Ibid, 148–49.

58. Civilian deaths were tabulated from obituaries in the *Gettysburg Times* from September 1918 through April 1919.

59. Eisenhower, *At Ease*, 149; Robert B. Roberts, *Encyclopedia of Historic Forts: The Military, Pioneer, and Trading Posts of the United States*, 1st ed. (New York: Prentice Hall, 1988), 677.

60. Commonwealth of Pennsylvania, *Report of the Pennsylvania Commission of the Seventy-fifth Anniversary of the Battle of Gettysburg*, 4 vols. (Gettysburg: Times & News Publishing Co., 1939), 4:341.

61. Ibid., 324, 341–42, 325. On page 444 there is an excerpt from the *Milwaukee Journal* that claimed that the youngest veteran was eighty-six, the oldest ninety-nine, and the average age was ninety-one.

62. *Gettysburg Times*, Dec. 26, 1941.

63. Beverly D. Eddy, *Camp Sharpe's "Psycho Boys": From Gettysburg to Germany* (Bennington, VT: Merriam Press, 2014), 9–29.

64. "The Prisoner of War Camps located in or Near Gettysburg, Pennsylvania, during World War II, 1944–46," No date or author, Historical Files at GNMP. Two POWs escaped shortly after arriving at the camp. They were captured eight days later in York County and returned to Gettysburg. *Gettysburg Compiler*, July 15, 1944.

65. Jay Luvaas and Harold W. Nelson, *The U.S. Army War College Guide to the Battle of Gettysburg* (Carlisle, PA: South Mountain Press, 1986), x.

66. Ibid., x–xi, One officer who attended the War College said that there "is something to be gained from walking those fields that will never be found on a computer terminal or Pentagon briefing chart" (xi).

67. Personal recollections of the author.

68. "August 2015 Gettysburg Staff Ride," Website of the Simon Center for the Professional Military Ethic, accessed March 23, 2016, http://www.usma. edu/scpme/SitePages/August%202015%20Gettysburg%20Staff%20Ride.aspx?

8. The History of Civil War Reenacting

1. Howard Giles, "A Brief History of Re-Enactment," updated Feb. 22, 2015, accessed May 2, 2016, http://www.eventplan.co.uk/history_of_re-enactment.htm.

2. Bruce Venter, "Ex-Union Officer Leads Re-enactment," *Washington Times*, Feb. 26, 2005.

3. Steven Sylvia and Michael O'Donnell, *The Illustrated History of American Civil War Relics* (Orange, VA: Moss, 1978), 185–86; Stan Cohen, *Hands across the Wall: The Fiftieth and Seventy-fifth Reunions of the Gettysburg Battle* (Charleston, WV: Pictorial Histories, 1982), 22.

4. See chapter 7 of this volume.

5. See Bradley S. Keefer, *Conflicting Memories on the "River of Death": The Chickamauga Battlefield and the Spanish-American War* (Kent, OH: Kent State Univ. Press, 2013).

6. John A. Paige and Jerome C. Greene, *Administrative History of Chickamauga and Chattanooga National Military Park* (Denver, CO: National Park Service, U.S. Department of the Interior, 1983), available online at https://www.nps.gov/parkhistory/online_books/chch/adhi.htm.

7. Sylvia and O'Donnell, *The Illustrated History of American Civil War Relics*, 182–84; John B. Wilson, *Maneuver and Firepower: The Evolution of Divisions and Separate Brigades* (Washington, DC: U.S. Army Center of Military History, 1998), 25.

8. *New York Times*, July 2, 1922. According to the *Times*, "After facing death a thousand times with the Marines at Chateau Thierry, St. Mihiel, Belleau Wood and in the two Meuse-Argonne offensives, Captain George Hamilton returned to this country and peace times to die a few days ago while piloting an airplane in a sham battle at Gettysburg. His machine crashed to earth from a distance of 400 feet above the historic battlefield." Hamilton is buried in section S W, site 4585, Arlington National Cemetery.

9. Sylvia and O'Donnell, *Illustrated History*, 186–88.

10. "North-South Skirmish Association," Washington Blue Rifles Web site, accessed March 25, 2016, http://www.washingtonbluerifles.com/nssa. htm; Jay Anderson, *Time Machines: The World of Living History* (Nashville: American Association of State and Local History, 1984), 137–38.

11. Anderson, *Time Machines*, 142.

12. Harry Roach, "Re-enacting: A Retrospective," *Camp Chase Gazette*, July 1986, cited at Wes Clark, *Jonah World*, accessed Mar. 25, 2016, http://wesclark.com/jw/roach.html

13. Quoted in Edward Linenthal, *Sacred Ground: Americans and Their Battlefields* (Urbana: Univ. of Illinois Press, 1991), 100–101.

14. Quoted in John Bodnar, *Remaking America: Public Memory, Commemoration, and Patriotism in the Twentieth Century* (Princeton, NJ: Princeton Univ. Press, 1992), 215.

15. Cited in Anderson, *Time Machines*, 143.

16. *Battle of Antietam Centennial and Hagerstown Bicentennial Official Program and Historical Guide, Aug. 31 through Sept. 17, 1962* (Hagerstown, MD: Antietam-South Mountain Centennial Association, 1962), viii–ix.

17. Ross M. Kimmel, "My Recollections of the Civil War Centennial, or Confessions of a Blackhat" Wes Clark, *Jonah World*, accessed Mar. 25, 2016, http://wesclark.com/jw/k_1963.html.

18. "Gettysburg Remembered," accessed May 14, 2012, http://gettysburg100yearslater.weebly.com/centennialcivil-rights.html.

19. Anderson, *Time Machines*, 143.

20. Conversation with Richard Cheney and his daughter Liz during a tour of Antietam Battlefield in 1999.

21. Mark L. Shanks, "Who Wears the Blue and Grey? A Survey of Civil War Re-Enactors," accessed June 14, 2007, http://www.geocities.com/living-history/bluegrey.html (site discontinued).

22. Interview with Kyle Pfalzer, Shepherd Univ. history major, June 18, 2007.

23. "Our Organization," 54th Massachusetts Volunteer Infantry Regiment Company B Web site, accessed May 2, 2016, http://www.54thmass.org/our-organization.

24. Shanks, "Who Wears the Blue and Grey?"

25. Ibid.

26. Ibid.

27. Jack Barth, "The Red Badge of Make-Believe Courage," *Outside Magazine* (May 2004), accessed Mar. 25, 2016, http://www.outsideonline.com/1886036/red-badge-make-believe-courage.

28. Susan Reimer, "Some Men Play Soldier and Forget It's Just Play," *Baltimore Sun*, Aug. 10, 1997. Cited at Wes Clark, *Jonah World*, accessed Mar. 25, 2016, http://wesclark.com/jw/fem_rant.html.

29. Barry Mackintosh, "Interpretation in the National Park Service: A Historical Perspective, *Visitor Fees in the National Park System: A Legislative and Administrative History*, accessed Mar. 25, 2016, http://www.nps.gov/history/history/online_books/mackintosh2/directions_living_history.htm.

30. Kimmel, "My Recollections of the Civil War Centennial."

31. Mackintosh, *Interpretation in the National Park Service.*

32. Quoted in ibid.

33. Shanks, "Who Wears the Blue and Grey?"

34. Roy Turner, "Bloodless Battles: The Civil War Reenacted," *Drama Review* 34 (Winter 1990): 130.

Epilogue

1. Jim Weeks, *Gettysburg: Memory, Market, and American Shrine* (Princeton, NJ: Princeton University Press, 2003).

2. The CWPT produced this film in 2010 by as a public awareness campaign to fight the casino's developers. It featured well-known historians, preservationists, actors, a Medal of Honor winner, and President Eisenhower's granddaughter.

Index

Camp Colt, training camp for Tank
  Corps, 6–7, 151–53
Camp Sharpe, 155
Camp of the U.S. Troops, Gettysburg,
  137–51
Capehart, Charles, 83–84, 108
Capehart, Henry, 83
Captain Bell's Independent Cavalry
  Company, 15–16, *17*
Carlin, John, 73
Carroll, Samuel, 78–79
casino, proposal to build, 181; film
  opposing, 179, 182–83
Casler, John, 75–76, 79, 84
casualties, 29, 63; from artillery battle, 80; in Battle of Hanover, 77, 95;
  burials of, 62, 114, 177; in cavalry
  charges, 76, 106; Civil War songs
  lamenting, 117; in Confederate retreat through Maryland, 84–85; in
  Farnsworth's Charge, 82–83, 104–6,
  110; in Pickett's Charge, 81, 125; in
  reenactments, 165–66; in Second
  Battle of Winchester, 72–73; from
  Spanish Flu, 153; transportation
  for sick and wounded, 57, 59–60;
  wounded left in Gettysburg, 63, 130
Catton, Bruce, 166
cavalry, 58; in Battle of Hanover, 33,
  38, 77, 81; casualties in charges,
  76, 106; clashes between, 76, 81;
  expense for reenactors, 171; horses
  and mules for, 54, 61; roles of,
  55–56, 59; timing of attacks on
  infantry, 98–99, 100, 105
cavalry, Confederate, 70, 94, 109;
  roles of, 76, 83; (West) Virginians
  in, 84–85
cavalry, Union, 51, 76, 82, 93, 106;
  leadership of, 76, 92–93, 98;
  mounted *vs.* foot attacks by, 98;
  need for aggressive leaders in, 93,
  110; planning attack on Army of
  Northern Virginia, 63–64, 70–72;
  reorganization of, 92–93; routed
  near Fairfield, Pennsylvania, 81–82;
  terrain as obstacle for, 97–98;
  trying to catch Army of Northern
  Virginia, 83–85

The Cavalry at Gettysburg (Longacre),
  104
Cebula, Larry, 179, 182–83
cemeteries: Gettysburg National
  Cemetery, 80–81, 114–16, 131; Holly-
  wood Cemetery, 3; Meuse-Argonne
  American Cemetery, 6; Soldiers'
  National Cemetery, 3
Cemetery Hill, 78–79, 85, *86*
Cemetery Ridge, 79–81, 85, 161
Chamberlain, Joshua, 129–30
Chambers, John W., II, 9, 84–85
Chambliss, John, 77, 94–95
Chancellorsville, Battle of, 30, 70, 80,
  106, 162
Chancellorsville campaign, 51–52, 92
Chew, Roger Preston, 74, 81–82
Chickamauga and Chattanooga
  National Military Park, 7, 162;
  creation of, 138, 162; living history
  at, 172, 174–75
Chickamauga Battlefield, 138, 162
"The Children of the Battle Field"
  (Clark), 120
Civil War, 31, 170–71; author visiting
  battlefields of, 7–8; centennial of,
  163–67, 172; living history of, 172–
  77; logistics in, 25, 41–42; Northern
  defeats in, 29–30; 125th anniversary
  of, 170; slavery as cause of, 27–28,
  32; York County trying to avoid,
  27–29; York County's commitment
  to, 34, 40
Civil War building plaques, 1, *2*
Civil War Memory blog, 179
Civil War Trust, opposing casino
  construction, 179, 182–83
Civilian Conservation Corps, 155
civilians: filing claims for losses, 18;
  Jennie Wade as only death of, 74,
  117–18; reenactors as, 171–72
Clark, James G., 120
Clarke, Henry F. "Ruddy," 49, 52, 57,
  63, 65
Coble, Max J., 122–23
Coddington, Edwin B., 103–4, 106
Cole's Maryland Cavalry, 122
Collins, George, 77
Colt, Samuel, 151